The
Way to
Wexford

The Way to Wexford

George Baker

The Autobiography

headline

First published in 2002
by HEADLINE BOOK PUBLISHING

10 9 8 7 6 5 4 3 2 1

For permission to reproduce copyright material the author
and publishers gratefully acknowledge the following:

A.P. Watt Ltd on behalf of Michael B. Yeats for
'He Wishes for the Cloths of Heaven' by W.B. Yeats,
from *The Wind Among the Reeds*; The Society of Authors
as the Literary Representative of the Estate of
A.E. Housman for 'Eight O'Clock' by A.E. Housman.

A CIP catalogue record for this title is available from the British Library

ISBN 0 7472 5381 1

Typeset in Granjon by Palimpsest Book Production Limited,
Polmont, Stirlingshire

Printed and bound in Great Britain by
Mackays of Chatham plc, Chatham, Kent

HEADLINE BOOK PUBLISHING
A division of Hodder Headline
338 Euston Road
London NW1 3BH

www.headline.co.uk
www.hodderheadline.com

DEDICATION

To Mummy

ACKNOWLEDGEMENTS

My grateful thanks to my family both in England and abroad; to John Moffatt for all of his help; to Sally Hale for all of her hard work and supportive laughter; but most especially to my wife Louie Ramsay for her understanding, patience and encouragement through the dark times and the light.

1

'TO BEGIN AT THE BEGINNING: WHERE WERE YOU BORN?' Edie Napean Smith of *The Picture Goer* sat on the edge of the sofa, determined to get all the facts down in the right order.

'I was born in Varna, Bulgaria.'

'Ah, so you're Bulgarian?'

'No. My father was Yorkshire, my mother Irish.'

Her copy read: 'Dark, vivacious, Bulgarian-born actor, George Baker . . .'

After fifty-four years in the theatre, we still get 'Bulgarian-born actor'. 'Dark, vivacious' has long gone.

The house in Bulgaria stood overlooking the golden sands of Varna. No. 27 Boulevard Ferdinand was a small house with bulbous, curled iron gratings covering the bottom windows. A veranda with wrought-iron railings ran the length of the first floor; French windows from my parents' bedroom opened out on to it. From here you could see the harbour and the approaches to it from the Black Sea. A very suitable place for the British Vice-Consul to live: he could see every ship that entered or left the port.

My father was a Yorkshireman, born in Wetherby in 1884. He was christened Francis Pearson Baker like his father before him. I belong to one of those irritating families that always christen the eldest son after the father, causing infinite problems for strangers and the need to call people Frank senior or junior. The family had been farmers for generations, and my grandfather was a notable breeder of Cleveland

Bay horses. By some quirk of nature, my father loved the theatre and loved poetry – Robert Browning in particular who was, after all, a contemporary of sorts. Father was five when Browning died.

It was my father who passed his love of theatre and the English language on to me. His sister, my Aunt Ethel, told me that he had confided in her that he would have loved to have become an actor, but there was no question of his ever doing such a thing as a living. 'It wouldn't have done,' Aunt Ethel said to me many years later. Perhaps that's why he did everything he could to encourage me to be an actor. It is one of the sadnesses of my life that he didn't live to see me on the stage.

As a small boy, I stood at the foot of my parents' bed and recited Robert Browning's 'Pippa Passes' as a birthday present to my mother and to reassure her that the Second World War might not happen. That's the nearest he got to a performance of mine.

My father went to Bulgaria via Moscow, Siberia and the First World War. It was planned that he should go to Leeds University to read Medicine, but at the age of nineteen he took himself off to the recruiting office to join the Boer War. His father was having none of that, and insisted that he should join the family business.

His maternal uncles, the Medd brothers, had set up an import/export business with offices in Moscow and St Petersburg and in 1905 my father was sent to work with his Uncle Robert in Moscow. He arrived in Moscow and settled down to learn the language and the business. The company imported cotton yarn from Lancashire and exported wheat and, rather strangely, eggs from Russia. I've never known the exact nature of the friction between uncle and nephew but they didn't get on and Father decided to come home. He left the office that day. The parting was acrimonious.

He had had to write home for his fare but, as he didn't want his landlady to know that he had left his job, he had his breakfast and left the house at the usual time each morning. There were about 330 churches in Moscow and he saw them all. As he walked the streets, the rumblings of disquiet, the threat of strikes and revolution must have been all round him, but especially in the working-men's cafés where he drank endless cups of tea. To return to Yorkshire would have seemed the sanest decision to have taken.

My father's fare home arrived at the same time as a customer of the Medds knocked on the door of his Moscow lodgings. The proposition was put to him that he should take over an import/export office in Bokhara, a district in Tsarist Russia. He was also offered the agency for a German sewing machine company, a company that was in direct competition with Singers of the USA.

Having established that the contract would allow him to trade privately, my father used his fare home to travel to Bokhara and here, in May 1905, he established his office and started his own business trading in Bokhara rugs. He opened another office in Tashkent and a few years later in Siberia as well. The firm of F. P. Baker was appointed buying agent for many British and continental firms, including the carpet section of the State Museum in Vienna. According to a letter he wrote to his sister, he found it easier to send his shirts to be laundered in Vienna than to have them done in Tashkent.

It was in January 1906 that my father became personally involved with the 'revolution'. Strikers on the Trans-Siberian Railway took control of the stations between Chelyabinsk and Irkutsk. One of the stations en route was Omsk and it was here that the train Father was travelling on was stopped. He was to stay here for six weeks before being allowed to travel on to Irkutsk – a profitable six weeks since the station master invited him to stay at his house. There was a good library and, with time on his hands, he was able to learn Russian properly. The other passengers fared as best they could. Some found rooms in the town, but a great many tore down the sides of the train and made makeshift shelters against the sub-zero temperatures. Everything on the train that could be burnt was burnt. Food was scarce. Water and milk were sold as frozen blocks which then had to be thawed.

I remember listening to my father telling me and my brother stories of maudlin, drunken Russians singing, dancing and fighting round the timbers of a vandalised railway carriage late into the night; of phenomenal vodka consumption and of murderous fights between strikers and passengers, between passengers and passengers, strikers and strikers and so on. Apparently, it was the peasant women that were the most formidable and the most to be feared. Father would tell us these horrifying stories with a wonderful twinkle in his eye, especially the one about the vast woman who put an arm round her drinking partner's neck in a friendly way and crushed his head. When she let him go, he fell down dead. She didn't even notice, just walked away and helped herself to another vodka.

The siege lasted for six weeks before it was, at last, broken by the Imperial Army. Passengers were left alone but strikers were taken away and shot without trial. Having finally reached Irkutsk, he seems to have been there for six months before returning to his base in Bokhara.

It was in 1907 that he became a British spy. He was approached by an officer from British India. Apparently, they had been monitoring Father for months before deciding he would suit their purposes. They wanted him to collect information while on his business travels and pass it back to British Army Intelligence in India. By this time, his main office was in Tashkent and the firm of F. P. Baker flourished, his business acquaintances grew, and his territory expanded; he was moving and trading in a region that was politically sensitive. He was asked to join because two English officers had been murdered and since Father was accepted in the region as a trader his chances of success were greater than the soldiers and the danger less.

The British Army in India wanted to know of tribal developments. When and where were the Russians planning an attack on Afghanistan, for instance? What was the local Uzbeki feeling against their Russian conquerors? He was to report to a safe rendezvous. The obstacle of getting information through to the Indian frontier was that foreign nationals, including my father, were not allowed to board a train for any of the crossing points. So, while he could get the information, getting it to its destination was a problem. The difficulty was solved by a Turkman acquaintance who lent him his horse, promising that the horse knew what to do. The horse was trained not to go into towns; it halted beside broad mud walls at night, knew various stops along the way where food could be bought and finally arrived at the appointed place. The Turkman friend was without doubt a regular smuggler. My father undertook these expeditions under the cover of trading.

The news of the war in Europe took some time to reach Tashkent.

My father got the news from his uncle in St Petersburg. Business to Europe had practically come to a halt. The Medds' business was in chaos; for instance, thousands of eggs which they were exporting to Hull lay bursting and sulphurous on the docks of St Petersburg because there were no ships to carry them.

Father shut up shop, sold his horses and his house and set out for England early in 1915 to enlist in the army and that September he joined the Leeds Officers Training Corps. In July 1916 he was commissioned as a Second Lieutenant in the West Riding Regiment and shortly after he was in the front line at the Battle of the Somme. He was there only for three weeks before he was wounded on 3 November, a fortnight before that most awful battle of all battles ended with 420,000 British dead, to say nothing of the French and Germans. He was invalided back to London and hospital with a serious shrapnel wound.

While the war against Germany raged, another war was being played out on the eastern side of the continent. If Churchill had not so disliked the Bulgarians, they might have joined the Western Allies at the outset of the 1914–18 war. However, inept diplomacy and apparent dislike drove them into the arms of Germany and the Central Powers. On 12 October 1915, Bulgaria declared war on Serbia. Five days later, Britain, France and Italy declared war on Bulgaria. The war was cold and cruel. My father joined General Milne's Staff as an Intelligence Officer in April 1918, fighting through the last campaign. The war in Salonika ended with the capitulation of the Bulgarians in May 1919 at the cost of over 4,000 British lives, 1,350 Greeks, 1,700 French and 200 Serbs. I don't know how many Bulgarians died.

The Armistice had been signed in Paris and the Russian Revolution was a certainty. General Milne ordered immediate demobilisation; the men had to be got home as quickly as possible. My father, by then Captain F. P. Baker MBE (agent 2nd class, twice mentioned in dispatches) was the demobilisation officer. That done, he became part of the military mission that was, in effect, the Army of Occupation. As a member of the British military mission, he was to oversee the terms of the Armistice.

What to do with himself after demobilisation? It would be difficult to re-open his business in Russia as it was now certain that the Bolsheviks would gain control. To return home to England and set up an export business would be too expensive for his meagre resources. What to do?

The following is an extract from Telegram No. 139 from Sir Arthur Peel to Lord Curzon (Foreign Office).

> If it is not possible to appoint salaried Consul immediately for Varna, where British interests usually require protection, could the services of Capt. Baker, Intelligence Officer of the mission, now at Varna, be retained for the present. His admirable commercial and consular work render application to the war office in the above sense most desirable.

Sir Francis Rodd of the Legation asked Captain Baker to apply for the post and suggested to the Foreign Office that they offer him the Lloyds Agency for Bulgaria. What to do after demobilisation had been sorted out for him? My father had become British Honorary Vice-Consul in Varna, Bulgaria, and to the Lloyds Agency added some old friends he had done business with before the war.

And so it was that my father came to settle in Varna.

My mother, Eva McDermott, was born in Eskdale Street in Dublin on 8 September 1903. Her father was Joe McDermott, a solicitors' clerk; her mother, Bella Turner, was the second of three sisters. The eldest, Eva, was to play an important part in my mother's life. For some incomprehensible reason, the Irish side of the family decided to call all the female children Eva or Eve.

Theirs was not a Dublin of slums nor the Dublin of Georgian squares and Anglo-Irish high society. The McDermotts were Protestants; they belonged to the Presbyterian Church and the children attended Sunday school. Joe McDermott ran for the Dublin Harriers and sailed in Kingstown harbour. He wanted nothing to do with Ireland for the Irish. Bella's work was to look after her children.

Bella's sister, Eva, was a staunch Republican. She did not believe that John Redmond, the leader of the Irish Party in the English Parliament, could ever achieve Home Rule and she wanted the

Republic of Ireland. She had married Jack Morris, a junior manager at Heaton's Coal Merchants of Dublin; he was a man full of humour and music, and was a fine amateur photographer. His political stance was 'what comes, comes'. By 1912, Eva and her brother George moved with their parents to the Quinsborough Road, Bray, not far from where Jack and Eva Morris lived.

The next two years were idyllic for George and Eva. Endless explorations of the Wicklow Mountains, visits to Powerscourt. The whole family was in the choir of the Presbyterian Church, and the children attended Sunday school. Eva loved the stories of the Bible, but even at a young age she became fascinated by church history. All of her life, Mother was to study comparative religion. Just as my father passed a love of poetry and horses on to me so my mother passed on a profound sense of a universal and metaphysical deity – actually, an almost child-like belief in the goodness and love of God.

By 1914, there was conflict in the McDermott and Morris families. Joe was preparing to go to war while Eva Morris was very outspoken in her Republican sympathies. 'What's the matter with you, Bella?' she would ask. 'Have you no tongue in your head? Tell him you won't have it. He's not to go over to fight.' My grandmother merely replied, 'He'll do what he thinks is best.'

The shot that killed the Archduke was heard from Tashkent to Dublin. From Berlin to Peking. From Auckland to Sydney, and from Gallipoli and the Dardanelles. In 1914 Joe McDermott went to war for England. Two years later, Joe, then a corporal in the Ordinance Corps stationed at Woolwich, became worried about Bella whose health was giving cause for concern, and brought the family over to married quarters in Eltham and, for the next two years, my mother continued her education in Woolwich.

Bella was fading fast; she died in 1917 just as Joe was posted to France. He buried his wife in Eltham cemetery and sent the children back to Dublin to live with Eva and Jack Morris.

After the war ended, one would have expected the family to have been reunited. But no: after a few months a letter came from Joe – he had found a new love and was emigrating to Australia. And that was that. My mother seems to have sustained this crushing double loss with fortitude. Or did she bury it all? Certainly she seldom mentioned her parents and only three photographs of them have survived.

The bond of love that was forged between young Eva and her Aunt Eva, however, was strong and endured to the end of Eva Morris's life.

For me to be born in Bulgaria necessitates the second of my parents to go there and my mother's journey to Varna was as full of colour and coincidence as my father's. I sometimes think of them being guided to their destiny. Or are we just shoved along to our end game willy-nilly?

My mother was a worker and it never dawned on her to take the world for granted. When she had lived in London, she had taken a part-time job with Kodak in Kingsway, working there on Saturday afternoons. Returning to Ireland, she found herself a job at Kodak in Dublin. She went to evening class to work for her Higher School Certificate which she accomplished by the time she was sixteen. Her diploma in business studies, shorthand typing and book-keeping took her another year. At seventeen, she looked round for a better job than Kodak and found it in the Land Registry Office which was looking for clerks. The office was housed in the Four Courts on the banks of the River Liffey, but she was not happy.

She had worked there for a year when she contracted an infection of the throat that would not be moved – gargling, painting with iodine, nothing would shift it. She was sent by her doctor to see an ENT specialist, Sir Horace Law, at the Adelaide Hospital. The hospital was founded and endowed by Queen Adelaide and kept up by Protestant subscription; it was the teaching hospital for Protestants. As soon as she stepped into the hospital, the first she had ever been into, her vocation became clear, and in 1922 she applied to become a probation nurse there.

While there wasn't too much overt friction between Protestants and Catholics in Dublin, there was a considerable division. Eva was entered and waiting to be enrolled in a year's time when the civil war flared up again. This was 1921 and the treaty was on its way to being ratified when the IRA occupied Jacobs factory in St Peter's Street. The fight was hard and a great many public casualties were brought into the Adelaide. There were not enough beds, so makeshift beds were erected in the corridors. There were not enough nurses, so the hospital authorities called in all their waiting probationers and gave them just six weeks' theoretical training before putting them on to the wards. Eva was on her way to being a nurse.

The IRA had occupied the Four Courts. They waited from Wednesday to Friday for the Army to fire the first shot. One evening, Eva was sitting in a probationer's cubicle at the end of the ward. There was a tremendous explosion outside and, looking out of her fifth-floor window, she could see right across the Liffey. The English Army's artillery was blasting the Four Courts. Dramatic explosions continued, and flashes and flames mingled with the setting sun and the sky was filled with burning or blackened papers being blown across the town on the light evening air. Eva realised that had she not been recruited early by the Adelaide, she would certainly not have a job: the papers that were flying through the evening sky came from the Land Registry Office, years of work escaping towards the Wicklow Mountains.

Eva won the silver medal on passing her nursing exams. She was in competition with all the nurses from the eleven teaching hospitals in Ireland. The Adelaide was delighted with her and she was, actually, delighted with herself. Off she went to the Rotunda to take her place for the midwifery course – the Rotunda was Dublin's famous midwifery and gynaecological hospital. While the Rotunda's matron was congratulating Eva on her success, she happened to look at Eva's papers.

'Nurse, you can't come in here yet, you're a year too young. You are not yet twenty-three and I can't have anyone here who is not twenty-three.'

'But I'm a trained nurse and have already been accepted,' replied my mother.

'I'm sorry, but those are the rules.'

Now, that sort of remark was like a red rag to a bull to my mother and she walked straight out of the Rotunda and sat down to write a letter to the Mothers' Hospital of the Salvation Army in Clapton and was in due course accepted.

She arrived in London and took a taxi to the hospital, in the East End of London. The driver didn't really know where it was and they were even more confused when they realised Clapton was full of Salvation Army buildings. Finally they saw a large redbrick building with 'Salvation Army' in brick relief above the large oak doors. This had to be it. The taxi stopped and out stepped Eva. She went boldly to the front door and rang the bell. A formidable woman in Salvation Army uniform answered it. This was obviously the right place and Eva asked to see the matron.

'Matron can't see you now. You've no appointment.'

'Yes, I have. I've come all the way from Dublin to see her. Of course I've got an appointment. I've come to see Colonel Castle. I'm entered for today. I repeat, she is expecting me.'

'Colonel Castle? Oh, you're for the Mothers' Hospital?'

'Of course I'm for the Mothers' Hospital. What did you think? I'm a nurse from Ireland.'

A smile of triumph broke across officialdom's face.

'This is a home for unmarried mothers. Keep your cab. We'll soon have you on your way to the Mothers' Hospital.'

It was a splendid teaching hospital and she was extremely happy there. So much so that she came back to have her first child there: my brother Francis was born within the sound of Bow Bells. When she had finished her training, she had two months to wait for the Central Midwifery Board exam. She was found a nursing job with Alfred and Kate Birks, to look after Alfred's father in a lovely house in Broadlands Road, Highgate. Here began a friendship that was to last all their lives. Kate Birks was like a mother to her, and their daughter, Catherine, became a special friend and my sister's godmother.

During the General Strike, Eva became very political. Demanding to know what was to be done, Mrs Birks replied, 'In situations like these, you remain extremely calm, get some tissue paper and re-line all the drawers!' It is not what Eva meant, but it's what she had to do.

In the spring of that year the young Irish doctor, Jack Stuart, whom she had met at the Mothers' Hospital, jilted her. She was used to being the instigator of such decisions, so this came as rather a shock; the only thing to be done was to get right away from it. So it was that she applied to the Royal College of Nursing for a job abroad.

The Secretary at the Royal College of Nursing said there were no jobs to be had abroad in January. But just as Eva was leaving the interview, the Secretary had a thought and asked her to hang on for a moment. She then telephoned someone, and holding her hand over the mouthpiece, she asked Eva if she would like to go to Bulgaria. Eva nodded her head vigorously in assent – Bulgaria was a long way from young Irish doctors.

The result of this telephone call was a preliminary interview with Dame Sarah Swift of the Red Cross. Dame Sarah had never been to Bulgaria but had been assured that the most important item of clothing to take was a pair of Wellington boots.

'Absolutely essential in that terrain,' she said. 'What's your size in gumboots?'

From this exchange, Eva assumed – correctly – that she had passed the first hurdle and was now to go on and be interviewed by the relevant committee, which consisted of a brigadier general, Dame Sarah Swift, Lady Muriel Paget and a working Red Cross lady who had been to Sofia. She told Eva: 'I can assure you that Dame Sarah is absolutely right: gumboots! Gumboots are essential in the interior.'

Eva asked her if she had been to Varna, where the British Red Cross mission was to be stationed and from where they would set up the welfare clinics. The Red Cross lady had not been there but said she'd heard it was not more than a fishing village. She added that a delightful young man at the legation had told her that most of the transport into the interior would be on mules. 'So you see, my dear, gumboots are absolutely essential.'

Between the two interviews, Eva went to the Chamber of Commerce. She bought a book which told her about all the consulate districts abroad. She read that the Bulgarians had a national theatre and opera in Sofia, which toured all the main towns, while Varna had its own theatre and opera companies. And that the Bulgarians had their first railway in 1895, built for them by the British: it ran from Sofia to Varna. She mentioned during her second interview that it was from the port of Varna that the Light Brigade had embarked for the Crimean War, that the port was an ancient one and had 75,000 inhabitants.

There was another contender for the post but she got the smallpox so Eva had the job and, almost simultaneously, an anti tetanus jab which reacted badly. She returned to Broadlands Road feeling unwell and was put to bed by Mrs Birks.

Eva was appointed head of the Red Cross mission which was not difficult since, so far, she seemed to be the sole member. She was given leave and took the opportunity to go home to Dublin.

Eva asked Jack what he knew about welfare centres. He advised that she should go and talk to the Little Sisters of the Poor and ask their advice. The Little Sisters of the Poor was a Catholic sisterhood, an order that fed a great many poor children in Dublin, and she was to profit from their advice in the years to come.

Back in London, she was joined at the mission by Hermione Whitehead at the last moment. At thirty-two, Hermione was older than Eva. She spoke fluent French and German, and Eva wondered what on earth she was doing going to Bulgaria. The answer was familiar: she too had been jilted. Hermione christened them Britain's blighted buds.

In Sofia there was a considerable reception to meet the British Red Cross mission. There were representatives from the Bulgarian Foreign Office, the Bulgarian Red Cross, and a Captain Kanutsen of the Danish Guards who was the Official Director for the International Red Cross of all refugees. There was even a representative from King Boris. And so the train set off for Varna and divine providence had played its part into putting my parents into the same country at the same time and as they were going to be in the same town there was every chance that they would meet.

2

EVA AND HERMIONE WHITEHEAD ARRIVED AT VARNA STA-
TION WHERE THEY WERE MET BY REPRESENTATIVES OF THE
BULGARIAN RED CROSS AND ESCORTED TO THE SMALL HOUSE
WHERE THEY WERE TO LIVE. They settled in and the next day
started work.

Varna may have had golden sands and a picturesque harbour but,
due to the massive influx of refugees from the Salonika campaigns
and the thousands of White Russians fleeing from the Revolution,
there was widespread disease. The town itself was healthy enough
but on the outskirts there was serious overcrowding, the sewage
system barely functioned, children playing in the dusty roads and
near the open drains looked pinched and hungry – most of them
had rickets. If Eva and Hermione had thought their job would be
virtually non-existent they were quickly disabused. They were driven
around the province and it became obvious that their work was going
to lie with the great flood of refugees.

They had been in Varna for a few days when Eva told Hermione
that she had to find a bank in order to deposit her money, part of
which she was carrying with her while the rest was unsecured in the
chest of drawers in their house. She had letters of authority to open
a bank account in the name of the British Red Cross with herself as
signatory but, because she wanted to know how the banking systems
worked in Bulgaria before she went to see the manager, she decided
to call on the British Consul.

The two women had been invited to their first ball, to be held at the Officers Club. It was held on the evening of the same afternoon when they called on the British Consul – Frank Baker. He answered Eva's question about banking but appeared more interested in the fact that they were going to the military ball that evening. He asked if they would join him and a friend. Arrangements were made for Eva and Hermione to be picked up in a *droshki*, a two-horse sleigh. How more romantic can it have been? It was quite obvious that Frank Baker had fallen head over heels with Eva McDermott at first sight. She, too, had found him extremely attractive.

The following week was a busy one for the British Red Cross mission as they prepared for their first clinic. A local doctor had said that he could get them a nursery in the district they wanted. When they arrived they were surprised to see that it was a long, low, glass building – a nursery for young grapes. But choice was not on the agenda so they moved in with their crates of equipment and began to prepare. The drawback was that the British Consul was so interested in their work that he was there morning, noon and night, lounging about on the crates and drinking tea from the samovar.

At this time, Eva was twenty-four and Frank was forty-four, but the age difference didn't seem to matter. As much as she wanted to see him, Eva was not able to get on with her work when he was around, and they struck a bargain. She and Hermione would come to his house on a Sunday morning, have a bath in a civilised bathroom, have lunch and spend the day with him. In return, he was not to call on them during the week, disrupting their work. It wasn't long before the two women realised that there were perfectly good bathrooms at the hospital which could be used. Hermione opted for the facilities at the hospital but, unsurprisingly, Eva decided to stick to the Sunday arrangement.

The courtship of Eva McDermott and Frank Baker progressed apace. In a letter to her Aunt Eva dated 6 March 1927 she wrote:

We are very busy and get up very early and work till sunset. After that we have accounts and book-keeping. But the British Consul, Mr Baker, is awfully good to us. When we are so tired that we cannot drag one foot after the other, he hauls us out in his car, and rushes us out along the coast for a couple of miles and then we go back to his house for supper. He has a lovely house with beautiful Persian carpets, rugs, books and open fireplaces ... a very English house. He has done it all himself as he is not married. He has trained his maids etc. in English ways. You can even get an English breakfast there. Bacon, eggs and tea.

Frank Baker's office was in the market district of Varna and after Eva had done her shopping she would often slip into his office, taking with her a cup of Turkish coffee. One morning, it was different: she took in two cups of coffee and sought out the British Consul. Finding him in the warehouse, they sat side-by-side on a bale of cotton yarn and proposed. She always swore that she could not remember who had proposed to whom. But whichever way round it was, they accepted each other.

A second letter to her Aunt Eva, dated 21 April 1927, contained important news for the family.

I don't know what to say to you about this. I have not tried to tell you about it before because I was not sure of myself. I have always been sure of him since we came. I have known one other real love. I know that he loves me dearly, quite madly enough even to satisfy Jack Morris. We became engaged last Sunday evening ... Frank has given me a very beautiful little gold watch with a 'second hand' for taking pulses.

I am utterly and entirely and deliriously happy with no misgivings at all. I am sorry he is not younger only because we shall have less time together. That is the only reason. The whole English colony in Sofia is charmed about it. I will have my ring in a couple of months, because I feel I must see home first before I take it.

A few days later, Frank wrote formally to Jack Morris to ask for Eva's hand in marriage.

Eva has told me that she has written to you and told you that I want to marry her. I can quite understand that this news will have caused you very great anxiety, as you do not know me – and Eva has known me a very short time. I understand also how very dear she is to you and Mrs Morris as she has told me of your constant care and love and how deeply she loves you.

I very much regret that I cannot go to you in person and ask you for her – it would be much easier than writing. In the first place, and the most important, I do ask you to believe that I love Eva very dearly. I am utterly devoted to her and I shall consider it the greatest happiness to be able to care for her always. I shall also very greatly appreciate the honour of being accepted into her family.

You will naturally want to know about me. I have been for the last six years in business here in Varna, and am also our Consul here, and the Lloyds Agent. My position is well established and I think I shall be able to give Eva a home where she will be happy. I have given her a ring and hope that you will not be angry that we have given our promises before she has been able to talk with you. I shall be very, very happy to have your consent as soon as possible. I do not know what else you would wish to know about me, but we shall be writing again, and I will write to you unreservedly about everything.

Frank arrived in Dublin in the middle of June. The Customs man in Kingstown looked with interest at the silk topper nestling in its box. 'Are you going to a funeral?'

'No, I'm going to my wedding.'

'Ah! God help us!'

Frank Baker and Eva McDermott were married on 2 July 1927. They went to Glendalough for their honeymoon and then round the north of England, visiting relatives. They returned to Bulgaria to settle down to married life – he to his business and she to the Red Cross. Presumably because of his age, they decided to start a family straight away, but things started badly when, in 1928, there was a miscarriage.

In the spring of that year, Frank and Eva were sitting having supper when suddenly there was a dreadful noise. They rushed outside and stood in the middle of the rose garden. Papa told Mummy to look at the lamps in the house – they were swinging backwards and forwards. They were close to a very big earthquake which did considerable damage, making many people homeless.

The Bulgarian Government, in conjunction with the Plovdiv Earthquake Organisation, appointed Eva Baker. She was gazetted as a lieutenant in the Bulgarian Army. When asked what rank a nursing sister would hold in the British Army, she said the first thing which came into her head. 'Nursing sisters in the Queen Alexandra's Royal Nursing Corps always hold the rank of lieutenant,' and was duly commissioned. She was to spend the next three months up in the mountains. She had a sergeant and fourteen men under her command.

The tremors continued for about two months. Thankfully, the cold weather kept away any threat of a subsequent epidemic but there were more than enough patients to keep everyone very busy. Another twenty men were placed under her command. One advantage came out of this – she had been struggling with the language but now she began to speak it well but slowly.

Eva was twenty-five years old when King Boris of Bulgaria acknowledged her work with the Red Cross, first with the refugees and then with the Earthquake Relief organisation, by decorating her with the Royal Humanitarian Order of Bulgaria. It was gazetted in *The Times* in October 1928 with King George V's appended 'Permission to wear'.

My brother Francis was born in January 1929 and my mother returned to the Mothers' Hospital in Clapton to have the baby.

I was born on 1 April 1931.

Extraordinarily, April that year was extremely cold and there was snow on the ground. Father and little Frank both had whooping cough, lying in adjoining rooms. The Russian doctor decided that the house was much too cold and got the manservant, Sergi Ogolkoff, to pile wood on the stove. So there you have the picture. My mother upstairs, her room immediately over the fire, Father in one room, whooping away, and Frank in another, also whooping away. The birth was imminent. Then the chimney caught fire. The Fire Brigade was called, and Ogolkoff tried to put out the fire with the garden hose. When smoke gushed up into my mother's bedroom, Ogolkoff panicked, thinking the fire had spread, and sprayed water up through the window which the doctor had flung open to release the smoke. All the sterile blankets laid ready for the birth were soaked. Using blankets from the whooping cough rooms was out of the question so my mother's winter coat was brought up from the hall and thrown over her and a screen put round her bed. In the meantime, the firemen had arrived with their hoses and pounded in through the window.

In the middle of all this, I arrived and was handed to my mother who had not felt a thing so distracted was she with the fire. She used to say that she could not recommend it as a sure-fire way to painless childbirth.

My parents had five children. My elder brother was, of course, called Francis; he is *now* known as Frank senior and his son is Frank junior – quite tedious, really. I came next and after me Eve (of course), Patrick and Terence.

When I was just eighteen months old, Mother took brother Frank on three months' leave to Dublin to see the Irish family and then on to Scotland to stay with friends, leaving me with my father. Can three months at so tender an age make such strong bonds between a parent and child? They certainly did between my father and me. We seemed to have the same sense of humour and became each other's folk. It was summer and Papa removed himself and second son to a villa called Poplars which he had bought soon after his marriage. The villa was tiny, rather like a Swiss chalet made of hand-carved wood and glass. It commanded the most spectacular view of the bay. It was built on a hill, with terraces running down to the main road; on the other side of the road were the golden sands of the Black Sea.

It was in these idyllic surroundings I spent three months with my father and a nursemaid. The villa was only six miles from Varna so it took Papa about twenty minutes to get to his office. He returned each evening to spend time with me. I can remember little but I do recall holding his hand and standing in front of the marigolds and delphiniums. I think he must have filled the house with roses that summer – no matter where I have lived, I have grown roses.

Later on, he instilled in me a love of poetry and horses. Recently I saw an epitaph in a Suffolk church: 'He was a good man. He loved his children and his horses.' Add 'poetry' and I would be enchanted if anyone would carve that on my gravestone.

Whatever happened in those three months, it has informed much of my life and rarely a day goes past when I don't think about my father. My mother was, undoubtedly, the greatest influence in my life. When times were bad, I was cast in the role of the oldest daughter and family housekeeper – and times did become bad. But there was a Bulgarian childhood to be lived through before the bad times happened.

Nothing in that Bulgarian childhood could possibly have prepared me for life in England. The summers were hot and the swimming was good; I learned to swim when I was very young and my father taught me to ride when I was three.

On one of the terraces leading down from the villa grew an old fig tree. Frank and I would lie in the shade under its large leaves waiting for a ripe fig to drop into our mouths. Not a single one ever did. There were eating grapes, too, all at a good height for children to pick on their way down to the beach. There was a Turkish fountain on which floated a small blue boat and in this we sailed the seven seas. Pirates, renegade men-of-war, steel-hulled German battleships, we fought them all and won. If we stood on the fountain wall we could pick cherries from the overhanging branches. One other vivid early memory I have of myself is lying near an ants' nest, getting the ants to walk into a shallow cup, pouring water on them and drinking them. This peculiar pastime doesn't seem to have done me any harm. I think I was learning to cook.

Papa's potting shed – surely one of the most English of all buildings – was under the house. It was a shed redolent of smells and memories – mud floor, gunshot, raffia and wine casks. When brother Frank lived in Montreal he recreated a shed where he made his cartridges, stored wine, and bundles of raffia hung from the beams. When I went to visit him, the first thing he did was to take me into the shed. 'It smells exactly like it, doesn't it?' I knew at once what he was talking about.

I was four when my sister Eve was born in the house in Varna. Papa, Frank and I had been sent off to the villa for the duration but the day came when we were driven back to Varna to see our sister. Bye Shteru, our gardener, odd job man and friend to children, came with us.

It all seemed odd and unfamiliar. My father's study had been turned into a bedroom. The sofa, from behind which I would perform puppet plays, had been shunted into the dining-room to make room for the bed and here, lying beside my mother, was this tiny creature with blue eyes. It was even more surprising when Bye Shteru took a silver coin from his pocket, spat on it and put it beside the baby's head. For good luck, Papa told us.

While the fire at my birth had been an accident, Mother decided that if she wrote a blow-by-blow account of Eve's birth, it might take her mind off the business in hand and make a good article for the *Trubie King* magazine. The article was published but the birth was not painless.

The Bulgarian diminutive for George is Jora and that's what I was called, both at home and at school. School for me was the kindergarten of the German School in Varna. Frank was in the senior school. I think he quite enjoyed it; he liked discipline and he liked to learn. I was and still am a little dyslexic. In those days you were considered backward or stupid if you were dyslexic, and if you had a teacher like Fräulein Bertha, you were automatically dubbed 'insolent'.

'At Assembly, you will sing *Deutschland, Deutschland Über Alles* with the rest of the class.'

'I can't sing so I won't.'

'You will hold out your hand.' Two sharp smacks of the cane. 'You will sing.'

'I can't sing.'

'You will stand in the corner for the rest of this morning.' Better than looking at your silly face, I thought. She then talked about the arrogance of the English and I looked at the wall. There has always been an independent streak in me that, unfortunately, hasn't always stood me in good stead.

The winters were cold, the snow plentiful. Christmas was joyous, except on the occasion when a girl was attacked by a dog outside the house on Christmas Eve. I remember my father rushing out of the house with his gun. There was a shot, then silence. Papa brought in a very frightened girl of about fourteen. While we waited for the doctor, my mother cleaned and sterilised the wound.

'What happened to the wolf, Papa?' I asked.

'It was a dog, Jora. Just a dog.'

Some pedantic people called this tendency to exaggeration lying. I always enjoyed colouring a story and acting it out. When I was at prep school in Yorkshire I had an English teacher who understood the problem exactly and explained it to the class.

'It is not that Baker is lying but that he is given to exaggeration. If he tells you that he has just seen a giant you must interpret it to mean that he has just seen a tall man. Lying can harm or hurt; exaggeration should be enjoyed for what it is.'

God bless you, Miss G. Butler. I have fond memories of the small, squat woman in blue skirt and cardigan, with nicotine-stained fingers and nicotine-stained grey hair.

'Baker, write me a poem about a railway viaduct.'

'Baker, write me a poem about a bridge.'

Yes, fond memories of someone who did not think me a fool.

Although my father had a great love of the theatre and a secret yearning to act, passing this gene to me would not necessarily have fed my desire to be an actor. However, there is no doubt that my mother had an irrepressible desire to be centre stage and she, passing that gene to me (it is typically the case that a person receives a gene from each parent), made it impossible for me to escape. We are doomed from birth.

This is the only explanation I can give for knowing from my earliest childhood that I had to be an actor. The nice thing is that I know exactly who to blame.

And so it seemed quite natural that, at the age of six, when the National Theatre of Bulgaria opened a drama school in Varna, I should want to join. Having worn my parents down, they finally let me have the fifty leva, about five shillings, to pay my subscription fee. I took myself off to enrol. The school was in a room up a small flight of stairs. I sat on the step outside the door and listened to the talking inside. Then screwing up my courage, I went in. I told them I wanted to be an actor. They were very kind to me, but were firm about my being too young. I offered them my money but they wouldn't take it. I went home and, according to family legend, explained to my parents that the school was for 'grown-ups with notebooks and pencils'.

I didn't have much time to be disappointed because a number of exciting visitors came to stay that year. First of all, Negley Farson VC stayed with us for a few days. We were allowed to sit at the top of the stairs in our pyjamas to listen to the story of how he won his medal. I didn't understand much of what was being said, but it was very thrilling to be allowed to stay up and listen to the grown-ups. Much later I got to know his son, Dan Farson, at the Bunch of Grapes pub on the Isle of Dogs. Dan was very unlike his father. He had a sharp tongue and wicked sense of humour. We saw each other occasionally over the years, the last time being at the Groucho Club with Jeffrey Bernard. Jeffrey had praised my performance in *Little Lord Fauntleroy* in his column. As soon as they saw me, they both went into extravagant mode, heaping me with compliments. It was all very flattering until Dan said, 'You're such a splendid actor and so lovely, why haven't you got further – Hollywood and such?'

'Have another glass of champagne, Dan,' I replied.

In the spring Paddy Leigh Fermor arrived on his bicycle (he was cycling around the Balkans) and stayed for some days. Now, here was a hero. He was brave and gallant and blond and brown, what a role model for us boys. He spent hours talking to us, and used to take us swimming. He and my mother kept up a correspondence until her death and whenever he was in London he would call on her.

A German destroyer, the *Deutschland*, called into Varna harbour for a visit. Some of the German Senior School visited the ship and my brother was in the party. I was incensed that Frank should go round the ship and I was not allowed to and threw the most dreadful tantrum. I had the most appalling temper, aimed always against myself. I would hurl myself to the floor in a fury and, taking my head in my hands, I would bang it against the floor or the walls. I have never quite understood why I had to take myself by the ears when the head could have managed quite well on its own.

Frank, who enjoyed bullying me, would wind me up into a state of homicidal frustration, then stand and watch triumphantly as I damaged myself. 'I'll be in to separate you when the blood flows under the door,' my poor mother would say. She put up with a great deal from us. The temper has followed me through a good part of my life.

In order to appease me, I was taken to see the captain of a British merchant ship which had also just come into harbour. I was allowed to go up to the crow's nest and look down on to the deck of the *Deutschland*. A sailor followed me up the ladder and tried to help. '*Sam, sam*,' I shouted at him. Being interpreted, 'I'll do it my way.' Why is it that these appalling traits of nature form so early in one's existence? It would have taught me a lesson if I had fallen off the ladder. I have always wanted to fight life my way and, in consequence, have made a pretty appalling fist of it. Anyway, Frank didn't see me waving from on high so the pleasure wasn't entirely complete.

The ship was out of Liverpool and I remember admiring the mahogany furniture of the captain's cabin and the neatness of the bunk. A sailor brought tea and rock cakes and something for me to drink. I transfixed when the captain brought out a tin from which he took a compact brown square smelling strongly of tobacco. He held it in the palm of his left hand. He opened a pearl-handled knife and cut two slivers of tobacco, which he popped in his mouth and began to chew. The palm of his left hand was entirely stained and calloused.

The captain came to dinner that evening and we boys were allowed to stay up while they had drinks. On hearing that I wanted to be an actor he gave a shout of glee, and stood on his head. From that position he recited 'You are old, Father William, the young man said . . .' You can imagine my delight, and I went to bed dreaming of the day I would be able to be an actor and recite poetry whilst standing on my head. Whenever I hear people say, 'He could play the part standing on his head', it always reminds me of that delightful evening.

I had no idea what actors did. The closest I had come to acting was watching some reels of Mickey and Minnie, which you popped into a pistol and moved the frame by pulling the trigger. My first experience of real acting was an outdoor, evening showing of the film *Blossom Time* with Richard Tauber and Jane Baxter. It was 1938 and I was seven. We set off from the villa in the open Fiat; it was a wonderful evening, the sky was clear and full of stars. Before the show, we were treated to ice creams in the botanical gardens. The whole town seemed to be there. I remember Tauber's beautiful voice and I fell madly in love with the leading lady. Only twelve years later, I was working with Jane Baxter at the Bedford Theatre in Camden Town.

I was beginning to build up a picture of England. The fact that the film was set in Austria didn't seem to matter very much. Father and Mother told us a little about the England and Ireland where they had grown up, but our horizons were short at that time and I was happier playing in the Roman catacombs on the way back from school than trying to read *Hansel and Gretel* – books had to be read to me because I couldn't read a word of English, German or Bulgarian. In the summer of 1937 Aunt Ethel came to Varna for three months. She brought with her two books, which were to become favourites, *Silver Snaffles* and *The Wednesday Pony*. From these books I learned about an English village and a place called Exmoor. I learned that beautiful, blonde English girls rode across the moors and saw wonderful stags guarding their herds. I also learned that if you stood in the corner of the stall of the butcher's pony and fed him carrots, he would lead you through to a land where ponies talked and taught you how to ride properly.

My parents found a German governess called Greta to teach us. She was harsh, spoke loudly, and would literally bang my nose into the book, endlessly repeating words, hoping, no doubt, that some would go in through the skull. We didn't like her but much preferred Leonid, a young student who had taken a summer job with us, teaching us to swim and box. Apparently, Mother thought that we might need to know how to box when we got back to England. Little did she know how right she was.

Leonid's brother, Stefan, was 'walking out' with Greta. He was a communist and Leonid told us he was a suspicious character who had bad friends who wanted to kill King Boris. One summer evening, Stefan came up to the villa and, finding my father on the terrace, started cursing and swearing and shouting about the fate of bourgeois capitalists. He shouted that the communists would take power in Bulgaria and then the purges would start. King Boris would be the first to go and then it would continue until we were all dead.

Frank and I were listening, open-mouthed, from a distance. I was terrified, I thought Stefan was going to kill my father and then murder the rest of us. Finally Papa cooled him down and sent him on his way. Words like Buchenwald and Nuremberg came to us across the ether. We heard there was going to be a war. We picked up talk about how much the Germans hated the Jews. Greta even told us about things called concentration camps.

I would sit in the kitchen and watch Kounka, the cook, plucking game my father had shot, roasting meat and baking cakes. Soon she let me make the stuffing for the peppers or wind the forcemeat through the grinder into the sausage skins. Papa always made the Christmas pudding and the marmalade and was pleased that I wanted to help. I felt at home in the kitchen and, unknowingly, I was learning to cook – but I still wasn't learning to read. I found it very difficult even to focus on the letters. I was sent for an eye test and it was found that one eye was stronger than the other. I was given glasses – but they didn't improve my reading either.

Stefan came up to the villa to see my father. Leonid took us to the orchard and tried to distract us but we could still hear him shouting about British imperialism versus communism. When he left, he took Greta with him. This made things very difficult for Mother because sister Eve was two and brother Patrick just one year old; there is only eleven months between them.

We heard a great deal of talk about the coming of the war. As young as we were, we knew it was something to be feared. Frank and I were taken away from the German School and sent to a Bulgarian school. This was a move that pleased me because I was seated next to an enchanting blonde-haired girl who wore a blue pleated skirt and white blouse. I would put my right hand as near to the hem of her pleated skirt as I decently could and sit in contentment, not listening to a word that was being said. I am still very susceptible to blue pleated skirts and white blouses. There was one teacher there who I greatly respected. He tried hard with me and gave me extra lessons but much as I wanted to please him I still couldn't see the letters.

We were taken to a musical concert at the National Theatre and this was the first live theatre I had seen. I was bowled over. At the end of the show, I sat staring at the red and gold curtain and had to be prised out of my seat.

At the end of 1937 I contracted double pneumonia which, at that time, was often terminal. Without penicillin or other antibiotics, it was just a question of constant nursing. My mother and Nurse Condova took it in turns to nurse me day and night.

Again my heart was deeply affected and I fell in love with Condy. Crisis point came one morning in January when, outside, it was snowing and there was a bitter wind blowing in from the sea. I turned purple and could not breathe. My mother and Condy wrapped me in a blanket, opened the French windows that led to the balcony and stuck my head into the wind. I was forced to take a deep breath and I lived. Many thanks to them both.

When my health was fully restored, Father took us with him on a business trip through Bulgaria. Frank was then nine and I was seven. It was a wonderful journey in the open-topped Fiat. We went through small villages set on the side of the Danube; the houses were built of mud and painted in pastel colours. The family would live above the cattle in stalls below. Some villages had mosques with tall minarets and we occasionally heard the muezzin call the faithful to prayer.

We went to Sistov, to Pleven and to Plovdiv, and it was this last town that really captured my imagination. It was a market town with a river running through it. Bullocks, guided by small boys sitting on their backs, towed the barges. The ruins of a medieval fortress guarding the approaches from the plains of Asenovgrad brought to life the battles and the invaders and the history we were being taught about in school which in no way featured Great Britain in its curriculum.

We stayed in a hotel in the square, and ate at a table on the pavement outside – which we thought was a very swell thing to do. Papa entranced us by telling us about how meatballs were cooked in this part of the world: having minced and seasoned the meat, the chef would roll it into balls, then, sifting flour on to his naked and perspiring belly, he would roll the balls down his stomach and into the frying pan. We did not believe him and told him so. When the waiter came for our order, Papa pretended he had forgotten the name of the meatballs and indicated his order by rolling his hand down his stomach. 'Mr Baker, this is a respectable hotel!' came the sharp answer. I think I had stuffed peppers.

While we were away we also had a picnic with my old nurse Condy and her family. There were a few ladies of varying ages and I suddenly realised how much my father loved women. I watched him being attentive, solicitous, flirtatious, with a wonderful twinkle; and I watched them enjoying his obvious understanding and enjoyment of their company. It was the best part of the picnic for me. I had always thought women were quite wonderful and now I knew it.

The war was getting closer. Klaus, one of Frank's best friends, was under strict instructions not to speak to or acknowledge us in the street – he was German. The great excitement was the arrival of the 3rd Mediterranean Cruiser Squadron, complete with submarine, which sailed in for a four-day visit. There were parties at the King's Summer Palace, on board ship and at our villa. I remember my father rolling out all his wonderful Persian rugs on to the terraces; long tables ran the length of the top terrace and lights hung in the trees gave the scene a feeling of Oriental excitement.

The Munich Crisis was on top of us. I couldn't really understand what was happening although Mother tried to explain. She was quite sure there was going to be a war. Apparently a Mr Chamberlain had achieved nothing, never mind about 'Peace In Our Time'. She and Papa would discuss the pros and cons of leaving then or staying until the last possible minute. I told her I didn't want to go anywhere, particularly not back to England since this Mr Chamberlain obviously didn't know what he was doing.

There was considerable diplomatic excitement when HMS *Delhi* came into harbour. This was definitely a British mission to King Boris. The likelihood of war was now being openly discussed at school. We heard that the communists were going to throw out King Boris and join forces with the Germans. There were anti-Jewish slogans appearing everywhere. The British were not popular. This was all murmured at classroom level but obviously had roots in the national psyche.

The aristocratic family of the Stancioffs had become friends of my father when he first arrived in Varna. Old General Stancioff had been Bulgarian Ambassador to St Petersburg, Paris and to the Court of St James. His son, Ivan, had married a beautiful American heiress, Marion Mitchell. They took my mother to their hearts and she and Marion were to be friends for life.

There was no summer journey in 1939 with Papa. Instead, I made a nuisance of myself by dressing up and stamping about in high heels as my poor mother tried to pack up the villa for our return to the town house six miles away. Everything seemed to be a game and all of it out of control.

On 3 September 1939 I was standing with Frank and Mother on the steps of the villa. We saw Papa drive the Fiat past the gates. Mother said she couldn't understand what he was doing back in the middle of the day. He drove the car to the garage and came down to the terrace. 'The Bosche have gone into Poland,' was what he said.

I remember my mother's face, the tears were running down her cheeks. 'Well, that's it, my darling,' she said.

'Just let them come! Just let them come!' I cried, fiercely. 'We'll shoot at them with Papa's guns.'

My father put his arm round my shoulder. 'Why don't you both go and have a swim. I want to talk to Mummy.'

We went and sat under the fig tree. Frank tried to explain to me what was happening in the world and what might happen in ours. We would go back to England and we would go to school there. Papa would join us as soon as he could and we would all live in Yorkshire.

Yorkshire? That meant nothing to me at all.

3

WE STAYED IN VARNA UNTIL THE BEGINNING OF MAY 1940 WHEN WE TRAVELLED TO SOFIA. The next day we were to travel by the Simplon Express to Paris and from there to London. The party consisted of Mother and her five children – baby Terence was just one year old. We were looked after by an eighteen-year-old nanny, Irinka. We had personal luggage only, all the rest was to come by sea.

I had seen the station at Varna and the goods trains down near the harbour, but the station at Sofia was magnificent, awe-inspiring. Noise, bustle, steam and hundreds of people who had come to say their farewells to Mother: she was very much admired for all the work she had done with the Red Cross. Our carriage was bursting with flowers and chocolates.

There was little time to take anything in. My memory is of a scrum relentlessly moving forward but in the middle of the movement are two clear pictures. When Frank and I were much younger, Papa had taught us a silly game of trying to catch the thumb on your left hand with your right hand. You present your thumb and as the right hand makes to grasp it, you slip it down below your fingers and show it again as the right hand passes over it. At breakfast in Varna one morning, we were playing this game when Mother appeared. She took it in at a glance, copied us – and caught her thumb. 'My God, she's caught it!' said Papa.

Now Papa looked at her and caught his thumb. He smiled. It must have meant something special in their personal language of love. She was laughing and the tears were streaming down her cheeks. His eyes were twinkling.

He called me over to the carriage window. 'Jora, remember: always take a woman by the waist and a bottle by the neck. That way you'll never go wrong.' There was still the teasing twinkle in his eyes.

The train pulled out of Sofia station. I stood at the window and waved goodbye to him. My mother took my place and waved and waved and waved, long after the platform was out of sight.

That was the last time I saw my father and my mother her husband.

The family prepared itself for the journey – it was to take five days to get to Paris. In the event it took much longer. At first, it was a wonderful adventure, especially walking along the corridors of the swaying train to get to the dining-room. It was quite inconceivable to me that someone could be cooking while the train rolled along at such speed. The conductor took me up to see the galley where they were cooking on coal-fired stoves.

Frank read his book. Irinka looked after Eve and Pat, and Mother fed and cared for baby Terence. Each evening, the bunks were made ready for the night. Whenever we reached a border, customs men came in and checked the passports. I was frightened when we came into a station: Italy had begun to mobilise and there were soldiers on all the platforms.

There was a problem in Milan because Irinka did not have a diplomatic visa and Italy had decreed that these were necessary for anyone travelling on via the Simplon Pass. We were told to get off the train and a large Italian representative of Cook's tours told us to follow him to the hotel. He picked up baby Terry and, putting him on his shoulder, set off across the square in front of the station. Mother ran after him, calling to us to keep up: she said he was as drunk as a lord.

I seem to remember that we were in the hotel for about three days. There was a great deal of '*La signora irlandese con cinque bambini*' floating around, and gushing smiles, but I think they gave Mother a hard time before allowing us to get on our way to Paris, through Turin and Lyon. The large Italian tourist guide, who was no longer drunk as a lord, took us to our train. He waited courteously until the train was leaving and, choosing his time carefully, put his hand in through the window and took all the money out of Mother's handbag.

This part of the journey was very different. We were travelling in an ordinary train which had no dining car – which didn't worry us very much because we had no money to pay for food. But neither were there any bunks, with lovely white sheets, in which to sleep the night away. We sat up on the hard benches in the very overcrowded carriage. We were in the process of becoming refugees. We were soon very hungry and very thirsty. This was not something that we had ever experienced in our lives before.

At Lyon we changed trains. This time, it was even more uncomfortable and we weren't all together. At least, Mother, Irinka, Pat and Terry had found seats in a carriage together; Eve and I sat on the floor of a sort of guard's van, and Frank was in a similar van further down the train. The train was full of French servicemen; we couldn't of course understand a word they said, but their tone was kind and their eyes smiled at us. This was very much the beginning of defeat for them and they must have known it.

I am unsure of exactly when we arrived in Paris but I have a letter from my father written to my mother dated 22 May 1940.

Eve dearest, Your two dear letters came by this morning's post – the one written on the train and the other from the hotel. They had been ten days on their way. I was afraid you would have a rotten time with the trains from Milan onwards, especially in Italy. Damn them, I'll never eat an ice cream off the street again . . .

So, we must have been in Paris around 12 May, staying in the Hôtel Cambri. The hotel was deserted except for the manager, his wife and the chef. Everyone else had gone, running from the advance of the German army. The manager had kept the hotel open since he didn't want to let us down, Papa having booked so well in advance. We had food, we had baths and I remember going up and down in the lift with undiminished joy. It was one of those particularly French lifts, fronted with a black iron grating pulled to and fro by brass handles.

The next morning Frank and I accompanied our mother to the British Embassy where we stood in a long queue of people trying to get visas for England. I think the clerks were only too delighted that Mother only wanted to cash a promissory note in order to get some money for the onward journey. The Nazis were in Belgium. The siege of Dunkirk was about to begin.

In the afternoon we went shopping *en famille*. The streets were deserted, the shops showered us with gifts saying that we may as well have them before those that would soon be in their city most certainly would. That evening our mother did a remarkable, a seriously bizarre thing – she took her eldest sons to a nightclub, the Bal Tabarin. She wanted us to have a real feeling of Paris in case there was no Paris after the war. The waiters were delighted with the small party, my elegant mother and we in short pants. We were shown to the best table by the floor. I remember girls dancing and being astounded by the dexterity with which they kept the tassels turning on their nipples. I remember people laughing a great deal; I became very excited and then very sleepy.

The next day we left for London. The windows of the train were criss-crossed with tape, the carriages were crowded but at least we managed to get seats. We saw soldiers marching and convoys of trucks being driven along the tree-lined roads. There were horses and carts and bicycles, all loaded with the family's belongings. At Calais, Mother kept us very close to her so we should not get parted. Gangplanks everywhere, myriad languages and Terry crying.

I can't remember the Channel crossing but I can remember the customs house at Dover. Irinka was not to be allowed in because she was Bulgarian. I can vividly see the fat red face of the official in his light blue uniform. I can remember my mother's calm tone as she explained that Bulgaria was a neutral country and that the visa in Irinka's passport was issued in the British Consulate. For the first time, I felt frightened. Was my invincible Irish mother going to be beaten? I longed for my father. My father was all things to me. I was near to tears. I hated the man with the red face. If England was going to be like this, I didn't want to be here.

A little man with a pinched face came along, looked at the passport and waved us through. We were on our way to Euston – wherever or whatever that was – and so started the last leg of our long journey.

We were met at Euston by our Aunts Mamie and Ethel. They were accompanied by Olga and George McCloran, two friends who had been married from our house in Varna. It was wonderful to see Olga; she was tangible proof that the world we left ten days ago still existed. George was a captain in the Black Watch and stood well over six foot. He was an imposing figure in his kilt and stockings, sporran swinging and the dirk nestling against his calf. I had never seen anything quite like this before.

We must have made a strange crocodile as we wended our way across the Euston Road to the Endsleigh Court Hotel which was where the aunts had booked us in. I felt immediately at home here: the hotel had polished mahogany panelling and a semi-circular staircase leading out of the hall. It was the England of the merchant ship and the tobacco-chewing captain.

Mother asked the waitress if tables could be put together so that we could have breakfast as a family. The waitress refused, saying, 'No, you can't. Don't you know there's a war on!' Mother flew into one of her more spectacular Irish rages, which progressed into hysterical sobs. She had stayed strong for us on the difficult journey, but this stupid piece of bureaucracy was too much.

George McCloran immediately decided that the 'chaps' should go to the pub. When the publican said he thought we might be under age, George told him that we were Bulgarian midgets and were dying to try a half pint of his bitter. Frank and I spoke out bravely in Bulgarian and so we drank our first half pint of English bitter. When we got back to the hotel, we found all was calm and serene. The manageress had administered smelling salts to Mother who, she assured George, was a very brave lady. The tables were together and the family reunited.

That afternoon, Aunt Ethel took us to the London Zoo. The next day we set off on the last lap of our journey home. Home was to be Ireland. I remember very little of the eleven-hour journey to Holyhead; trains had become a way of life and I can't say that I was excited by the scenery we passed. I had seen stunning Alpine landscapes, then sadness and refugees on the hot summer roads as we travelled through France. The self-protecting mechanism of this nine-year-old refugee was to close down his mind, block out memories and pray to God that there would be an end.

We arrived at 42 St Helen's Road in Booterstown, Dublin on 3 June 1940. That was the day Hitler dropped 1,100 bombs on Paris and eleven days before France fell. We had made it by the skin of our teeth.

Five children, a mother and a nanny moved into a three-bedroomed, semi-detached house in a Dublin suburb, sharing it with two of the most enchanting people in the world – my Great Aunt Eva and my Great Uncle Jack who had been my mother's surrogate parents and now became ours. The rest of our belongings from Varna finally caught up with us.

We were introduced to a whole new world – one of peat fires and Bewley's barmbrack. Eva taught me how to cut crosses on the top and bottom of tomatoes, then pour boiling water on them so that they peeled easily. Jack taught us draughts and another board game called halma. We went to the Presbyterian Church and Frank and I began to understand that not only were we English/Bulgarians but bloody Proddies – a mixture not easily acceptable to the basic Roman Catholic mind.

I don't know how long we stayed at St Helen's Road but long enough to go to Elvery's and buy some tennis rackets and balls. I played tennis against the garage doors all day, at least all of the day that I wasn't swimming in the Blackrock swimming pool. Frank began reading avidly; he became almost reclusive, hungrily devouring 'Rockfist Rogan of the RAF' and piles of paperbacks. English books for boys had been in short supply in Bulgaria.

Poor Mother – her second son was over nine and still couldn't read. She would sit with me for hours, she was patience itself, but I really could not divide the letters. My concentration span was nil and the distractions formidable.

The house was obviously much too small for four grown-ups, five children and a terrier bitch called Gippy. Better accommodation had to be found. Uncle George had married the niece of a rich builder and property developer, Uncle Fraser, whose properties were mostly in Bray and he had a house in mind for us. No. 4 Putland Row was a tall Victorian house with a basement and an attic and large rooms in between. There were no beds, we slept on mattresses on the floor. Orange boxes were good bedside cupboards and were to become a feature in our lives.

Our mother set about finding a school for us and chose Avoca School on the outskirts of Dun Laoghaire where we were to be boarders. I think Mr Parker took me as an act of charity. There was a great deal of bullying, physical with Frank, verbal with me. Frank fought a number of fights for me as well as for himself. They liked to wind me up by calling me a Bulgarian spy. I was born in Bulgaria therefore I was Bulgarian. Mother came to my aid with 'If kittens are born in a biscuit tin they're not biscuits.' I felt much stronger armed with that. These were not happy times.

It began to dawn on Frank and me that money was not coming through regularly, that our mother was not the best of managers and that Uncle Fraser wanted his rent. We had to move again. Uncle George and Auntie Avie divided their house so that they had the ground floor and we had the top floor and the attic.

Avie had worked as a voice coach at the Abbey Theatre with Lennox Robinson and now gave singing and elocution lessons. She had a splendid soprano voice and was well known at all the music and poetry festivals. When she discovered I had a love of poetry, she decided to give me elocution lessons. She had to teach me the poems line by line as I couldn't read. I think my love of poetry and my desire not to shame my mother, coupled with the good teaching at Avoca School, began to make me aware that there were certain words I could read and slowly the battle was being won.

I learned 'The Fiddler of Dooney' by W.B. Yeats and was entered in the Under Tens section of the Father Matthew Feis (the best and biggest of the Irish music and poetry festivals). I spoke the poem three times and was declared the silver medallist. The judges asked me down to their table and, giving me a book, asked me to read a poem. While I calmed my beating heart, I came up with a brainwave – I had forgotten my glasses and was quite unable to see the page.

The judges conferred, then waived the reading and I went home with my medal.

There was a local fleapit in Bray and we went as often as we could. William Boyd (Hopalong Cassidy) was usually showing in twice weekly matinées. We saw Errol Flynn in *The Adventures of Robin Hood* and *Captain Blood*; Arthur Askey in *Calling All Stars* – I tried desperately to sing 'I'm A Little Prairie Flower', but to no avail. There were Fred Astaire movies and I fell madly in love with Ginger. I dreamed I was a swashbuckling hero, riding a white horse and rescuing damsels in distress.

But there wasn't much money for the cinema, and none for Abbey Theatre which Mother longed to visit. She was going through a very bad time as none of Papa's letters came through for five months, then she got seventeen in one day.

I had been to a poetry and music festival at Rathmines and I had heard the voices of the boy trebles, the tenors and basses, the sopranos and contraltos and I was mortified: I couldn't sing. It broke my heart. One evening shortly after this I slunk behind the laburnum bushes and talked to God.

'Even if You won't let me sing in tune all the time, would You at least let me sing in tune in church?'

There is a perversity about the Deity; he stuck to the bargain exactly. In church in tune. Everywhere else, deep distress to all around. It keeps me in the Christian fold, that and a strong belief in the goodness and love of God.

My father had left Bulgaria just after the legation quit Sofia and in March 1941 he took a job as president of the United Kingdom Commercial Corporation which was based in Cairo. He was in charge of the British merchant ships that went through to the Black Sea and on to the Russian ports. He wrote to my mother saying that he hoped his money would now get through to her regularly.

Mother was a political animal and she found Ireland stifling. She wanted to do something for the war effort. Every letter she wrote to my father contained some political observation or other. We were subjected to Mother's political opinions which naturally differed from those of anyone we spoke to or, rather, ours had a more colourful hue.

She had scant respect for governments. In her opinion, there wasn't a government in the world that knew what it was doing, particularly an English one. After all she was a good Irishwoman.

Frank and I were sent to a farm near Roscommon for a two-week holiday. Mother told us that we would be staying in an old farmhouse which had its own ponies and a lake where we could boat and swim. When she spoke to the farmer's wife, who sounded quite ordinary, she learned that there would be other children of our age staying there at the same time.

I was ten and Frank twelve and a half. Off we went. Mother put us on to the train in Bray, the rest was up to us. We crossed Dublin and took the bus. It was a four-hour journey. An old fellow driving a jaunting cart met us. Up went the luggage and away we went through Roscommon and out into the leafy lanes beyond. Nothing could have prepared us for what we saw as we rattled into the farmyard. There were the inevitable chickens and pigs, there were ducks, geese and cow shit in abundance, but the farmhouse looked positively derelict. The porch leaned one way and the door the other. There were gaps under the windows, there were boards missing in the passageway and on the stairs. Our room was damp and musty.

It didn't appear there was anyone else staying. Mrs Gregg told us to come down and have our tea as soon as we were unpacked. 'Ravenous you must be. Ravenous.' We were hungry, we were tired and now we were dispirited. We went down the stairs and found the kitchen quite easily. The smell of stale cabbage was so foul it knocked you over. We settled down to boiled bacon, boiled cabbage and cold potatoes. Then rhubarb and cream. I had milk to drink; Frank was going to have tea but the mouse droppings in the sugar bowl put him off. He was always very fastidious.

Mrs Gregg was of indeterminate age, veering towards elderly. The ginger-grey hair was covered by a knitted cloche hat. I am sure she always wore the same red blouse because the many stains seemed to be in the same place every day. She certainly wore the same grey tweed skirt, the thick brown knitted stockings and unlaced boots, the latter easy to leap out of and into the folded-down wellies. She now kept up a steady commentary on the delights of the place, and suggested we should go for a walk round the grounds. Frank opted to go to our room and see the delights the next morning. He flung himself on his bed and read 'Rockfist Rogan'.

I sat for a while and then went for a walk. I went downstairs very quietly, but opening the front door was a formidable achievement and a noisy one. Even when I was outside, the place was terrifying. I was glad to get back to our room.

That night we were woken by the most appalling howling. Frank said it must be a fox, but we had heard wolves and this was much worse than that.

There were ponies of sorts. We rode down to the lake where there was a boat with most of its planks missing. Mike, the odd job man, said, 'She shouldn't advertise like that, it's daylight robbery.' That evening we had tea, cabbage, bacon and cold potatoes, rhubarb and cream.

Again in the night we heard the howling. It was terrifying. The next morning we rode down to see Mike. He looked surprised to see us and asked if we would like to have tea at his cottage. 'Yes, please.'

We put the ponies away and walked round the farmyard. We came across a loose-box with a half-door and grating. We looked in. A man with a dog collar round his neck was pacing across the stable; the collar was attached to a chain which was linked to a wire stretched across the stable. We fled to our room. This was where the howling was coming from.

Frank decided to stay in his room but I went to Mike's cottage and had a great time. There were young people and old, and everyone was full of laughter. But I couldn't get the man in the collar out of my mind. When I got in, Frank was waiting up for me. 'I've spoken to Mummy, and we're going home tomorrow.' There was a lot of banging from the kitchen.

In June 1941 Hitler mounted a massive attack on the Soviet Union stretching 2,000 miles from the Arctic region to the Black Sea, and on 6 July Mother wrote my father one of her more eccentric letters.

I can get Frank to St Peter's and Jora, too, at reduced fees. I think I'll take them over and send them as day boys but as soon as they come back from the farm I'll send them up for tutoring,

English and so forth until they can go to York. It was lovely for them at Avoca and absolutely necessary for me to have them off my mind, but now I am happier and very rested in fact and so relieved by Hitler's Russian adventure.

She was delighted that Hitler had invaded Russia because she knew there was no hope of success. 'He's safe there for another ten years,' she wrote and, 'oh, the joy of seeing Hitler going deeper into the mire.'

We children had a wonderful summer. The weather was good and we spent most of the day on the beach. I was enrolled at the Bray Cove Swimming Club and entered myself for the Round the Head race, a distance of three and a half miles. As I was only ten years old, I was given a handicap and an accompanying boat. It was tough but I finished the swim and was by no means last. While I was drying off in my cubicle I was asked to go to the club house. Here I was given three cheers and invited to play water polo later in the evening. A day to remember!

Under Avie's tuition I was learning more poetry. We recited Herrick and Thomas Moore. And, more importantly, I was at last beginning to read.

Things were not good between Avie and our mother. They were constantly sniping at each other – as they were to do all their lives. It was very difficult for two such strong women to share a house and the childless Avie found five children difficult to cope with. It all came to a head one lunchtime when, returning from the cove, I threw my bike against the fence and damaged a rose. Avie rightly gave me a ticking off, making sure that every word she said would annoy my mother, standing at the open door, beyond endurance. She then stomped back into the house. Mother flew into a rage, producing one of her angular fits (as I had come to call them). She took me by the ear to drag me into the house. When I resisted and pulled away, she slammed the door and the Yale lock hit me on the eyebrow above the eye. For a second she was concerned for my eye but, seeing it was unharmed and the blood was gushing from above, she again took me by the ear and marched me down to the chemist.

'He'll need a stitch in that. Send him back when you've done with him.'

Mother was now anxious to get to England and she was relieved when a letter arrived from St Peter's, York saying they would take Frank and that the preparatory school, St Olave's, would take me. Irinka, the Bulgarian nanny, was found a place with a family in Galway. Frank went to stay in London with Mother's good friends from Highgate, Mr and Mrs Birks, and the rest of us packed our bags and went off to York.

4

I CAN'T REMEMBER IF MOTHER HAD ALREADY BOOKED DIGS OR IF SHE HAD TO FIND THEM WHEN WE ARRIVED IN YORK. As always, she was lucky. She had a way with her that made people love her and while she needed them she used them. Mrs Rawlings took us in at her house, Southlands, in Russell Street: my mother, Eve and Patrick slept in one big bed, Terry was in a cot and I slept on a put-you-up.

My mother was desperate for money and equally desperate to find a job, but it had to be a job to which she could feel that she was making a significant contribution. It was out of the question that she should get a nursing job which would pay for us to have a small house, allowing us to have a normal family life and attend the local school. In retrospect, I'm glad she did what she did. It was a mad world but worth it.

She borrowed money from the Birks to buy Frank's uniform for St Peter's, and she pawned her jewellery to pay Mrs Rawlings and buy my uniform. She borrowed money from Jack and Eva in Dublin to buy uniforms for Eve and Patrick who were going to a boys' prep school, Red House at Marston Moor, a few miles out of York. Eve was six years old (and the only girl among thirty-six boys) and Patrick was five years and two months old when they went to boarding school.

Mother was on the march to achieve the goal she believed she was destined for. On 11 January 1942 she wrote to my father from York.

It is like timing in boxing – or rhythm in life – you can be as clever and as strong and as courageous and good as you like but if your timing is wrong you are nothing. I timed my flight from Bulgaria and I timed my re-entry into England and since last May I have timed other things. But once my 'intuition' tells me that the rhythm of outside life coincides with mine it should result in some action which should be timed for a certain moment. Then, I'm afraid I'm utterly unscrupulous who gets in my way or what happens because as most of my actions are connected with leaving this world a little better – kinder and more courageous – the ends justify some means. Not all means as Hitler thinks. But some means as I think.

So we were being parcelled up and put away to give her greater freedom to operate.

Frank travelled up from London and joined us at Southlands; an extra mattress was put in my room for him.

I don't think there was ever a period in my life when I was more unhappy than my time at St Olave's. I used to see Frank occasionally, crossing the quad or playing rugger. We didn't speak much.

My reading was coming along slowly but my writing was not making the same leaps, quite the contrary. Fear froze the pencil in my hand. A diminutive creature, Miss Rowe, bullied and hectored, called me names and stood me in the corner, 'in order that shame will drive you to overcome your inadequacies'. Then there was the headmaster, Mr Ping. He was a thickset man of uneven temper – although this was not entirely his fault. He had been badly wounded in the foot during the First World War. A spring attached to the toecap of his boot was fastened to a strap at his ankle and this device made his foot bend as he walked. It must have been intolerably painful. He had a way of passing the pain on to us. He had two canes called Hengist and Horsa and he used these as frequently as possible.

As small boys do, we talked after lights out. On one occasion when we had been caught, Ping called the whole dormitory, all eighteen of us, down to his study from where the pyjama'd queue wound from the door and up the passage. We were each given three strokes of Hengist – or was it Horsa?

I learned the Second Collect, 'For Peace', but particularly one sentence: 'Defend us, thy humble servants, in all assaults of our enemies; that we, surely trusting in thy defence, may not fear the power of any adversaries, through the might of Jesus Christ our Lord.' It was my mantra, its repetition comforted me and its words held me together.

With four of us settled and out of the way, Mother found herself a job with a wartime resident and day nursery attached to St Stephen's Orphanage in York. She was able to have Terry there with her. She pitched into the work and made herself indispensable, so much so that Miss Marshall, the orphanage's supervisor, virtually allowed my mother to run the place. She was very happy there until she discovered a case of flagrant dishonesty and flouting of the rationing laws. She was up in arms. She fought a good fight – and lost her job.

Her ambition to stand in the forefront of endeavour was overwhelming her – at one point it was politics, the next it was the BBC. She fervently believed that Bulgaria, her adoptive country, should have been wooed by the Allies, and in her mind this tiny country was in some way central to the winning of the war.

That first unhappy term at St Olave's came to an end. Frank went to London to spend Christmas with the Birks. We moved back in with Mrs Rawlings, and the walls of her house stretched again. Aunt Ethel arrived from Leeds, bringing gifts from Papa; perhaps he thought she would have more time to shop than his wife who was coping with four children. There was money from him, too, and Eve and Pat were able to have dressing gowns (fawn dressing gowns were *de rigueur* at Red House but, of course, Mother didn't check and bought the poor little sods blue ones). Frank sent a food parcel from London. I made up a murder play in which Eve, Patrick and I took part. It went well and received great applause from the rest of the family and the long-suffering Mrs Rawlings. Ethel took us all back to Leeds where we stayed with her for a few days. While we were there, we went to *Mother Goose*; this was not only the first pantomime we had seen but it was the first live theatre I had been to. I thought that to be part of the theatre would be a joyous thing.

All too soon, the Christmas holidays were over and we had to return to our respective schools. Now that Mother had lost her job at the nursery, she needed somewhere to put Terry and found a very good nursery school in Harrogate, Pannell Ash College for Infants. Terry was just two years old.

Mother was free. In a letter of 13 January, she wrote to Papa:

The 20th sees me through here and off on my work (DV). I must get established so as to cover or help with the Red House fees – at all costs those two must go on there, they love it and they've put on pounds. They are out of the way of bombs and are in lovely country air and are getting a good start in education into the bargain. I may have made a mistake but what was the good of settling down in some house outside York, tying myself down so that I couldn't work. Everyone here lives from hour to hour – any night may end one's life so one must just do the best one can ...

About this time, there was a daylight raid on York – to remind us all that there was a war on. Before leaving for London to look for a job, she found a school which took boarders during the holidays. It was St John's at Green Hammerton, about twelve miles from York. St John's was run by Primrose Ware, a woman from a good Yorkshire family whose war effort was to keep her school open for children whose families were either serving or stationed abroad.

When the Easter holidays arrived, therefore, Frank went down to London to stay with the Birks in Highgate, Terry stayed in Harrogate, and Evie, Pat and I made our way to Green Hammerton. I could not believe our luck: unlike St Olave's, here were civilised people who laughed and smiled and treated us with kindness.

Prim was a cultural force. It was not a question of learning and following, as with Avie, but of looking and appreciating the whole. Pictures, artists, music. We read books – even me, and I began to read Shakespeare. I was frightened by the plays so I read *Venus and Adonis*. I thought it wonderfully romantic.

The holidays passed quickly; there was so much to do. I used to take Evie and Pat to the River Ouse near Kirk Hammerton. In a shallow stretch we could, with a great deal of patience and luck, catch small eels, flinging them out on to the bank with great squeals of delight.

A little further downstream was a pool deep enough to swim in. I frequently bicycled to Harrogate to see Terence and I was allowed to ride a pony on the neighbouring farm. It was here that I had my very first proper kiss, from Ruth Johnson, the pony's owner.

We didn't see Mother at all that holiday. She was living with the Birks in Highgate and had a freelance job with the BBC. She augmented her income writing articles for the *Nursing Times* and night-nursing private patients.

She sat a series of tests in oral and written Bulgarian and obviously satisfied the examiners because, on 22 April 1942, she was able to write to Papa:

> I have signed up with the BBC and go down to Evesham on the 1st of May. The salary is £340 a year but with living allowances and so forth I shall receive £360. All outside literary work must be submitted to my immediate superior – so I hope he enjoys my articles on breast feeding and midwifery anaesthesia for the *Nursing Times*.

York was bombed again and we all sat under the stairs. Eve, then seven, was simply terrified; she went into catatonic shock which lasted some weeks. She would walk about in a daydream then suddenly come out of it and be as bright as a button, then back she would go. We were told she would recover. Both St Peter's and St Olave's had been bombed and we couldn't go back to school for some weeks. Mr Hardwick at Red House took us in. Our mother was not exaggerating when she told Papa that this was a happy place for Eve and Pat. Lawns and fields ran down to the river; and there was a stable-block full of ponies. It was a lovely place.

Unfortunately, we were only there for two weeks before Frank returned to St Peter's and I to St Olave's. The foul Ping was still in charge. I hated him all the more when he told me that, as I was so good a swimmer, I could only enter two races at the swimming gala.

There was an allotment near the house, which grew vegetables to augment the rations. On their way up from the cricket field, a fair-haired boy called Nicholson and a dark-haired boy called Jackson picked some peas and ate them. We were in the changing-room, jumping in and out of the bath in turn, when the door burst open and Ping, stick in hand, bellowed at the boys that they were thieves and he would show them what happened to those who stole. He laid about him indiscriminately. I don't know how many times he hit Nicholson and Jackson, but all of us got a stroke or two as Jackson and Nicholson ran round the showers trying to avoid the blows. After he had finished, Matron came in and took the boys away. They were put to bed.

I wrote to my mother telling her how unhappy I was. She got leave from the BBC as soon as she could and came up to Green Hammerton. She did some investigating which included talking to a boy from St Peter's who assured her that I was not exaggerating the situation. She moved with dazzling speed. I was out of St Olave's and into Red House and she back to Evesham in forty-eight hours.

Here was happiness — watching the bats swoop round the eves of the house and skim over the roof of the chapel in the evenings, roller skating in the locker-room, learning English from Miss Butler. My inability to see the letters properly still hampered my reading but I was getting better.

I was growing: I was not yet twelve and was over six foot. My height, however, was sometimes a disadvantage. I had a diminutive friend who was always spoken to nicely if we broke the rules whilst I was spoken to severely and told, 'You are big enough to know better.' I felt Tom Hardwick, the headmaster, didn't like me being taller than he was and I am sure that, when he once beat me, my height was a contributing factor. I forgive him. He was a wonderful, generous man. He quite often let me off organised sport and allowed me to ride the ponies through the woods.

During the summer holidays at Green Hammerton, I helped with the harvest, leading the horses to the farm and back to the field. Work began early each morning and continued until the light faded. Old men, land girls and small boys. Frank had gone to a farm camp, picking potatoes. His was very hard work and he was paid a penny-halfpenny an hour. In August he went to London to stay with the Birks and he saw Mother when she came up from Evesham.

When he returned, he told me that things were not going very smoothly for her at the BBC. With hindsight, it was most probably her own fault. As far as she was concerned, the King of Bulgaria and the Bulgarian nation as a whole were both grossly maligned and misunderstood by the British Government. In 1939 she had been at a dinner with King Boris who had apparently sought her out and talked to her not only about the war but also about how Bulgaria would cope with a German invasion. She took it that she had been given a personal mission to alert Winston Churchill of this conversation; she was to tell him that King Boris would be prepared to put his army at the Allies' disposal. She did not stop to wonder why on earth the King should confide in her rather than go through the proper diplomatic channels.

Working as a Bulgarian monitor at the BBC, she decided that Bulgarian Radio was sending out coded messages. She even managed to wangle a meeting with Mr Churchill for half an hour. She found codes and messages in almost every bulletin. She bombarded her superiors with her supposedly greater knowledge of Bulgarian affairs. Mr Burns, the head of the monitoring service, was sent for by 10 Downing Street to answer questions about one of his monitors; he had known nothing of my mother's visit to Churchill. After the meeting, he travelled down to Evesham to see this Mrs Baker. He asked Mother to explain herself, listened patiently to her fervent outpourings, then told her that her job was not to interpret her bulletins but to pass them to experts. This was not what she wanted to hear: she thought the head of her unit was an ignorant fool and often told him so. Not surprisingly, he put in a dreadfully bad report. Mother resigned.

She had a breakdown after this and spent some time in the BBC's convalescent home. My poor mother, she could not help giving her advice or voicing her opinions. Everyone in the entire world was a fool and she the only wise one. Frank spent most of his holidays in Highgate with the Birks, and from here he was able to see more of our mother than the rest of us. He travelled down to Evesham to visit her when she was ill; he rowed her up the river and walked with her in the gardens.

This first breakdown was the beginning of a fifteen-year period of Mother's obsession with Bulgaria that would dominate and, ultimately, change our lives.

*   *   *

Mother came up to York in September and we had a fortnight in Scarborough. It was the first time we had been properly together since Ireland.

There was, thankfully, a constant in our lives to make up for our lack of maternal attention. This was Aunt Ethel who visited every fortnight, trudging the two miles up the lane to Red House once the bus from Leeds had dropped her off. In a way, she became a sort of an anchor for Mother who knew she could rely on her sister-in-law's good common sense. Things would have been a great deal worse without her.

Mother had met and made friends with Major Gene McQuatters, General Biddle's secretary. Mother left Evesham and she and Gene decided to share a flat in Maida Vale. The flat was part of a house owned by Lady Reid-Dick. One wing of it was Sir William Reid-Dick's studio, the other wing was their home and the flat joined the two together. At this time, Sir William was working on his statue of Lady Godiva for Coventry. Lady Dick – as we called her – remained in my life until her death in the 1970s.

Christmas 1942 was spent at St John's in Green Hammerton. Terry was brought over from Harrogate and Mother came up from London. Frank joined us from York. The family was together. It was a jolly time, and it was especially good to have Mother with us. There were about fifteen children in the house and Winnie Harboro seemed to be able to produce food out of nothing. There was a huge Christmas tree, mistletoe and music.

After Christmas, Frank and I went to London with Mother. It was a strange and wonderful time. We went to the cinema to see *Yankee Doodle Dandy*, James Cagney dancing as no one had danced before. We also saw *Pride of the Yankees*, and *Forty-Ninth Parallel* with Eric Portman, Laurence Olivier, and a very young Glynis Johns. We went to the theatre to see *A Quiet Weekend* which also starred Glynis Johns. During the play, she had to remove her dress which had got wet in the rain and needed to be dried by the fire; she finished the scene in her petticoat. I fell head over heels in love.

Many years later I met Glynis in Monte Carlo. We were sitting on the terrace drinking with that great cameraman Georges Perrinal when I told her that I had fallen totally in love with her in *A Quiet*

Weekend. She seemed quite pleased but said, 'You must have been very young?' 'Oh, yes,' I replied, 'I was twelve.' She turned away and didn't speak to me for some time. However, we got to know each other well over the years and when I last saw her in Hollywood in 1998, she had forgiven me.

Kate Birks took us to a matinée of *A Midsummer Night's Dream* at the Haymarket, starring Robert Atkins and Leslie French as Puck. I particularly enjoyed this since we had already performed the play at Red House. We also saw *While the Sun Shines* with Michael Wilding and Ronnie Squire. After this exhilarating time in London, I went back to school knowing beyond doubt that I must be an actor.

I wrote and told my father so. He wrote back that he was delighted and told me that I must pay especial attention to English. Shortly afterwards, we put on a production of *Macbeth* and I played the Third Witch.

Mother had the opportunity to rent Lady Dick's cottage outside Wisborough Green in Sussex. She leapt at the chance and from now on we were to be together during the holidays. I went to Harrogate to collect Terry and take him back to St John's. Terry was now three and had not seen his mother for nearly a year. He had developed a wonderful Yorkshire accent. Four of us left St John's since Frank had gone ahead. We took the train from Marston Moor, changed at York and caught the Flying Scotsman. Mother met us at King's Cross. Sitting in the train at Victoria, waiting to leave for Sussex, Terry suddenly turned to me and asked, 'George, is she really my mummy?'

Westlands was a paradise. It was a cottage with thirty acres, mostly woods, a vast tithe barn and a yew tree reputed to be a thousand years old. It was also cloud-cuckoo-land since there was hardly any money with which to pay the rent, never mind about buying food. 'God will provide' was the motto.

There were four bedrooms and a bathroom; the water supply for this and for general household use had to be pumped by hand. Frank and I took it in turn, two hundred strokes each every morning. There was a kitchen with a solid fuel cooker. There was a big hall, a dining-room and a sitting-room. There were books; there was a gramophone and records. We had found ourselves in a proper house with proper furniture.

There was a generator that produced sufficient electric light for the kitchen and one light in the main bedroom. All the other lighting was by paraffin lamps, from smart Aladdin lamps with delicate mantles that became white-hot and gave off a shining, brilliant light, to mundane little lamps with small wicks and tiny globes. All the wicks had to be trimmed and the lamps filled every morning. Frank and I did or did not do these jobs every morning as the mood took us.

We were three miles from Wisborough Green, the nearest village. Mother had bought a 1938 Hillman and our ration gave us enough petrol to go shopping once a week. We explored the woods and we found the way through them to the bus stop that would take us to Petworth.

In due course, we met Mr Stemp who was the gamekeeper for the neighbouring estate and who also looked after our woods. He wasn't a man of great humour but he was certainly a man of great kindness. He showed me how to set snares for rabbits and how to skin them – a great bonus because they augmented our meat ration. Every now and again, we had a pheasant or a partridge, courtesy of Mr Stemp.

When the Easter holidays came to an end, Mother warned us that we might have seen Westlands for the last time since she didn't think she could continue to afford the rent. She took us to King's Cross and off we all went on the five-hour journey back to Yorkshire, a journey which never took less than seven.

She very seldom wrote letters *per se*; she preferred to stand in the post office and whiz off four or five letter telegrams. In this way, we learned that Papa had been knocked over by a Canadian Army truck during the blackout in Cairo. We knew he had been out of hospital for some weeks so it was with some surprise that we read the telegram from Mother saying he had been re-admitted.

It was a beautiful early summer afternoon. The trees were putting out their leaves of softest green and the baby bracken was fighting through the dark loam of the woods. I was lying on my back, watching the rooks and waiting for the bell to call us to fire practice when Tom Hardwick sent for me. He was standing by the big window which looked out over the meadow and the cricket pitch. There is no easy way of telling a twelve-year-old that his father has died and Tom Hardwick did it as well as anybody could. He told me that Matron was telling Eve and Patrick.

I stood beside him, staring unseeingly at the green and white cricket pavilion outside. My father was my father and very precious to me. I was not going to show anyone how I felt. 'Thank you, sir,' I said and left as the bell rang for fire practice.

I talked to Eve and Pat and we all had a cry. 'We don't really remember him, you know, George,' said Pat.

But I remembered him. I remembered him saying goodbye to me at Sofia station. I remembered the letter he had written to Mother in May 1940, in which he said: 'And that leaves Jora. He wants his Papa and how his Papa wants him.' I asked Tom Hardwick if I could go and have a swim. I sat on the banks of the Ouse and knew that I could not be separated from my father. In that knowledge, I slid into the water and swam.

5

AT THE END OF THE SUMMER TERM WE GATHERED FOR THE JOURNEY TO WESTLANDS. Mother had conjured the money from somewhere – or Lady Dick was being kind. We had fetched Terry from Harrogate the night before and Tom Hardwick travelled with us as far as York. Brother Frank was on the platform with three friends and made it quite obvious that we would be an embarrassment if we were to insist on travelling with him.

Tom Hardwick saw us on to the train. I don't know if Frank and his pals had reserved seats, but they were certainly sitting very comfortably in a Pullman carriage while we struggled down the train to find seats. There was none to be had. Soldiers sat the little ones on their kit bags; they made us laugh and we sang songs and I'm sure we had a much better time than the four 'grown-ups' sitting at the other end of the train.

There was a moment on that journey which still makes me shudder. Pat suddenly needed to be sick; indeed, he started to be sick. I picked him up and, slapping my hand over his mouth, I rushed him to the loo. I took my hand away and he was violently sick into the pan. By the grace of God he had not choked when I held the vomit at bay with my hand.

The instructions from my mother were that, on arrival at King's Cross, we were to take the Underground to London Bridge and from there a train to Billingshurst. Frank sloped off with his friends, leaving me to look after the three young ones.

I carried Terry on my back; Evie held my arm and Pat the tails of my macintosh. As we were boarding the Underground train at King's Cross, the doors closed, leaving a startled seven-year-old out on the platform. I decided we should get off at the next station to see if we could see Pat on the following train. We stood near the front of the platform and gazed into the carriages of the train as it came through but we couldn't see a Patrick anywhere.

We went back to King's Cross, but Pat wasn't waiting for us on the platform. Standing on the platform, watching the trains go by, the enormity of what had happened dawned on me. I had lost my seven-year-old brother. The memory of that moment lives with me still.

We went to London Bridge, explained to the ticket collector what had happened and were taken to the stationmaster's office. Patrick was not there and they had received no news of him. I was desperately trying to think what to do next when the door opened and Pat was led in by a porter. The story was that he had taken the next train and got off at Cannon Street where he was caught trying to go through the barrier. When questioned by the ticket collector, he replied that his big brother was lost but that he was on his way to Billingshurst.

Thank God we were reunited. We were escorted to the train and found a seat near the guard's van. We had to change at Three Bridges. The guard was kind and helpful and saw to it that there was someone on the Three Bridges platform to see us on to the right train. When we arrived at Billingshurst, we found that the taxi Mother had sent for us had been taken by Frank.

I bought some pork pies and lemonade and we set off to walk the short distance into town to catch the Petworth bus. The final leg of our momentous journey to Westlands was the three-quarters of a mile walk through the woods and we finally arrived home at about eight-thirty that evening.

As we stood, exhausted, in the hall, Mother came sweeping past us, an old brown blanket hanging round her shoulders and a cigarette dangling out of the corner of her mouth. 'Ah, there you are, George. Feed the children. I'm writing a novel.' And she swept on up the stairs.

It was the first time we had seen our mother since Papa died.

I didn't think about the sequence of events until much later. There was no one Mother could speak to about her grief at losing her husband two months earlier. She had recently suffered a breakdown and had been dispensed with by the BBC and now five children aged between four and fourteen were descending on her for their summer holidays.

I had made the scrambled eggs with egg powder and dried milk when Mother came downstairs and busied herself with being a mother. We told her about our adventures crossing London and we laughed a lot. It was her spirit that always made the home wherever we were. Somehow we knew that although there was no money, sometimes not even enough for food, she was giving us other things. She felt that the human brain had a capability as powerful as any force in the universe and that it was wasted, hardly used by man.

I have no right to speak for my brothers and sister, no right to make it a collective experience. They have their own impressions of their childhood just as I have mine. Quite separate delights, hurts and frustrations. This is my memory of those times.

I had started writing poetry. 'Poets have a pot-au-feu on their shoulders into which the universe tips the brightest and the best of its ideas, and they spill out on to the page as poetry. Listen to the universe, darling,' said my mother. My poems had a rhyme or two but not much content. The main thing was that I was reading. The Reid-Dick library at Westlands consisted of a collection of holiday reading, books not wanted in the London house, books outgrown by the Reid-Dick children. *The Cloister and the Hearth, Dr Doolittle, Vile Bodies*, books by Angela Brazil, Margaret Irwin, 'Saki' – they all lived in the sitting-room or in a bookshelf on the landing.

Our nearest neighbours lived in three houses on a small piece of common ground the other side of the wood. The Hassells lived in Cheesmans, an old, pretty cottage, well ordered with weedless flowerbeds and a close-cut lawn. They kindly invited us to tea. Our poor mother – she tried to tidy us up and pass us off as a normal family. I remember clearly seeing the absurdity of us all taking tea in the garden, looking for the entire world like ill-kempt gypsies. We did try very hard to do the right thing. Mummy was busy charming Mrs Hassell. Frank fell into immediate teenage lust with either Jennifer or Jane, I can't remember which. He sat staring at her, beetroot red with embarrassment. He told me later that he had a hard-on all the way through tea and was dreading having to get up and go home.

Mother cried a lot and we were perplexed how to cope with it. She made great efforts to achieve some sort of normality for us but, being refugees from Bulgaria, we had no idea how normal people in England lived. I think the normal people around us thought we were very peculiar. But they were all wonderfully kind.

One afternoon during that hot summer, two maiden ladies were due to come to tea. At ten to four there was nothing ready, no dainty Shippam's paste sandwiches, no bread and jam, no table and no tea.

Even Frank stood mortified in front of his mother. 'Mummy, four o'clock is teatime.'

'They'll just have to take us as they find us.'

'They're not going to find me. It's too humiliating.' Frank was not prepared to stay around to be humiliated. He disappeared for the rest of the afternoon.

His phrase passed into the family language. If anything was 'proper', we reminded each other that 'four o'clock is teatime'.

'Put the kettle on, will you, Jora?' said my mother calmly as we heard a knocking on the front door.

I heard Mother spilling over with charm. 'You found it? Well, why wouldn't you? You've known Lady Dick for years. Shall we go into the garden?'

I laid the table and did my best with the Shippam's paste and the jam sandwiches. The Misses Berkley obviously thought it was all right for despite of (or maybe because of) the eccentricity, they were steadfast friends to us.

Mother and I took the Hillman and went shopping in Wisborough Green. Rationing was at its worst and the manager of the Forest Stores decided that he could not honour the emergency cards we had brought from school. Mother tried to reason with him but he was obdurate. They had not enough provision to meet their own needs, he told her.

I was terrified as I could see my mother beginning to get angular. However, she was very restrained and said she would take her own rations and shop somewhere else with the emergency cards, but that they would be hearing from her. Although she was seething with fury on the way back, she still let me drive once we were out of the village. Both Frank and I had driven the Fiat in Bulgaria.

Once home, she rushed for the telephone and the lines to the Ministry of Food sizzled. I sat on the stairs and listened. The headlines seemed to be that 'widow of British officer left without food for her five children because the emergency ration cards had no value in the country' – or was the shopkeeper right? Was the food shortage so acute that there were no provisions to be had? she asked. If so, should not the country be told that we were in a national food crisis, and would they like her to make it her business to write to *The Times* informing them of the emergency?

The next day, a young man in striped trousers, black jacket and bowler hat arrived at our front door. He was dripping with sweat as he had walked from the Hawkhurst crossroads. We sat him down and gave him orangeade to drink. He assured Mummy that there would be no need to write to *The Times*. He had spoken to Mr Forest who had told him that the whole thing had been an unfortunate misunderstanding and that if we were to return to his shop, the rations would be waiting for us. The Ministry of Food had been in touch with the Forest Stores and extra rations had been delivered.

The arrival of the provisions was important to me since I was doing most of the cooking now. We had even tried to resurrect the vegetable garden; it was too late to plant anything for the summer, of course, but we managed a few leeks and Brussels sprouts for the winter.

Irinka had come over from Ireland to be with us and was a wonderful help looking after the little ones but not much help in any other way. She did not appear to consider that helping in the kitchen or with the cleaning was part of her job. Nonetheless, I felt that my mother was treating the girl rather badly. She had found the Bulgarian girl very useful on the journey back to England and for a little while in Ireland, but she certainly didn't see that she had any ongoing responsibility for her – until, that is, she needed her again. On the other hand Irinka looked on us as her family.

Mother was weeping more and more. Through Lady Dick, she had met Charles and Minnie Cousins, Christian Science practitioners. She had willingly embraced Christian Science and the philosophies of Ouspensky. She was on the telephone to Charles Cousins at all hours of the day. Sometimes Frank or I would be deputed to talk to Min or Charles. Mother would mutter, 'There is no life substance or material in matter', or 'God is love and there is no pain', wherever she went. At night, she would eerily cry out for 'Frank, darling Frank', screaming my father's name into the night.

She retreated to bed. Brother Frank sat patiently reading Ouspensky's *New Model of the Universe* to her. I read the Bible to her or Mary Baker Eddy's *Science and Health*. Frank had made it quite clear that he was on for Ouspensky but Mary Baker Eddy was not on his reading list.

I cooked whatever there was to cook and presented it as palatably as possible; I decorated her tray with flowers. While she remained in bed, I cooked for the family and Irinka looked after the youngest children.

There was a memorable night when Mother was shouting her husband's name into the darkness and in between her sobs Terence's small voice piped, 'Evie, what's two and two and four is . . . ?' Evie didn't answer, any more than anyone answered Mummy.

I remember that night because Irinka came into my room, ostensibly to make sure that I was all right and that I was not worried. She stroked my forehead and then she kissed my mouth. Her tongue played on my lips and parted them. Her breasts were warm through her nightgown on my body. She took my hand and put it between her thighs and there we lay, she kissing me and stroking my head while I stroked her breast with my free hand. We lay there until Mother had stopped shouting and Terence had stopped catechising Evie. Irinka gave me a last kiss and returned to her bed.

I suppose that now that would be considered child abuse but I consider that the only abuse about it was that it never happened again. Although she was sixteen years older than me, I think she was very frightened by her loneliness in a strange country, by the war, by the collapse of the woman she considered her guardian in her new life. Like us all, she needed comfort.

For two days Mother was delirious, shouting in Bulgarian about King Boris, calling for our father; she was alternately hot and cold. In a lucid moment she told me to get a bowl of cold water and sponge her forehead with a flannel. Frank, Irinka and I took it in turns to sit with her through the nights. After three days, the temperature and the delirium went.

We were all weak and exhausted, the kitchen was a tip, there was a pile of washing on the floor and a pile of ironing on the kitchen table; the little ones roamed about looking anxious and bewildered.

Into this astonishing mess came a saint in Canadian uniform. Corporal Bill Simpson had been Gene McQuatters' driver when she and Mother shared the flat in Maida Vale. Now he was driver to a Canadian colonel stationed outside Billingshurst and thought he would call on his old friend Eva Baker. He knocked on the cottage door at the height of the domestic chaos that had grown during Mother's illness. Although he told me he was an old friend of my mother's, I couldn't help wondering what a corporal of the Canadian Army was doing visiting her. He said he wouldn't stay long.

I went up to her bedroom and told her Corporal Bill Simpson was downstairs. She had to think for a moment before she remembered him. She told me to make him a cup of tea and that she would come down.

I found Bill looking round the mess in the kitchen. When he asked if we had any help, I told him Irinka looked after the youngest children while I did the cooking and washing up and, I should have added, the washing and ironing. No, we didn't have any help.

Mother had made an effort with herself but she had been very ill. Bill told her that she should have stayed in bed but she insisted that they should have some tea together in the sitting-room. I made the tea and some sardine sandwiches. True to his word, Bill didn't stay long. When he left, he told me to look after her and that he would call again.

Since my mother had become ill, I had driven the Hillman into Wisborough Green to do the shopping. I was still only twelve and, although I was six foot two, I was certainly not eighteen and the holder of a driving licence, so I was not very surprised when the local bobby flagged me down. Could I give him a lift to the village? I have never been so frightened. He got into the car and I drove off smoothly. I remembered to slow down, indicate and stop at the main road. We arrived at the stores and I parked. I waited for the axe to fall. No licence and no insurance.

'Does your mother know you're driving the car?'

'She's not very well,' I said. 'I didn't tell her, but I had to get some groceries. Bread and milk are delivered but not the groceries.'

'Yes. I know your mother's been poorly. Just till she's better you can come into the shop and out again, but don't ever let me catch you driving anywhere else. Just till your mother's better, look.'

He went into the shop and I turned away.

When I got home I was surprised to see Bill Simpson in the kitchen. With the help of Irinka, I had made small inroads into the washing up and ironing – but here was a professional on the job. Bill was stacking the dishes in the order they were to be washed: the glasses stood on the draining board nearest the sink, then the cutlery and the plates, the saucepans came last. He handed me the drying-up cloth and we set to work. It was amazing how quickly the job was done. While he worked he told me that he had gone back to barracks and asked his commanding officer for compassionate leave to help us while our mother was ill. He was granted leave for six days. He bustled us about, organised Irinka, and even had Frank up a ladder gathering plums. He taught me how to make a proper stock for soups. We cut the grass and even did some weeding.

He fell in love with Mummy. In the evening while Frank lit the oil lamps, I did the cooking and Irinka put the little ones to bed, he would sit with her and we could hear them laughing in her bedroom. Then they would come down and we would play bridge. Bill knew how to play the game but his calling was wild and erratic, more designed to confuse than inform his partner. Flag flying, Mother called it.

One evening Bill and I got on the bicycles and pedalled into Wisborough Green. I had my first pint of beer sitting outside The Cricketers. I had my second at the Kirdford Camp NAAFI. Cycling home sobered me up.

On the day before he was due to leave us, he and Mother stayed upstairs rather longer than usual and there was no laughter. I was irrationally jealous. I banged about in the garden. I was quite certain they were making love. Finally they came down to eat and play bridge. My mother's face was radiant and I didn't have to be told that I'd been right. That night I went down to the kitchen to get some water, or did I just want to check if Bill was on the sofa in the sitting-room? The sofa was empty and my worst fears were confirmed. I sobbed myself to sleep.

The next morning I got up very early and went for a walk in the woods. I sat in my special spot by the stream and recited 'Down by the Salley Gardens', one of Aunt Avie's favourite poems. They were both going to be 'full of tears' and serve them right. That uncharitable thought made me feel much better. I went back to the house to make tea and found Bill in the kitchen, behaving as if nothing had happened.

I felt the need to get out of the house, so went over to a neighbouring farmer and asked if he needed any help with the harvest. He offered to pay me a shilling a day for an eight-hour day. I agreed to start the next day. My mother was up and about when I got home, looking her old self. I told her what I was going to do and have always marvelled at her reply. 'Good, darling, you deserve a holiday.'

The day stretched for ever. Bill was going to catch the last bus and because of the late hour, Mother asked me to go with them so that I could walk her home. We took a torch. They walked a little way ahead of me, his arm round her waist and hers around his shoulder. We stood by the bus stop and they kissed lightly, as friends might, before they parted. When Bill said goodbye to me, he told me to look after her.

On the way home, my mother took my hand and tried to tell me how desperate she was, how lonely since my father's death, and the nightmares she had lived through. 'The fool BBC and the worse fool Government that wouldn't believe me and couldn't anyway see a yard ahead of their faces. If only they had listened to me Hitler would never had got into Bulgaria or run across the Balkans and Papa would still be alive.' She was crying. 'It was just that Bill was so sweet and gentle.'

For my part, I was just glad he had gone.

We never heard from him again, but the little Canadian corporal did leave an indelible mark on my life since I am meticulously ordered in the kitchen. I try and bring order to any job before I start to do it.

I honoured my agreement with the local farmer, and went to help with the harvest. The harvester went round the field from the outside, and the wheat was cut in swathes until the centre was reached. Land girls, wives and anyone who could be coerced did the stooking. At the end of two weeks, the farmer gave me fourteen shillings and a seven-shilling bonus. He must have thought I put in a man-sized job.

I cycled into Billingshurst and bought a pair of agricultural corduroys which were exempt from coupons for 4/6d, and a 4½-lb axe for 12/6d. I was delighted with my purchases, and when I got home I left the trousers in the kitchen and went into the barn to split wood. The axe was a triumph, just the right weight for me and very sharp. Now to try on the corduroys, my first pair of long trousers – which, for a boy of my height, was not before time.

Frank had applied for extra clothing coupons to replace the clothes he had lost in the bombing of St Peter's, York. The coupons had recently arrived but here he was sitting at the kitchen table, in my corduroys, discussing with our mother what she might need in the way of clothing.

'Those are *my* trousers!'

He sneered at me and didn't answer. I lost my temper. It was a foul, murderous temper and would arrive, uncontrolled, out of nowhere. I wanted him dead and hurled the axe at his head. Luckily he ducked and it missed. My throwing the axe didn't faze him at all but it achieved the right effect since he took off the trousers and threw them at me without a word. Then he sat down again and resumed his conversation with his mother from the point at which he had been interrupted by a flying axe.

'Now what else do you need?'

'I need some knickers and a bra –'

'Articles, Mummy, please, just articles.'

Frank was a cold character and didn't pull his weight in the house or with his younger brothers and sister. I loved and hated him. I loved him because he was so strong, nothing and nobody could ever get the better of my big brother. I hated him because he was cold and distant and had no sense of fun.

Frank was fighting his own battle with the journey we were making. Otherwise, why would a fourteen-year-old sit in a cupboard eating apples, reading a book and sucking his thumb most of the day?

Mother decided that Eve should go to a boarding school in Petworth and that she would keep Terry with her at Westlands. Irinka had found herself a job near Billingshurst; she never came back to live with us again. Frank, Pat and I were off to Yorkshire on the all-too-familiar journey.

I was at Red House for two years and it was the closest I had got to any stability in my life. It was a wonderful school; there were woods and there were ponies and, instead of organised games, I was allowed to take one of the ponies out on my own. I had favourite tracks through the woods, one of which led through to the Ouse at Nun Monkton. The ferry was here, a flat-bottomed barge pulled across the river by a chain.

There was a boy at school, Willy Palmer, who had had polio which had left his leg emaciated and crippled. He was a wonderful musician and often played the chapel organ, either to practise for the Sunday service or for his own pleasure. I would creep into a pew and listen to him playing Bach, sometimes some Handel and Purcell. It was the beginning of my pleasure in listening to music. We had no gramophone at home and the poor wretched wireless was too busy crackling round the dial trying to pick up coded messages from central Europe to be much use as an instrument of pleasure.

Although I was still reading with some difficulty and was quite unable to spell, my concentration continued to flag because of eye strain and my schoolwork was poor. Despite all this backwardness, the teachers at Red House made me feel an average sort of pupil and by no means a fool. They gave me a confidence for which I was to be immensely grateful in the very near future.

Mother sorted her life out by taking the position of matron at a local preparatory school in Wisborough Green. She was able to have little Terry with her, costing her nothing. This was his second school and he was not yet five. Eve was safely at North End House, five miles away in Petworth. It must have been good for her to be among girls instead of being the only girl among three dozen boys as she had been at Red House.

Christmas 1943 was by courtesy of Aunts Avie, Mamie and Ethel.

Avie sent a goodly cheque, and Mamie and Ethel contributed by sending each of us postal orders for ten shillings a few days in advance of Christmas so that we could go into Petworth and buy our presents.

It was a very cold Christmas and my axe did sterling work. The big open fireplace in the dining-room burned brightly all day. We cut a Christmas tree from the woods and stood it in the hall; everything was as normal as could be. Papa had only been dead seven months and this was the first Christmas after his death. He had always made the Christmas pudding in Varna and now I was in charge. The three youngest were given first go at cleaning out the bowl with their fingers.

We sang carols with the wireless and were invited out by neighbours to children's parties. Well, Frank wouldn't go, of course, and I think I only went twice. There were games like pass-the-parcel and charades and I was quite hopeless at them all. Anyway, there was always a pile of washing, ironing or washing up waiting at home, to say nothing of the cooking.

Mother and I were a good team and more or less kept the chaos at bay. She was a good cook when she wanted to be and, having been to and given ambassadorial parties in Varna, her knowledge extended beyond plum duff. Every now and again, we would have a flight of fancy and make puff pastry, rolling the sheet of pastry thin and covering it with a layer of lard or margarine before putting the next sheet on top of it. We would leave it in the cold pantry overnight and then use it as a lid for a vegetable pie or, in September, a blackberry and apple pie. Soda bread was a staple, and a muslin bag of top-of-the-milk dripped into the pantry sink and turned into cream cheese.

But for all our ingenuity, we were often hungry. The rations were insufficient and the money non-existent although there always seemed enough for Mother's Gold Flake or Churchman's Number One. She was about to start what turned out to be a long, long fight to prove probate on my father's will. Being an Honorary Vice-Consul did not entitle him to a pension from the Foreign Office. The two houses and land in Bulgaria were in enemy hands – although, anachronistically, the Germans who occupied them paid rent into our account right through the war. It was quite worthless, however, as there was no financial exchange. I can't think why the various schools we attended were so patient.

When we returned to Sussex for the Easter holidays, the woods surrounding the Hawkhurst crossroads and running up to Bedham and on to Fittleworth were occupied by troops, some British but mostly Americans. There was considerable racial tension because the white battalions had been stationed beside the black. The latter were stationed by the side of the road along which we walked to get the bus to Petworth, and were well dug in. The men were big and friendly. They had put up makeshift road signs in their camp: Georgia Forever Road, Alabama Crescent, Savannah State Highway. Even individual tents had names: God's Acre, Seven Days from Death, The Mississippi, and other strange names. The battalions of white men were stationed further into the woods, near the common.

Then, one night, they began to move out, five-ton trucks carrying supplies and soldiers, Bren gun carriers, amphibian troop carriers, staff cars and jeeps rolled past the cottage all night. Frank and I sat on his bedroom windowsill and waved them goodbye. After the Normandy landings on 6 June, someone told me that the American troops had left our area that April night in order to move closer to the coast.

I can't remember how long we kept our vigil before we fell asleep. By the evening of the next day, the woods were still and quiet; only the dugouts and the road signs remained. The army had erected Nissen huts in Bedham for their headquarters and the huts are there to this day, overgrown with briar and morning glory.

6

THE SUMMER TERM OF 1944 WAS MY LAST AT RED HOUSE. Fate now began to play strange tricks with my life. I happened to pick up a book about public schools which was knocking about the classroom. At the top of the left-hand page at which I opened the book was Lancing College. I saw that it was near Worthing and as I had often bicycled from Wisborough Green to Worthing, I knew it was near home. If I could go to Lancing, I thought, it would mean I would never have to do the dreadful journey from York to Billingshurst again. I wrote to my mother and pleaded with her to try to get me into the Sussex school.

Somehow, my mother and Tom Hardwick managed to get me accepted – mainly, I think, because Lancing was evacuated to Shropshire while the College was given over to the navy. The school authorities were, apparently, taking anybody, as they needed the fees. They picked the wrong one here, of course; my mother could certainly sweet-talk and as certainly she couldn't pay the fees.

Lady Reid-Dick decided that she needed to sell Westlands and Mother was in search of somewhere for us to live again. She found Cheesboys, a small wooden bungalow set in the middle of a field on the same common where the Hassells had lived. When they moved to Fittleworth, a retired grocer, Colonel Knight, bought their cottage, Cheesmans. Before the war, he had owned three grocery shops and was quite well-to-do. Not only did he buy the Hassells' cottage, but also the bungalow across the way, Cheesboys. And this is where we spent the summer holidays of 1944.

He was a kindly man. He had a good singing voice and had at one time thought of going into opera. Snatches of *La Bohème* – 'Your tiny hand is frozen', 'The time for parting is when roses blow' – was as near as he got to grand opera but I am eternally grateful to him for letting me know that Puccini existed. Franz Lehár and Gilbert and Sullivan were more to his taste. While at Red House we had been taken on a school outing to the Theatre Royal York to see *The Mikado* and I would ask Colonel Knight to sing 'A wandering minstrel, I'.

It goes without saying that this lovely man and his wife fell under my mother's spell and she was able to lease the bungalow at a peppercorn rent. It was small, far too small for the family. There was a largish bedroom, just about big enough to squash four beds into, and I slept there with Evie, Pat and Terry. Mother and Frank occupied the other two very small bedrooms. There was a living-room and a small kitchen with a copper in the corner, a Valor Perfection paraffin stove against one wall and a clothes mangle up against the other. The larder was a long tin box with a mesh front screwed to the outside wall. The bungalow was lit entirely by oil lamps.

The family washing was done in the copper, rinsed in the sink and then put through the mangle. A big galvanised tub served to hold the clothes after they had been mangled, while a small one caught the water that poured out of the clothes as they went through the rollers. Having hung the washing out to dry (in winter months, wooden clothes horses littered the living-room and fought with the humans for a space by the fire), we kept the copper boiling and one after another leapt in and out of the big galvanised tub which then served as the bath.

The cramped accommodation was a nightmare but, as ever, luck was on our side. Evelyn and John Parry lived at Blackboys, a big house set deep in the woods not far from the Reid-Dicks' cottage. The Parrys also had a bungalow called The Holt which they lent to Mother. During a couple of holidays, Frank and I used The Holt as an annexe to Cheesboys, walking back there each night to sleep. It was about a mile and a half through the woods.

To prepare me for Lancing, Mother and I had to go to London to buy the uniform of grey flannels and a grey herringbone tweed jacket; we couldn't run to the blue serge suit. However, Papa's trunks arrived by sea from Cairo at about this time; they had been nearly six months on their journey. Mother asked for them to be delivered to The Holt. We opened them together and grief enveloped my poor mother as she laid her cheek on his shirts and held his ivory-backed hairbrush in her hand. I joined in with the blubbing but Frank was stoic and his example brought us back to the business in hand.

I tried on one of Papa's suits, a green serge affair which fitted here and there. Mother and I decided that by letting down the trousers we could have a passable suit for church on Sundays. Can you imagine arriving as a new boy at a public school in an ill-fitting suit, which had belonged to your dead father? No? Well, boys are not nice.

The lane leading from Cheesboys up to the Wisborough Green road had very few houses on it. On the left lived some Seventh Day Adventists; we hardly ever saw them and as they were expecting the imminent second coming of Christ, I thought it better to avert my eyes and study the flora. At the top of the hill lived a woman called Joan Dane. She was small and dark-haired with pretty blue eyes and a smashing figure. Her husband, having fought in the desert, was now in Italy. She hadn't seen him for three years. I suppose that my being over six foot made her think I was rather more than my thirteen and a half years. I only learned what she was expecting when some friends invited me to a party at the Petworth Town Hall. She picked me out from the edge of the dance floor and instructed me in leg-to-leg turns and close body harmony. It was wonderful. She told my hosts that, since I lived nearby, she would drive me home.

We sat outside her house. She undid my flies and put her left hand inside my trousers. Her dress was very low cut and her breasts were readily accessible. I can still remember her low groan and the sudden relaxation of her body. She withdrew her hand, kissed me very gently and said, 'You'd better go now.' I think it was later that night that I learned the joys of masturbation.

What with me not looking at the Adventists and Joan Dane not looking at me, I spent a great deal of time with downcast eyes when walking to the bus.

Eighteen years later when I was playing in *The Glad and Sorry*

Season with Juliet Mills at the Theatre Royal in Brighton, the stage door keeper brought me a note from Joan Dane. She wondered if I remembered her. She would come to the stage door in the hope of having a word with me. She was going grey but the eyes still twinkled. We talked in the dressing-room for a while but neither of us mentioned the evening of the Petworth hop.

I took her to a nearby pub for a drink where I was to meet Madge Ryan. Madge was in the play and her wonderful sense of fun and sense of humour captivated me; we had become great friends and were to remain so until her death. She thought me slightly mad and called me Kook.

When Joan had gone, Madge said, 'OK, Kook, what's the story?'

When I'd told her, she burst out laughing. 'How old were you, for God's sake?'

I replied, making good use of the dramatic pause, 'Thirteen – but I was very tall.'

Also at the top of the lane lived Biddy White in an old gypsy caravan, her beautiful Sussex farmhouse with its splendid antique furniture being closed for the duration. Biddy, the widow of a naval commander, had befriended my mother while we were still at Westlands and walking over to get a few eggs from her was always a pleasure. If she was able to spare us a chicken, I had to wring its neck when I got there.

She entertained the American Army, or as many as could fit into her caravan. Sometimes she opened the house on a Sunday, and the Americans brought the food and drink. She had a fine disregard for the so-called county ladies. When taken to task about her cut-down wellies, the men's shorts that she wore and the cardigan done up with different buttons, she was quick to reply that 'each of these buttons comes from the flies of my soldier boyfriends'.

Biddy played a part in my life until she died in the 1950s.

One bright September afternoon, I arrived at Ludlow station wearing, as did many other boys, the grey flannel trousers and grey jackets of our uniform. There were buses to take us to the different houses. My house, Seconds House, was at Canham Court. Canham is a splendid Georgian house some miles out of Ludlow and eight miles from Moor

Park where the main school was. We bicycled to Moor Park every morning for classes and then back for lunch. The person in charge of feeding us apparently thought that one piece of toast with a sausage or a rasher of bacon was quite sufficient to sustain growing boys, especially in winter weather.

There is no doubt about the fact that, educationally speaking, I was a dunce. However, there were some compensations: Mr Neville-Smith, my English master, was kind and friendly and may even have seen some spark of intelligence. I heard later, through his daughter Jennifer, whom I came to know well, that he had talked about the Bulgar new boy with friendly interest.

Then there was the history man, 'Tiger' Halsey, an eccentric and gifted teacher. He illustrated Disraeli's purchase of the Suez Canal by placing a column of copper coins on a desk. 'You, profligate boy, represent a profligate Egypt.' He then swept the coins to the floor, declaring, 'You are bankrupt. That's what you are, bankrupt! If you are the Khedive of Egypt, what do you do? You turn to your French partners and put your shares up for sale in Paris. But Benjamin Disraeli, the Prime Minister, has other ideas.' The column of coins that are now appearing on Tiger's desk transfixes us all. 'Who are the richest bankers in the world, eh? Who are they?'

'Barings,' ventured a small voice, the owner of which got a smart clip on the top of his head with the tennis ball that lived at the end of the sleeve of Tiger's gown.

'Rothschilds?' queried another child.

'Rothschilds! Certainly, Rothschilds! The Prime Minister gives them a quick buzz on the telephone. Or does he?' Silence. 'Of course, he doesn't. This is 1875 and Mr Alexander Graham Bell did not invent the telephone until 1876. No, Mr Disraeli nips across the Channel on the packet steamer and borrows the four million necessary from his friends, the Rothchilds. Without a word to Parliament, without a word to anybody.'

Tiger then took all the money from his desk and handed it over to Egypt. 'There you are, Egypt, you're solvent again but we will have to move a few troops in here to protect our investment. England had bought Egypt. Now, boys, you can collect those coins off the floor for me, and don't fight over them. I know exactly how many

The Way to Wexford – 69

there are.' The class was in turmoil as we leapt about, scrabbling for the coins.

Tiger was now stamping about and tearing his hair. 'The French were livid,' he announced. 'Fit to be tied.' He laughed happily. And that was how I came to learn about how Great Britain came to own the Suez Canal.

Cycling back to Canham one rainy day, I reviewed the bleakness of the years ahead; I could see no light anywhere. I was frequently in trouble of some sort or another and either being beaten by a prefect or writing out lines: 'Armand Jean du Plessis de Richelieu, cardinal and chief minister of France, 1624–42.' Who cares?! I learned more about the man by reading *The Three Musketeers*. The other highly original punishment was to set ten to fifteen lines of poetry to be learned by heart and recited whilst standing on the table in the prefects' common room. I didn't mind this at all and learned endless verse, but I do believe it put hundreds of hefty soccer players off poetry for the rest of their lives.

Stone was a prefect with a squat body, red face and large, red, working hands. I suppose he did me as great a favour as anyone I have ever met. He punished me for the heinous crime of leaving two milk bottles in my locker, and I remember the punishment with intense pleasure. He set me Wilfred Owen's poem 'Anthem for Doomed Youth' to learn and, what is more, Stone sat and listened.

'You like poetry, don't you?' he said when I had finished.

'Yes, I do.'

'It makes sense when you say it. I wish it made sense to me.' There were no other prefects present. I presume that's why he was able to say that to me.

I looked out some of Wilfred Owen's other poetry and thought it just as wonderful. It lay in the back of my mind for many years until it inspired me to read about the man. This led me to write *The Fatal Spring*, a play about Siegfried Sassoon and Owen at Craiglockhart, the Scottish rehabilitation hospital where the two men found themselves during the First World War. The play starred Charles Dance and David Sibley and was awarded the United Nations Media Peace Prize, Award of Merit, in 1980.

I took to the hills and started cross-country running. Usually a couple of Woodbines and a match or two came with me. I was so downright miserable I even had a fistfight with a boy in the stable yard. It was a strange half-intentioned affair which neither of us wanted anything to do with. So we stopped, shook hands, got on our bicycles and cycled off to Moor Park.

The end of my first term at public school arrived and there was Christmas to look forward to, but where was Christmas to be? At the end of the summer holidays Colonel Knight had died suddenly. The luck of the Irish was still with us. The property was not long on the market and was bought by a London solicitor, Peter Glanville, and he was happy for Mother to keep Cheesboys, at the same peppercorn rent.

Peter Glanville was tall and dark-haired, very much the English gentleman. He played cricket for The Invalids, Sir John Squire's cricket team, which gave birth to *England, My England*. He used to come down to Cheesmans at the weekend with his friend, Pete Baker. Pete was a Cockney chorus boy and wonderfully camp. He wore gold bangles round his wrist. 'Name tag, dear. Doesn't do to die incognito, as it were. Some people go for the silver, but it doesn't suit my colouring.'

He told me wonderful stories of touring the army camps in the Middle East. 'Small shows, dear. They call them intimate reviews. You know, we all did a bit of everything. The soldiers loved it. They're so brave. I couldn't do what they do, not if you paid me. Like another gin, dear?' What with beer at twelve and gin at thirteen, life was going along splendidly.

Old Mrs Baker came down from Stratford East for Christmas. She had bowed legs, a round body and she and her son used the same hair colourist. She adored Peter. Whether she knew what the situation was between them, I don't know. She called them 'the boys'.

At Cheesboys life continued. We all chipped in with the chores that had to be done round the house. Frank was very good at digging the pit for the Elsan so long as he didn't have to carry the bucket. Otherwise, his contribution to the smooth running of the house was to sit and read by the open fire, putting a log on if it was getting low. I ruled the kitchen and was Elsan carrier; my reading was done sitting in the outside loo, a great place to read *Gone With the Wind*. Patrick, now about nine, did the important job of gathering kindling, using a ferociously sharp billhook, with which he once cut himself. There being no money for a doctor, Christian Science had to do. Mother took the precaution of cleaning his wound.

Christmas had an air of madness to it. Mother decided that we should all go out singing carols and persuaded 'the boys' to come with us. We trailed round the common visiting the houses. I kept my eyes firmly on the ground when singing 'Hark the Herald Angels' at Joan Dane's front door. She smiled a lot and offered us each a glass of sherry – and her husband, back from the war, was smiling, too. The Seventh Day Adventists slammed the door in our faces. Biddy was wonderful. We all trooped into her caravan, ate cakes, drank tea and laughed ourselves into great good humour and Christmas joy.

Christmas Day arrived. Biddy had given us a turkey and it had to be cooked, but where? There was no room in the oven or the Valor Perfection as all the other goodies had to be cooked on the two burners. We dressed the turkey at eight o'clock in the morning and I set off with it through the woods to The Holt bungalow. I lit the oven, popped in the turkey and went back to Cheesboys. At midday, I fetched the bird, wrapping it in greaseproof paper and an old towel for its return journey. I can't remember how we managed to cook sprouts and roast potatoes and bread sauce, but we did. The Christmas pudding was cooked in the copper. It was a good Christmas and a good New Year.

Some things were constant. Even in 1945, the wireless crackled incessantly as it emitted some incomprehensible language. Mother sat beside it, chain smoking and making copious notes. Then she would leap to the telephone for a long chat with Charles Cousins, her Christian Science practitioner. She was endlessly distressed by her Bulgarian friends not sending her the messages she was expecting nor, indeed, any messages at all.

Many, many years later, after my mother had died, I visited Marion Stancioff, her great friend from Bulgaria, in London. We had lunch and I made her laugh with snippets of theatrical gossip. As we parted, she said, 'You know, Jora, there never was a code from Bulgaria.'

The downside was the return to Shropshire for the spring term at Lancing. Nothing had changed except that it was cold and wet. Then the cheering news broke. The navy was moving out of Lancing

College which meant that the school could return to its own home. While the move took place, we were to have an extended Easter holiday – six weeks instead of four.

I didn't want to be at home all this time – too much washing and cooking – so decided I would get myself a job. I went to Horsham on the bus and made my way to the Labour Exchange. There was a possible job in Wisborough Green at the bakery. They weren't too happy about my being under fourteen but decided to turn a blind eye since it was only a temporary job. That evening I cycled in to Wisborough Green to see Mr Hew, the baker. I was to start at 3 a.m. the very next morning when he would tell me what I had to do. I was wildly excited that I had a job even though threepence-halfpenny an hour didn't seem much of a wage.

I set off at 2.30 in the morning and was in Wisborough Green with five minutes to spare. Mr Hew was already there. He was a big man with a broad face and little hair. He wore a white apron over his everyday clothes; his shirt had a front stud and a back stud but no collar. As I came in through the door, he was walking over to the proving trough and I realised that he only had one leg. His left leg was tin and had only recently been fitted. He was very proud of it. He had lost his own leg four days before the Armistice in 1918.

'Right, your first job every morning will be to grease the tins.'

A very large pile of tins stood on the work surfaces and the floor of the bakery. There were round tins for cottage loaves, there were 1lb tins and 2lb tins, and they all had to be greased. He handed me a tin with some form of oil in it and a grease-sodden rag. 'You want to cover all the surface but be sparse with the grease. There's nothing worse for the bread than too much grease in the tin.'

I set about my first task. We had more than a thousand loaves to bake a day. While I was greasing the tins, Mr Hew was taking the dough from the trough, banging it on the table in front of him, then cutting it with amazing dexterity to exactly the right weight. He would throw it on to the scales to weigh it, but he was never wrong. That first morning, while he was knocking back and kneading, he told me how to differentiate between the loaves. There was the coburg, with cross slashes on the top. When baked, the corners of the coburg became very crisp; these were easy to break off and extremely good to taste.

The cottage loaf, the crinkled loaf, the split tin, the Hovis that needed special flour and a special tin with 'Hovis' embossed on it.

'When you've greased some of those tins, you'd best put them in the proving oven for a minute or two,' I was instructed.

Then Mr Hew went on to tell me about the bloomer, a loaf with four or five cuts in its crust. 'Funny little loaf, the bloomer, bit like a woman. If you treat her nice and let her stand a bit, the bloom will come, but if you leave her on her own too long she's sure to wither. You've got a girlfriend, doubtless, so you'll know. You can't leave them to bloom too long or they'll be picked by someone else.'

At eight o'clock, Bob the deliveryman arrived; he was small, ancient and totally eccentric. Occasionally he would hit his pocket watch a smart knock on the table, pass my greasing cloth over it and pop it in the cooling oven for a few moments. He swore he had never had to have it cleaned and that it had kept regular time for upwards of fifty years.

Mr Hew and Bob had a wonderful bicker–banter relationship and were delighted to have me there to bounce off and, hopefully, embarrass. The running argument was normally the difference in merit, beauty and ability between Anne Shelton and Vera Lynn. Mr Hew was for Vera Lynn while Bob favoured Anne Shelton. The wireless was always on, tuned to the 'Light Programme'. So as well as the art of baking, I was getting an education in popular music and wonderful comedy – Rob Wilton, Flanagan and Allen, Jack Warner, Gert and Daisy. What a change from home where the wireless crackled interminably on uncommunicative wavelengths.

Sometimes I would accompany Bob on his afternoon delivery run and sometimes I coerced him into letting me drive the van. We would bowl along through the Bedham Woods, over the top and back through Kirdford. It was a very happy time.

But like all good things it came to an end and I had to go back to Lancing which was now ready for us.

However, the weekend before I went, Peter Glanville read some of my poetry and suggested he should send it to Jack Squire, literary editor of the *New Statesman*, and chief literary critic on the *Observer*. I was delighted that anyone should take the trouble to help me and sat back to wait for the reply ... days, weeks, months.

*   *   *

Lancing College is an extraordinary building, its tall chapel over-looking the sea and towns of Worthing and Shoreham. The school was built on three terraces, each separated by a quadrangle, each quadrangle surrounded by cloisters. The foundation was firmly rooted in Christian doctrine and we spent what seemed an eternity in prayer. The dining-hall was vast, panelled and gothic, its atmosphere redolent of overcooked cabbage and holier-than-thou tapestries. I was reluctant to admit to myself that the whole was imposing and really very comfortable. There was, of course, a good deal of spartan survival with cold showers every morning and games most afternoons. Again I opted for the solitary cross-country running. A good run to Cissbury Ring, a quick fag under cover of the wood and back to school through Coombes. I played soccer for the Colts and was in the school swimming team. Needless to say, my academic achievements remained firmly below average.

School hadn't been back for ten days when the great news broke: Victory in Europe – 8 May 1945. We were given a week's holiday to celebrate the end of the war. I went home to Cheesboys and Mother suggested that I should go up to London to see the celebrations. Like so many thousand other people, it is a day I shall always remember. I picked up a girl from Brighton Grammar School. We held hands at the Palace railings, we held hands all the way to the Bag of Nails pub on the corner of Buckingham Palace Road, where we had a drink or two. I remember being very grand and drinking a gin and bitters. At the end of the day, she got on the train to Brighton and I got on the train to Billingshurst, and that was that.

Three days later, our milkman from Bedham told us about the great bonfire chain which was to be lit to celebrate the country's victory. That night we walked to the top of the hill where the bonfire had been built as large as a two-storeyed house. People were singing 'All People that on Earth do Dwell' but, as the crier called, 'There goes Arundel! Dunkery next', everyone fell silent. Then a moment later, the crier called, 'Now for Bury'. The excitement was rising to fever pitch. We could see the fires already burning bright on the tops of neighbouring hills. 'It's us next!'

A farmer lit the torch and with a great swoosh our bonfire burst into flame and joined the magic of the flaring beacons proclaiming that Hitler was dead, and the war was over. Peace and victory blazed from hill to hill, past Horsham, past Croydon and on to Primrose Hill in London

Then it was back to Lancing, and the humdrum.

I was still academically dull but I was managing to hold on to some sort of self-esteem through games and perhaps being less bolshie. I began to think that one or two people might quite like me. It came as a complete surprise to me when I was asked to become the head of the 'settle' in Head's House. The settle comprised four boys who were a buffer state between the houseroom and the prefects. John Ewer was to be the senior prefect and it was he who had asked for me to join the new team. I was very flattered but somewhat puzzled. What could they be thinking about? I was a dunce, always in trouble, frequently beaten and always standing on the prefects' table reciting poetry.

Lancing Chapel is so tall that racing pigeons often stopped for a rest, dropping exhausted on to the shelter of its roof. Guided by our strange little housemaster, Mr Gordon, four of us made an expedition to the roof, climbing hundreds of stone stairs to get there. Once on the roof, it was not very difficult to catch the tired pigeons and pop them into a sack.

I christened mine Caesar and Ovid, and they lived in an old tea chest. I clipped their wings and very soon I could leave their door open all day, only closing them up at night to keep them safe from marauding cats. They often sat on my shoulder as I walked about my business. We became great friends but, with the thoughtlessness of youth, I did not consider what was to happen to them during the holidays.

My mother had become friendly with Nell Alderson who lived in a long, low cottage, Eventide, at the top of Bedham Hill. Nell Alderson was small with close-cropped hair, Savile Row suits, Beal and Inman shirts and bow ties, and hand-made shoes. She was very wealthy. She had built herself a studio in the garden where she wrote poetry that would never be published.

She persuaded Mother to take a lease on a small wooden bungalow a little way down the road. Little Farringdons belonged to a London dentist who had used it as a weekend cottage before the war. It stood in a small clearing surrounded by grass; there was no pretence at a garden. Dry leaves lay everywhere, nobody had been near the place for years. It had a glass-covered, wooden veranda where a store of logs and a pile of coal was kept. It had a living-room, a kitchen and three bedrooms. During the summer holidays, Mother and the three youngest were to live here while Frank and I would sleep in Cheesboys, a two-mile walk away.

Patrick, Terry and I arrived on the same day to begin the summer holidays. Frank was to join us the next day and Eve the day after that. We were to sleep that night at Farringdons and when Frank arrived the next day, he and I would move out to Cheesboys.

I didn't take an immediate liking to Nell Alderson, or she to me, but we had a strange mother who was doing her best for us according to her lights. After we had gone to bed, Mother went up to Eventide to have some coffee and a cigarette with Nell. After she had left, I got out of bed and found an old gramophone and some dust-covered records. I put on a record of Dame Clara Butt singing 'Abide with Me'. It made me cry so I played it again.

It had been an extremely hot day. Even the night was hot and still. I had a strange feeling about this place. The next morning, Frank arrived. He hit it off with Nell at once and I told myself that I was exaggerating my feelings of foreboding.

As a family, we had learned to adapt to whatever unusual circumstance we found ourselves in. Or had we? Perhaps we just smiled and accepted this mad way of life as our normality.

The next day was another hot summer's day so Terry, Pat and I went down to the river for a swim. We all had supper with Nell at Eventide, after which Frank and I walked down to Cheesboys to sleep. At about ten o'clock, we went outside to have an al fresco pee and saw the sky alight with fire. It never occurred to us that it could be anything to do with us. In fact, Little Farringdons was burning.

Mother had put the boys to bed and then gone up to see Nell. Patrick woke up, choking with smoke; a moment later, the wood and coal on the veranda burst into flames. He threw a blanket over Terry and, grabbing an ARP warning rattle as he went, he ran out on to the road. There he stood, rattling the rattle until Mother and

Nell heard and ran down to him. The fire was by now totally out of control and Mother needed little persuading not to rush in to try and save things.

They went back to Eventide to ring for the Fire Brigade. Like most telephones at this time, there was no automatic dial, and all calls had to go through the exchange. Mother sat tapping the phone rest until, finally, the postmaster came on the line. He was furious and, before Mother could speak, he roared at her for disturbing him and didn't she know that the exchange closed down at 6.30 p.m. except for emergencies?

'This is an emergency. I need the Fire Brigade,' she finally managed to get in.

'Ah, well, you should have thought of that earlier. Where did you say you were?'

By the time the Fire Brigade had come from Brighton, Little Farringdons was no more. All our clothes, all Mother's jewellery, her papers and her typewriter had gone; the only thing that survived was a badly charred file of my very bad poems. Mother kept one of them all her life.

You can still see the burnt-out shell of the bungalow on the Wisborough Green–Bedham road. It was never rebuilt.

We were refugees again. Mother and the three youngest crammed into Nell's cottage while Frank and I continued living at Cheesboys.

The day after the fire was horrendous. Most of the family had no clothes: Patrick and Terry had only their pyjamas, I had a shirt, trousers and a sweater, and Mother had what she stood up in. Frank had been prudent and taken the taxi from Billingshurst station to Cheesboys before walking up the hill to join us, so his clothes were safe. Evie was all right too since she was due to be fetched from school that day.

Mother, Frank and I went into Petworth and visited the council offices. She was determined to get emergency clothing coupons. Our mother was at her angular best, dismissing any comments of negligence with heart-broken indignation. 'I am a widow with five children, a catastrophe has been visited on the family, and everything was consumed in the fire. All the papers pertaining to my husband's estate, our ration books and clothing coupons, my cheque book and banking details have all gone. We are destitute – and you are trying to apportion blame and sit in judgement.'

The upshot was that we got temporary ration books, clothing coupons and sufficient money to buy the bare necessities of food and clothes. Uncle George came over from Dublin to hold Mother's hand and provide her with some money. He was the dearest man, gentle and benign. He stayed three or four days and was a tonic for us all.

Nell's property was extensive: the cottage had three bedrooms, she had her studio in the garden and there was another studio about five hundred yards up the hill. This long room had plate-glass windows that opened out on to a brick patio. At one end there was a wood-burning stove, a desk and a bed; a table and chairs stood in the centre of the room, and there was another bed by the door. Nell insisted that Frank and I should move up from Cheesboys and stay in this studio. The views were quite glorious and we could see all the way to the Chanctonbury Ring.

Frank and Nell struck up a gun culture friendship. Her father had been a great shot in the north of England and she had inherited her father's eye as well as his fortune. She put a target at one end of the garden and the two of them would sit for hours, shooting away at it. Frank was a very good shot and represented the army at Bisley some years later.

Back to school for the autumn term of 1945, to a new house and, I hoped, a better life. I went straight round to Seconds House to pick up the pigeons. I was not at all prepared for what I found. In their tea-chest house were the two skeletons of Caesar and Ovid. They had not gone out and foraged for themselves, they had not flown away. They had just died. I buried them and put up a little cross. To say I was heartbroken would be an understatement; I even woke up thinking about them in the middle of the night. It took a long time for the guilt and the pain to recede. It is no consolation to them that they taught me that animals must always come first and that if you can't look after them, don't have them.

There was a certain excitement in being one of the senior members in the reopened Heads House, which had been shut during the evacuation. I was captain of swimming and cross-country running, I was in the football and athletics teams, I scrabbled about in the cricket team and played squash. Our housemaster, Sam Jagger, was a squash Blue and coached us into some sort of shape.

My mother seldom paid my fees and we were terms in arrears. I prayed that the bursar would never stop and speak to me about it; I avoided him whenever I could.

While I was enjoying school a lot more, it can't be said that my work was improving. I was by now six foot two and still growing and I cheered myself up in the belief that I was outgrowing my strength and that not enough blood was getting to my brain. It was a good theory and I stuck to it.

It was during this term that something happened which made me resolve to leave Lancing as soon as I could. I had borrowed a pair of spiked shoes from 'Monkey' Chamberlain, housemaster of Gibbs House, who looked after the sports equipment for the school. I had worn them for my field event and then put them in my locker from where they were removed by someone else and used on a cross-country run which ruined the spikes. I knew who the culprit was and tackled him about it; he was mildly apologetic but shrugged it off.

Mr Chamberlain was called 'Monkey' because of his habit of tapping his chest with his clenched right hand when he spoke. It didn't help him that he had the forehead, eyes and jaws of a monkey, too. I took the ruined shoes back to him and told him what had happened but not who had done it. It was clear that Monkey didn't believe me, and said so, and later took great pleasure in humiliating me during an English class.

'You know, Baker is a dreadful liar and a cheat. Baker borrowed some running shoes from me and ruined them. He returned them to me saying that an unknown person had taken them from his locker and used them without his permission. Then, if you can believe such a thing, this unknown person returned them to his locker.'

There was a general laugh at this.

'Baker couldn't answer that simple question on parsing because he has no need to learn. He was born with a silver spoon in his mouth.'

Years later, I was appearing as the Earl of Warwick in the Old Vic production of *Saint Joan* when I received a note from the stage door. The note was from Monkey Chamberlain saying that he was seeing the matinée performance and would very much like to meet me after the show. I was flabbergasted.

I was sharing a dressing-room with Alec McCowen and told him the story. 'What are you going to do?' he asked.

'I can't pass up an opportunity like this,' was my immediate reply. 'I'm going to remind him of what he did and then tell him what I think of him.'

The man who came into the dressing-room was old and sad – a little, wizened monkey. He was full of praise for the production and our performances. Of course, I didn't say any of the things I had planned. I removed my make-up and took him out to tea.

When I got back to get ready for the evening performance, Alec was in high spirits. 'You told him. You really told him. I thought it was really cruel the way you called him sir and asked after his health, and then to cap it all you had to take him out to tea. That must have been the unkindest cut of all as far as he was concerned.' Then Alec lifted his left cheek off the chair and farted. A basic social accomplishment he had perfected over the years.

'God, Alec.'

He grinned happily at me in his dressing-room mirror.

Things were not going well at home. We spent our holidays in the usual ramshackle way, moving from one house to another. The friendship with Nell Alderson had become difficult for my mother to sustain as Nell was becoming more and more demanding of her time. Money had almost entirely dried up; Father's few insurances had matured and been spent. The year, 1945, was rolling itself up into a ball of misery and uncertainty.

Christmas at Cheesboys was cold and our spirits low and the wretched news that Peter Glanville was going to sell the cottages put us in a fine way of gloom. Where were we to live? As usual, we put up a spirited fight to pretend everything was as normal as could be. After all, what could be more normal than trudging a mile through the mud to get the milk every morning, or three miles through the snow into Wisborough Green to get the meat ration which had been forgotten?

Soon it would be 1946 and things were going to get better. The move I had been planning had to be made immediately.

On my return to school after Christmas, I laid the foundations by speaking to Sam Jagger, my housemaster, and telling him that I would be leaving at the end of term. I told him that I knew my mother would never get round to writing to the bursar, and failing to give a term's notice would simply add more money to the debt. Sam was a good, kind man from a normal middle-class background and could not make head nor tail of the mad world I lived in. He said that he was very sorry to hear of all the problems at home and that he quite understood the position. He would speak to the bursar himself.

For some terms now, I had had to borrow my fare home from Sam Jagger and he reimbursed himself when Mother's letter with my fare in it arrived, usually a couple of days after term had ended. I had to gamble that he wouldn't write to my mother to confirm the situation, and settled down to sit out the term, culling as much sympathy as I could from boys and masters alike.

Halfway through the term, Mother wrote to me to say that she and Nell were no longer on the happiest of terms and that she would be sending Pat and Terry to Prim Ware at Green Hammerton for the holidays, and Evie was to go to friends in Wisborough Green. She also wrote that Frank, having passed his Higher School Certificate, was going to join the army as a regular soldier. That left me. Apparently, Nell was quite happy to have me at Eventide until things were sorted out.

My original plan was to have gone home, wherever home was, at the end of the term and announce to Mother I had left school. This would no longer do as I didn't want to be at Eventide alone with her and Nell. There had to be another way forward.

At the end of term, I stood with Sam Jagger outside the chapel, looking out over the playing fields, over the estuary, and over the cement works to Hove and Brighton. He wished me well and asked me if I had thought of what I would do as a career.

I was far too cagey to tell him that I was going to be an actor. I said I had no idea. When we said our goodbyes, I could see that he was concerned for me but powerless to help.

Using the money he had lent me for the fare, I took the bus to Shoreham railway station and bought a one-way ticket to London. When I arrived at Victoria, I left my large suitcase in the left luggage office and, carrying my light overnight case, went out into Victoria Street. The first tram I saw was a number 36 to Lewisham and Catford.

7

I GOT OFF AT THE ODEON CINEMA IN LEWISHAM, AND ASKED THE WAY TO THE POLICE STATION. I needed somewhere to live, I told them. Having looked at my identity card and established that I was who I said I was and that I was fifteen and therefore over school-leaving age, the desk sergeant was extremely helpful. I was very tall and spoke with what in those days was called an Oxford English accent so it was assumed that I had money. In fact, I had £4 in the whole world.

The desk sergeant made a telephone call and then gave me the address of a Mr and Mrs Shepherd who were apparently willing to give me lodgings for thirty shillings a week, payable in advance, and for that I would get breakfast and supper. He told me how to get to 65 Quentin Road in Blackheath, not far away.

Em and Will Shepherd must each have been about fifty. She was tiny and round, Will was slim and sharp-featured and both were very Cockney. They seemed to be very kind people and made me feel at home immediately. Em showed me the spare room and I paid my thirty shillings. There, I was on my way! Making the excuse that I wanted to have a look round Blackheath village, I went to the nearest phone box and reversed the charges to Eventide.

I shall never know whether my mother was worried or not that I hadn't turned up when she expected me. Certainly there was no indication of concern in her voice. She just calmly asked me where I was. I hugely enjoyed telling her the whole story of my escape from Lancing, especially remembering to point out that, having given a term's notice, she would not have to pay a term in lieu.

Mother was always wonderfully calm in a crisis. She didn't scold or become hysterical; she simply asked me for my new address which, of course, I gave her. She said she would try and send me some money, but I told her I didn't need any since I was going to get myself a job in the morning.

When I got back, Em had made Marmite sandwiches and masses of strong black tea. Will asked me about my life, and what with he being so interested and I so garrulous, I was soon whizzing us through Bulgaria, Ireland, Yorkshire, Sussex – right up to this new adventure in London. He asked how I proposed to get a job, and when I said I thought I'd look at the advertisements in the local paper, he advised me instead to go to the Labour Exchange.

I was looking at a world so far away from the one I had been used to. I was in turn enchanted and dismayed. Enchanted because it seemed to offer such stability, dismayed because I could see a lifetime of captivity and no way out.

Will took my political education in hand, his ideas being far-flung from my mother's, especially on the subject of European unity.

When I dared to mention that Winston Churchill was all for a pan-European state, the explosion was ferocious and I was immediately put right about Mr Churchill's career: the Dardanelles, the siege of Sydney Street and a whole list of his other shortcomings, particularly his oppression of the British working classes. I had never met anyone who held such strong opinions or who had such disdain for the 'ruling classes'. If I thought about it at all, I assumed that everyone thought Mr Churchill was a wonderful man and that the Labour government under Mr Attlee was a joke; certainly Hugh Dalton's 'Ground Nut Scheme' seemed to be one of the best jokes around at the time.

After an invigorating evening with Will and Em, I went up to bed and, now alone, was suddenly very homesick for my mother. Having always been a believer, I knew what to do: I said my prayers, half orthodox, half Mary Baker Eddy, and cried myself to sleep.

The next morning I went to the Labour Exchange in Lewisham and was sent off to Elliot Machine Tool Engineers where I was taken on as a junior clerk in the despatch department at £2 10s a week. Having paid the rent, I would have a pound a week to myself. I went back and told Em the good news. She was very pleased for me, probably relieved since she could see the rent being paid.

I needed to go to Victoria to collect the suitcase I had left there, so I walked back to Lewisham and from there to Victoria. It was a good long tramp and that walk was the beginning of a lifetime's habit. Many years later, when playing in Noël Coward's *Look After Lulu* at the Henry Miller Theater on Broadway, I was staying in Brooklyn Heights and would walk to the theatre most days, a distance of about six miles. The Americans thought I was completely mad but, by crossing from avenue to avenue, I got to know that wonderful city very well. I got to know Sydney like this, Auckland and Madrid, Lisbon, Paris and Berlin, not to mention my continuing love affair with London.

I retrieved my case from the left luggage office in Victoria and caught the tram back to Blackheath. When I arrived at my new home, I found my mother sitting there. She had immediately stopped looking for somewhere else for the family to live at the required peppercorn rent, and had decided to come and stay in Blackheath. I was moved out of my little room and put to sleep on the put-you-up in the front parlour.

My mother's charm and brass neck had worked its magic. I was pleased to see her, of course, but somewhat dismayed that she had crowded into my new life. She wasn't slow in getting a job, either. She became a health visitor in Eltham and Woolwich.

One Saturday afternoon we went together to see her mother's grave in Eltham cemetery. I shan't forget that cold November day, an unkempt grave, a fading inscription and a very worn woman, crying gently in the soft rain.

She wrote shortly afterwards to her Aunt Eva:

I am now working out the fulfilment of the tragedy of Mamma's life in the same place as she failed to meet it. I need everyone's prayers to help me to stand in the very same place and denounce it all as unreasonable, otherwise it would be easy enough for me to give it all up as she did, but I have the consciousness of a loving husband beside me and behind me. However, don't let anyone imagine that it is either easy or amusing being without a home . . .

The family spent the Christmas of 1946 at nos. 65 and 69 Quentin Road. Emmie's brother, Frank, lived at no. 69 with his wife, Glad. Frank was considered very weird by the family because he'd had a vasectomy. 'It's that Glad,' they'd say. 'She put him up to it. Sinful, that's what it was.' Evie and I were in no. 65 and Pat and Terry were in no. 69 with Mother. Brother Frank was away in the army. Now a tall Irish Guardsman, he was stationed in Caterham.

It was not the best of Christmases. It was not the worst.

Throughout the war, Mother had been trying to get money out of Bulgaria where it had been frozen during the hostilities, but there was no trade between British and communist countries. Now, however, she had been told by the Foreign Office that she might try applying for compensation. Her world looked bright again; there was a fight to be fought.

I settled down to try to master the business of being a despatch clerk. With my record of academic achievement, this was not easy but I seemed to manage well enough to hang on to the job. I was told to enrol for the machine-turning course at Goldsmiths' College. Here I really proved to myself that I would never make a skilful lathe operator but help was at hand.

A production of *The Cradle Song* was looking for a chorus, so I went to see the producer, Philip Ryder, who asked me to do a piece for him. I trotted out 'The Fiddler of Dooney' and got the part. I enjoyed the rehearsals for *The Cradle Song*. My part was to give the narrator's speech in the opening scene. In those days, I had no idea that I should be nervous or frightened. I just got on with it and enjoyed it. Mother came over and saw me on the first night and said she was very proud of me, which was nice. Will's niece Celia came with a boyfriend. Em and Will didn't come; Will thought the theatre was for nancy boys.

Celia took to coming over on Saturday afternoons. She was a Comptometer operator in the City and about four years older than me. She was mildly myopic which I found very attractive. We walked on Blackheath and held hands. We went to the pictures and fumbled during *How Green Was My Valley*. As we walked home, I told Celia I was going to be an actor and fancied myself in the Walter Pidgeon mould.

We got home late and since Em and Will were in bed, we continued to snog in the kitchen. Celia was down to stockings, knickers and suspender belt when there was a knock on the kitchen door and Will's voice commanded us to go to bed. How tactful of him not to pop his head round the door. Talk about necking pains! We continued to see each other for some time but never reached such dizzy heights again.

There was a Sunday ritual in the Shepherd household that never ceased to delight me. After lunch, Will would have a bath while Em busied herself with the washing up. I was usually drying up so was in a good position to see her mounting excitement which rose to snatches of Scottish song. Then Will would come to the bedroom door and call to her. 'Em, where's my clean shirt?' 'Just coming, Will.' And they were not seen again until Wilfred Pickles was due on the wireless with 'Have A Go'.

Will felt there was no real future for me at Elliot's and that I would be better off in a job with a borough council. I think he saw me as a local government officer. He spoke to his sister-in-law, Celia's mother, who was Mayor of Poplar and an interview was arranged. I got the job as junior clerk in Poplar Borough Council's Baths and Washhouses Department, in the East India Dock Road. I was quite unsuitable for the job but, hey-ho for patronage!

With the advent of the new job I felt that I should spend the £5 I had saved on some new clothes: I chose a brown jacket with light red checks, a pair of grey flannel trousers, two semi-starched Van Heusen collars and a rather flashy red and yellow Paisley tie. That was it: the money had gone and new shoes would have to wait for another time. My current shoes consisted of a pair of highly polished uppers with disastrous soles made partly of rubber, part cardboard and part newspaper. The grey and black herringbone Lancing jacket, from which my hands and wrists protruded like a scarecrow, was taken by Em to a bring-and-buy sale and I got ninepence for it. With it sold, I felt that my old unsatisfactory life had truly gone.

I worked for Mr Walker, the chief clerk, who was small, bald and miserly but luckily I didn't have to spend much time in the office. My duties were simple enough: I had to check and refill the Brylcreem machines in the slipper baths, the Turkish baths and the changing rooms of the swimming pool, not only in Poplar but in Bow, Hackney, the Isle of Dogs, Stepney and Farringdon Road. Having refilled the Brylcreem and collected the pennies from the dispenser, I collected the money from the ticket sales to the swimming baths, Turkish baths and slipper baths. Under the baths was hell's cauldron — the collective washhouse. When you went down the steps to the washhouse you were met by hot steam and the sound of bubbling water. Large cauldrons full of washing were boiling and bubbling all day. Housewives without facilities at home could take their washing there and, having washed it, there was an ironing room. Or they could employ a washerwoman to do it for them. The washerwomen paid 1s 1d an hour for the use of the facilities. The name A. Weekes figured largely on the chitties from the Bow washhouse. Annie Weekes was a professional laundress and spent her days and well into the night in the subterranean hell. There was always laughter and wisecracks back and forth, insults that passed for wit and wit that was so much the stuff of everyday life that it went unnoticed.

One of the people I worked with in the department was Douglas Newman, gay, ex-sergeant in the Chindits, devoted to the theatre. A gentle, funny man, Dougie was a member of the Borough Amateur Dramatic Society, later becoming the Borough Entertainment Officer. I made no secret about wanting to be an actor. My colleagues ragged me about my ambition, promising that if I succeeded, they would come and see me. Many years later when I was playing in Agatha Christie's *Towards Zero* at the St James's Theatre in London, Annie Weekes and a group from the Baths and Washhouses Department came to see me. We had a wonderful party in the pub next to the theatre after the show, much to the bewilderment of the stalls and circle clientèle who had come in for a quiet gin and tonic before going out for a late supper.

Honest Stan, a fireman from Bow, gave his verdict: 'I never thought you'd make it. I thought you were a lot of piss and wind, but well done.'

In the meantime, things had been happening to my mother. She sometimes saw Nell Alderson and it was on one of their outings to the Cowdray Club that Mother had met Lady Hutchinson. Lady Hutchinson was recently widowed and was planning to go for a long visit to her daughter in Rhodesia. She was anxious about her house in Roedean Crescent in Roehampton which she didn't want to leave empty. Mother's quick wits came to the fore once more and she suggested that it should be turned into a maternity home and, when there was the need, a nursing home. To her delight, Lady Hutchinson agreed and Mummy moved out of the Blackheath house.

One afternoon, I decided to cross London to see what Mummy was up to. I finished work at twelve o'clock and set off to walk to Roehampton. The route I had chosen with the help of the office *A to Z* took me four hours. I soon found a better way to go and cut the journey down to two and a half hours. There was occasional entertainment on this route: one evening, with the dusk falling, I was crossing Barnes Common when I heard a disembodied voice from under a shrub say, 'You leave my body be.' I thought it better not to hang about and took to my heels.

The house in Roedean Crescent was a large, handsome, detached family home with an impressive hall, six bedrooms and three bathrooms. A large kitchen led to a splendid garden. Very suitable for a nursing home. Mother's partner, Major Nita Smith, had been a sister in Queen Alexandra's Royal Army Nursing Corps. She was a diminutive Welsh woman with a prodigious sense of humour and a heart of gold. She also happened to have money and she saved us many a time in the years to come.

I walked into the nursing home at about six o'clock that first Saturday evening. Mother's spirits were exuberant, she was taking everyone with her. She and Nita were the only nursing staff at the moment. Lady Hutchinson had taken in paying guests to augment her slender resources and some of them were still there. This helped the cash flow while the work required by the health authorities was done. The paying guests, too, had fallen under Mother's spell, particularly an Egyptian girl, Jackie Rollo. Thank God for her: she was very rich and Mother and the children owed many a meal to

Right Aunt Ethel: Small as we are,
a-hunting we will go...

Below Aunt Ethel as I remember
her – staunch friend to children

Grandpa Joe
of the Dublin Harriers

Playing the lead in
The Moonraker, with
co-star Sylvia Syms

Just for the fun of it!

Jackie. There was a splendid feeling of 'onwards and upwards'. I felt that Mother had come into a safe harbour and that her days of strife were at an end.

One afternoon a short time later, I was having a cup of tea with Dougie Newman. He was telling me to read plays as well as novels, when he suddenly changed the subject. 'Give in your notice and go. Go into the theatre.'

'But what would I live on?'

'Did you think of that when you ran away from school?'

'No.'

'How long did it take you to find a job?'

'A morning.'

'Well, then. And don't let anybody put you off. My mother put me off, and when I came home she was ill and I had to stay home and look after her. I shall always regret not having had a go. So, you take my advice.'

Before I took the plunge, however, there were one or two things that had to be decided – principally, where was I to live? All the rooms at the nursing home were needed for patients so Mother could not live in and she had found herself digs in East Sheen Avenue. It was only a short walk to the home across the common and suited her well. I rang her up and told her what I was going to do and asked her if there was room for me in her digs. And so it was arranged that I should move in with her at Mrs Gibbs'.

I gave in my notice to Poplar Borough Council and then told Emmie and Will. Will was pretty scathing about the whole thing. Acting was not a job for real men; in fact, acting was not a job at all. Notwithstanding, he wished me luck. Em and I had a big hug and she cried a lot. I told her I'd be seeing her, and that she wouldn't be rid of me that easily.

Mother, unthinkingly, played them a cruel joke. She invited Will to do the books for the nursing home. Will was a foreman-painter with little education and no knowledge of accountancy, but he decided to accept, saying he would go to night school and 'buff up' on it. So I was still to see them for a while.

I now started to look for work as an actor. Lady Hutchinson suggested

I went down to the Richmond Theatre and asked the man in the box office if there were any jobs going for actors. He turned his astonished gaze on me. 'Write in with your CV, and enclose a photograph. Address the envelope to Mr Miles.' He returned to his work. The interview was over and I left. I had no idea what a CV was, presumably something that actors needed. This business of getting a job in the theatre was obviously going to prove very difficult, particularly as I had no money. My mother was paying Mrs Gibbs for my room. Either I was eating at the nursing home or I just wasn't eating.

The next day I caught the 73 bus to Oxford Street. I was going to see an agent, Miriam Warner. I don't know where I got this information about agents, but I was sure that this was the proper thing to do. As I had no appointment, no experience and no training I was told to push off and not to waste people's time.

I wandered disconsolately down Shaftesbury Avenue and stopped to look at the front of house photos outside the Lyric Theatre. A hand fell on my shoulder and a voice said, 'Hello, Baker.'

It was Peter Beeny with whom I had been at school. Peter was a couple of years older than I but had left at the same time. He was in effervescent mood; he had just had the results of his first exam and was on his way to becoming a doctor. He had passed with flying colours and his father, who was a Harley Street specialist, was so pleased with his only son, that he was going to lend him one of the family cars to take himself off for a couple of days. Was I doing anything? Would I like to join him? He was going to Deal to see his prep school headmaster, Mr Harrison. Mother gave me £2 spending money. God knows where she found it, but it was wonderful of her.

We set off in a little Standard Eight, first to Canvey Island where we spent the night in a tent and then on to Deal. Mr Harrison was delighted to see us. We were offered some tea and then came the invitation that was to change my life. He told us that, although she was not of course a professional actress, his wife was sometimes persuaded to play an older part with the resident rep company at the Astor Hall in Deal and was, in fact, there now. He was going to see the play that evening and asked if we would like to join him. We jumped at it.

After the show, I excused myself and went backstage. I knocked on Mr Burke Onwin's door and asked if he had any place for an actor? Apparently I had picked an opportune moment: one of the company had been called up to do his National Service and I could replace him.

'How much experience have you had?' asked Mr Onwin, the company's producer/director and leading man.

'I've been at the Richmond Theatre for eighteen months,' I lied, effortlessly.

The next two questions were easy to answer. 'Have you got a suit?' 'Yes,' I lied again. 'Can you start next Wednesday?' No need to lie about that one.

Mr Onwin walked over to his dressing-room door and called for someone called Archie who was a tall young man with blond, wavy hair and moustache.

'Archie is not only an actor,' Mr Onwin explained, 'he does the money as well. Archie, this is George Baker from the Richmond Theatre. He can take over when Rupert goes. I suggest three pounds; what do you think?'

'I think that'll stretch us, Burke. Two pounds ten, how's that?'

'Thank you,' I replied, quickly.

'Be here at ten o'clock next Wednesday, then.'

So fate had sorted me. I was about to become an actor.

I went home and gave my mother first the glad news and then the bad. I had a job and was to be an actor but I needed a suit. Mother turned up trumps: the trump was Nell Alderson. I was to go to Morris Angel, the tailors, and be measured for a suit. They made it with one fitting in three days. I don't think it had ever occurred to Nell that we could have gone to the fifty-shilling tailors and bought one off the peg.

I went down to Deal a day early and found myself some digs with Mrs Lucas; they were just off the front and a stone's throw from the theatre. My room, breakfast and a light supper cost me £2, leaving me ten shillings for myself.

The Burke Onwin Players was unlike any other theatre company I have met with since. In effect, Mr Onwin had gathered together some friends who enjoyed amateur dramatics and by calling themselves professional had become so. They booked the Astor Hall in Deal for a season running from April to September; they did one play on Monday, Tuesday and twice on Wednesday, then another play on Thursday, Friday and twice on Saturday. Burke had trained, I believe, at the Guildhall but he had contracted polio and his left leg was withered. He wore a cork calf to even up his legs but he could not disguise his limp. He was a good actor with a splendid voice but overworked himself by always playing the lead. As we were staging two plays a week, it was almost impossible for him to learn the parts. That's where I came in. I was described as the ASM – assistant stage manager – on the books. I became a very good prompt.

Sometimes we had visiting actors down from London. I remember particularly an actress called Catherine Parr. She came down to play the mother in *The Silver Cord*. I had seen Olivier as Richard III, and as Oedipus in *Oedipus Rex* and Mr Puff in Sheridan's *The Critic*, a double bill at the Old Vic; I had seen Gielgud as Raskolnikov in *Crime and Punishment* with Edith Evans and Peter Ustinov. Therefore, I had some idea what proper acting ought to look like but I had not seen it at the Astor Hall until the coming of Catherine Parr. It was so unexpected that I remember the performance to this day. She also offered me some advice about trying to get myself into RADA and learning to act properly. There was not much point in trying to explain that a) I was a dunce and b) there was no money and I didn't want to get on to the merry-go-round of unpaid fees. I knew I would just have to pick it up as I went along.

The company was too poor to run to canvas flats so our scenery was made with hessian and sized. Size has the most awful smell and, I'm sure, was dangerously toxic. Burke had worked out a cunning scheme for the scenery which gave it a double use: the wooden frames of the flats were painted brown or black to represent oak beams and the hessian, on that side of the flat, was painted in cream. Immediately we had a period, rustic room, suitable for *Queen Elizabeth Slept Here*. On the other side, the paintwork was kept to a subtle colour above the dado, contrasting with something darker below. Thus we could play *Queen Elizabeth Slept Here* for the first half of the week and slip into Benn W. Levy's *Springtime for Henry* for the last three days.

I wish I had kept the first notice I received in the local paper, but

I didn't. Robert Morley had written a play called *Goodness, How Sad* which took place in theatrical digs in a seaside town.

The inspiration undoubtedly came from the rep company that Peter Bull ran at Perranporth. Peter Bull, perhaps one of the most loved and cherished of men – actor, writer and lover of teddy bears – in post-war theatre and films, started his career by gathering an astonishing cast to play a summer season at Perranporth. There was Pamela Brown, Judith Furse, Robert Morley, Michael Gough to act. Roger Furse, who later designed Olivier's *Henry V* and *Hamlet*, came down to design the sets. Robert Morley wrote *Goodness, How Sad* for the company and its premiere had been at Perranporth in that season of 1938.

Robert Morley had written himself a splendid part as a German seal trainer – not a very big part but very showy. I played it at Deal. There was a short but eye-catching scene when the trainer comes in to tell the company that his favourite seal has died. Tears coursed down my cheeks and my accent became ever more guttural with emotion. The house was enchanted, particularly the critic who said I played the part with great sensitivity. Only in rep could a sixteen-year-old, gangling and callow boy be cast as a fat, forty-five-year-old German seal trainer. As soon as I saw the notice, I rushed off to telephone my mother. I read her the notice and she was thrilled.

By looking through the spy hole in the curtain, I could watch the house come in and one evening I was ravished by the entrance of two beautiful girls. They were both blonde and were both wearing the height of fashion, the New Look. One was Archie's girlfriend, Tuppe, and the other was Pat Menges. It was on Pat that my heart settled. It was all so splendidly romantic and faintly Mills and Boon but the unconsummated love affair lasted for over a year. Pat, aged twenty-three, was married but was in the process of having her marriage annulled on the grounds of non-consummation. The non-consummation of the marriage led to the non-consummation of the affair. As the song has it, we went about as far as we could go.

It was a happy, tripping time and most of it with laughter.

Brother Frank came down to see me from Sandhurst where he was busy learning how to be an officer and a gentleman. Unfortunately, I wasn't playing as cast at the time so he didn't see his younger brother giving his art. He was puzzled about the Pat Menges business and concerned that I might get into trouble with the husband.

On occasion, an envelope would arrive from Mother with a couple of pounds in it. That meant a good blowout on fish and chips and a couple of glasses of beer. The culture of the pub was getting to me. They were welcoming, and they were warm. You could sit and clutch a half of mild and bitter, price sixpence, for nearly an hour. I could usually find someone to talk to and, being so tall, nobody questioned my age. Pubs became a habit – and there was an amazing forty-seven of them in Deal.

Nat Gubbins of the *Sunday Express* lived in Deal and frequently came to the shows. One memorable evening he brought with him the great comedian and actor Sid Field. Sid was supposed to be on a drying-out cure but was staying at the Royal Oak Hotel, which very soon defeated the object. They came to see *Life with the Carters*, a drama set in the East End and written by Burke Onwin. I was playing the son of the family, a bolshie, an apprentice motor mechanic suffering the pangs of unrequited love. I have an ear for accents and my Cockney is almost native so I flew into the part with gusto.

After the show I got a message that Nat Gubbins and Sid Field would like me to join them at the Royal Oak. I thought it was somebody pulling my leg but was assured by the front of house manager that it was genuine. I went to the hotel where the two men were waiting for me in the residents' lounge. I was very overawed because I had seen *Piccadilly Hayride* and thought Sid Field a great comic genius and here he was buying me a drink and showering me with praise. Had I come down from London to play the part? Where had I trained? I told him that this was my first job in the theatre and that I had no formal training.

He then did an astonishing thing: he wrote four letters of intro-duction – to Athene Seyler with whom he was starring in *Harvey*; to Kitty Black, managing director of the Company of Four; to the directors of the Richmond Theatre – Alan Miles, Andrew Melville and Freddie Piffard; and to Marjorie Hawtry at the Everyman, Hampstead. When the season finished at Deal, I was to take my letters and try my luck in London.

8

Having met Athene Seyler, Kitty Black and Marjorie Hawtry, all of whom were kind but unhelpful in the matter of employment, I finally saw Andrew Melville at the Richmond Theatre. He was happy to employ me as ASM.

Richmond was the proper beginning to my career, and a happy one. There were two companies interchanging with the theatre at Watford; in this way, each play ran for two weeks. Each company had a stage director, stage manager and three ASMs. The casts were strong and good: Leslie Sands, Terence Alexander, Harry Towb, John Le Mesurier, Henry Oscar, Winifred Melville, Jean Forbes Robertson, Bill Roderick, Jeffrey Segal and many others.

I had a couple of months to acclimatise myself as an ASM and also played some small parts before being flung into my first experience of a pantomime. There is nothing so glorious as watching a man rehearsing for Dame Trot or Widow Twankey. The steps and moves are indicated with a practised nonchalance and loose-limbed precision. Music is being played and songs sung, wonderfully silly lines are spoken with complete sincerity. The *corps de ballet* is stuffed full of amazingly pretty girls who have no time, sadly, to dally with drooling ASMs.

It all begins to come together and the great day of the band call comes. The rehearsal pianist has tinkled out the tunes for the actors to learn the songs. But now, a couple of days before the dress rehearsal, Bert Johnson brings in his orchestra. The orchestra tunes up and the Dame runs some of her numbers. Her dance routines are well illustrated by percussion and coconuts. Winnie Melville, as the Prince Charming, sings 'All the little trees seem to whisper Louise'. The transformation scene and the *corps de ballet* take their places in the Palace Ballroom to execute a couple of stately minuets before the entrance of Prince Charming and Louise who will lead the cast into the first waltz. The audience, the song sheet and the children singing make the whole evening into the magical stuff of dreams.

There is nothing so exhilarating as running from the bottom to the top of the theatre, knocking on every dressing-room door, shouting, 'Overture and beginners, please.' One evening I was doing just that when I heard a furious row going on in dressing-room four, the Baron's dressing-room, which he shared with his wife who was appearing as the Fairy Queen. It was surprising that he had a wife at all as he was 'a little light-footed' and certainly lisped. The row was about her pregnancy, for which he would not take the entire blame.

As I raised my hand to knock on their door and cry my cry, I heard him disclaim his responsibility, 'Well, if you hadn't wriggled, it never would have happened.' I decided to move on to the next dressing-room before calling out, 'Overture and beginners, please.' It was very difficult not to look at them both in a new light.

One minute from the stage door stood The Cobwebs, the theatre pub, run by Ma and Pa Carver. The Carvers were extremely good to me, often feeding me a big bowl of soup and a hunk of bread for free. They were used to me running into The Cobwebs to call the half hour to curtain up. On one occasion, we were presenting a play about Paddy Finucane VC, the RAF fighter pilot who fought in the Battle of Britain. I don't know if it was a good play or not but my education in theatre took a formidable step forward.

Henry Oscar was directing the play and playing Paddy's father. Michael Allinson was playing the hero. The substantial cast included Wally Patch and Mark Daly. Wally Patch was a large man with a big voice, a great capacity for drink and story-telling. He was also well into the black market with nylon stockings and ladies' dainty underwear. Wally would carry his make-up around in a matchbox, which contained a very small piece of eyeliner and a sponge. He would cut away some of the paint on the dressing-room wall and expose the brick, then he would rub the sponge on it and daub his cheeks, add a little line of black under his eyes and his make-up was complete.

'Sorry I'm late, boy,' he said to me one day. 'The good lady got a bit frisky after lunch and it ended with me table-endin' 'er and missing the bus.'

Wally went on to play in farce at the Whitehall Theatre where, I think, he stayed for the rest of his life. Mark Daly was a small, quiet man with a light tenor voice. He hummed happily through rehearsals, performances and when he was standing by the bar drinking. I've no doubt he hummed in his sleep.

These two were the bane of my life: they would slip out to The Cobwebs in between scenes, almost between pauses and I would have to run helter-skelter to the pub. 'You're on, Mr Daly! You're on, Mr Patch!'

'Don't take on, lad,' they'd say, calmly. 'There's all the time in the world.'

'Honestly, we're up to the battle scene,' I'd pant.

'Look here, boy . . . oh, all right. Put that scotch to one side, Bet, we'll be back in a mo.'

They would saunter through the stage door and on to the stage, making their entrance on cue. I was left a gibbering wreck.

I opened the play as a BBC engineer installing a system so that a reporter could send his commentary of the battle through to Broad-casting House. My lines seemed to consist of 'one, two, three, four . . . testing . . . testing'. Wally would stand beside me muttering in my ear, 'Here's your chance to upstage the oldest juvenile in the business. Walk downstage and slap your meat and two veg on the footlights, that'll get him.' There was never a flicker on Henry's face.

Of all the actors I met at Richmond, John Le Mesurier had the greatest influence. I would sit in the prompt corner listening to his laconic delivery and watching his impeccable timing. At that time he was married to June Melville, the boss's sister and herself an actress, so he seldom lacked for work. I also have to thank him for introducing me to jazz. There was a small jazz club in Soho where we would sometimes go after the show. I would then walk back to Richmond, both because of the lack of money and the lack of transport at that time of night. I tried all sorts of variations of the route but, in truth, they all took an hour and a half.

On one occasion, Henry Oscar taught me a salutary lesson. While in rehearsal, I had wandered across the stage about to change some props, a cigarette dangling from my lips and my hands in my pockets. 'Take that cigarette out of your mouth and your hands out of your pockets, and apologise to me and the cast for your behaviour.'

'I'm sorry.'

'You're sorry, what?'

I hadn't been to a public school for nothing. 'I'm sorry, sir.' I have never been able to smoke in rehearsals since.

It was coming up to Christmas 1948 and I had been at Richmond for the best part of a year. Because I was not going to be working on the pantomime, I was given a week off. Frank was due for some leave. Seeing an opportunity to have the whole family with her, Mother decided to take Christmas off and rent a cottage somewhere. The cottage she found was at Bignor, very near our old stamping ground in Sussex. This was to be the last time that all her children would be together under the same roof.

The journey to Pulborough was to introduce several exciting and unexpected dimensions into my life. I was sitting in the train waiting for it to leave Victoria station when an extremely attractive blonde woman came into the carriage. She was well dressed in a beautifully cut tweed suit and crocodile shoes, and was carrying a crocodile handbag. She sat down on the opposite side of the carriage by the door. She appeared to take no notice of me. When two more people got in, I stopped staring at her.

At Clapham Junction the other two got out and she immediately opened a conversation. 'I'm awfully glad they've gone, aren't you?'

'Er, yes.'

'You're a very *beau garçon*. What do you do?'

'I'm an actor.'

'*Tiens!* I'm Ginny Wharton and I'm divorced. What's your name?'

'George Baker.'

'Good straightforward name. Where are you travelling to?'

'Bignor, to spend Christmas with my family.'

'I'm going to Dell Quay near Chichester to spend Christmas with mine.'

She crossed her legs very prettily. They were not long legs. She had small feet and well-shaped ankles and the calves had just the suggestion of a bow.

As I had lately begun educating myself, I was full of Anatole France's *Thaïs*, Thomas Mann's *The Magic Mountain*, and dropped in a few quick references to the *Odyssey*. I don't know if Ginny decided to put up with all that rubbish in order to get some of the other, or whether she genuinely thought I was well read. She mentioned that this would be the last time she would be seeing her mother as her mother was going off to Mexico to the Ouspensky Foundation. So I launched into *New Model of the Universe* which seriously appeared to impress her.

We came into Billingshurst, next stop Pulborough where I was to leave the train.

'Have you ever been to Chichester?'

'No.'

'You must certainly come. The cathedral is wonderful. Well worth a visit.'

'Yes, I must.'

'Come on 28th December, when we've all got Christmas out of the way.'

'Well, I'll try.'

'Please do. There's a very good hotel called The Dolphin, just opposite the cathedral. Let's say midday. I'll be waiting for you.'

She had taken out her diary and had written her telephone number on a piece of paper which she now tore out and handed to me. 'Just in case you need to get in touch. But don't. Just be there.'

The train drew into Pulborough and I got out of the train and waved goodbye.

I set off down the road to Bignor and to another milestone in my life. It was a starry evening and the road quite bright. I was happily distracted by my train encounter and, anyway, three and a half miles was nothing to me. I would, however, be lying if I said that my thoughts were in the past, in the train; they were in the future, in Chichester.

A car drew up beside me and the man at the wheel asked me where I was going. 'Hop in. I can give you a lift.'

His name was Jack Evers and he drove me to the door of the cottage my mother had rented, and I invited him in for a cup of tea. Seeing him in the light of the sitting-room, I saw a handsome man with a strong face and blue-grey eyes that twinkled as he took in the chaos that surrounded my mother and my younger brothers and sister. He told us that he lived in Bury, which was not far away, wished us a happy Christmas and was gone.

It was a lovely cottage and there was enough room for us all without too much sharing. One of the first things I did after I'd unpacked was to look in my post office book. I had £2 7s 6d. Thirty shillings should be enough for my trip to Chichester.

I had walked slap into the preparations for Christmas. I lit the fire and we started on the decorations. I left Pat and Mother decorating the small Christmas tree with little balls of cotton wool while I dealt with supper. Somehow, through all the moves and adventures, Mother had kept some candleholders and a boxful of small hanging stars, shepherds, sheep and assorted cattle, which were now lovingly hung from the branches.

The door burst open and brother Frank joined the family. Even in mufti, the Sandhurst officer cadet appeared every inch the soldier. I looked at him and saw that my brother was grown up. The next day it snowed. Frank and I walked to the post office and I withdrew two pounds. We had a couple of beers and then walked home. Frank and I were closer then than we ever were before or since.

On Christmas Day, we had a turkey, courtesy of Biddy White, and all the traditional accompaniments. Then Christmas pudding with brandy butter. Mother looked radiant, all her children were with her and for a short time she was happy.

It was 28 December: I came out of Chichester station and walked through the town until I saw The Dolphin Hotel, painted white and blue. Would she be there? Did I have the courage to find out? I went in and there in the coffee room was Ginny.

'Hello, George. I've ordered us some coffee. Did you have a good Christmas?'

'Yes, thank you.'

I looked at her. She was glowing.

She took my hand. 'Sit down.'

We had some coffee and talked about nothing, looking at each other.

'I'm staying in room 27. I shall go up in a moment. Give me five minutes and then come up and join me. We don't want porters and people to be suspicious, do we?'

She got up and left. I began to panic: what if I was being set up as a co-respondent in the divorce case? Ah, well, I decided, not at seventeen, you're not.

I found Ginny in bed and naked.

These lines by Donne echoed in my mind:

> Licence my roving hands, and let them go,
> Before, behind, between, above, below.
> O my America! my new-found-land . . .

We had some champagne and, later that afternoon, I discovered that Chichester had a beautiful cathedral, too.

Life became a whirlwind of romance, unexpected turns and twists, great happiness and deep despair.

Having returned to London, refreshed by the break over Christmas, Mother had to admit that the nursing home was failing. The wonderful Mrs Gibbs made her house in East Sheen Avenue stretch so that it could accommodate the three youngest during the rest of the Christmas holidays. I have photographs of them – Eve thirteen, Pat twelve and Terry nine – walking across Richmond Bridge, following their distraught and hungry mother. It was the worried faces of the children and the desperate face of the mother that gives the lie to the life they were living: private schools and privilege and virtual malnutrition. Mother's world was full of pretension, the need to have background, the need for her children to be seen as ladies and gentlemen.

Her partner in the nursing home, Nita Smith, was well connected and introduced Mother to many who could feed the pretension and some who could help feed her children. Canon Hilyard of

Westminster Abbey was also chairman of the Royal Asylum of St Anne's Society. The society gave grants for the education of the children of army officers and Patrick and Terry were given a grant to help towards their education and school clothes. The grant intended for the clothes went a good way to help feed them. I would go over on Sundays and cook vegetable pie.

Mother's energy for schemes was boundless: 'God will provide' was her mantra but she found she had to do a lot of shoving. The money in my father's Bulgarian bank account came to the fore again. Mother was determined to get compensation from the War Commission. If she couldn't bring the money out in currency, surely she could bring it out in trade? But there was no trade agreement with Bulgaria, she was told by the Foreign Office. There was no interest in trade with Bulgaria, said Papa's old business associates. No, things were not good for Mother.

Jack Evers had kept in touch with me. As we had been driving to Pulborough that December night when he gave me a lift, I had told him I was at the Richmond Theatre as an ASM and playing small parts but that I hoped I would make it as a full-time actor. He had been out to the theatre once or twice when I had a part to play. He now rang to ask if I were due to play a decent part in a forthcoming production as he wanted to bring someone to see me. I was rehearsing a small but showy part in *Bats in the Belfry* which was the next play to open.

Jack brought with him a Mrs Barlow, a tall woman of central European extraction, with a vast chest and booming voice. She had married a wealthy man and, now that he was dead, she was going to indulge herself in some theatrical production. Her first venture was to be a play about the Boxer Rebellion, to be staged at the New Lindsay Theatre in Notting Hill in London. Jack told me that Mrs Barlow had been impressed and I was to go and see her at her home in Regent's Park. After the interview I was invited to join the company to play a small but important part, and to understudy one of the leads. Rehearsals started in a month and I was to be paid £5 a week. Riches.

On Sunday I took the bus to Barnes Common and went into the

Red Barn pub, hoping to see Sid Field and was delighted to find him at his usual place.

'Hello, Georgie, how you going along?'

I had seen him on several occasions since he had given me the letters of introduction in Deal. He was always interested in my progress and I now told him of the offer from Mrs Barlow.

'What can you lose? It will be wonderful experience.'

I gave in my notice at the Richmond Theatre. Andy Melville questioned if I was doing the right thing, saying he didn't think I had enough experience to do the understudying. But I didn't want to listen to sensible advice. However, I was reassured when he said that if the play didn't run, I was to come back.

Ginny had commented that my clothes were a bit drab and, with this new job, I took to looking in the second-hand shop next to The Cobwebs. I found a brown tweed suit that fitted me exactly and cost only five shillings. I bought it, and then a pair of shoes for two shillings. Ginny had some rich friend who was happy to discard three shirts from Beal & Inman: one of them was an open neck but the other two had stiff detachable collars. I became a dab hand at semi-starching with a little flour and water and a damp cloth. Some time later, Ginny's same friend discarded a pair of grey flannels and a blazer which she was fast to pick up on my behalf.

When *Bats in the Belfry* finished, so did my job with Melville, Miles and Piffard at the Palace Theatre, Watford. I was out of work but had the luxury of knowing that I had a job to go to.

One evening, Jack Evers asked me to go to the theatre with him and we saw *Harlequinade* with Eric Portman. Afterwards, we went out to Soho for supper during which Jack said that if I wanted to cut expenses, I could have a room in his flat at the top of 38 Chester Square for 17/6d a week. I would have the run of the flat except for one night every three weeks. Many houses in Chester Square and Eaton Square had been requisitioned during the war and divided into flats; Jack had one of these for a peppercorn rent. I never did find out what he did. He told me that he had worked in radar during the war and was now working for a chemical research laboratory near Cheltenham; I have often wondered if he had anything to do with GCHQ. His wife and daughters lived in Sussex and he simply had the flat to break his journey from Cheltenham to Pulborough once every three weeks.

Was I being propositioned, I wondered, and invited to pay for the favour of Jack getting me a job? He was a wing commander, the holder of the OBE: why should I think he was making sexual overtures? I looked at him and he must have guessed what I was thinking.

'My rent is thirty-five shillings a week. It would help me to pay less and it would help you to move into central London and also pay less. A business deal, nothing more. Come and see it tomorrow morning.'

And, I thought with pleasure, it would certainly help to have somewhere to see Ginny in comfort and privacy. I could afford it; after all, I was going to be earning a fiver a week.

The next morning I went to see the flat. It had a large sitting-room, kitchen, bathroom and two bedrooms in the attic whose dormer windows looked out on to the steeple of St Michael's church. It was all splendid and I couldn't believe my luck. But there was more to come. Jack took me to an office one floor down to meet his secretary: Fay Gordon-Hill was slight with shoulder-length auburn hair, a pretty face and a mouth that made a crooked smile. She worked for both Jack and a Norwegian diplomat who had the flat another floor down.

I turned up at the New Lindsay Theatre for the first rehearsal and met the rest of the cast for the read-through. I was to understudy Peter Cooke, and never was anyone so frightened as I was because his character never stopped speaking – and what was more terrifying was that Peter was playing him as an elderly Chinese mandarin with a slight lisp. I realised that Andy Melville was absolutely right – I wasn't ready for any of it.

Mrs Barlow sat in on the read-through. I can't remember who the director was but I was sure that he had reservations about me, just as I had reservations about myself. It didn't help that sheer panic made me read my small part badly. By the end of the week I was sacked but Mrs Barlow was kind enough to pay me for a week's work which, I believe, she need not have done.

I went home to Chester Square and heard the typewriter banging away in Fay's office so I knocked and went in.

'God, you look ghastly. What's the matter?'

'I've been sacked.'

'Oh, that's tough. What are you going to do?'

'Make a cup of tea. Would you like one?'

'Would you like the company?'

'Yes, please.'

'Let's go upstairs then.' And that was the beginning of a long friendship.

Later that evening, I went round the corner to the Royal Oak in Elizabeth Street and, having money in my pocket, treated myself to a full pint. I then walked through Eaton Square to the Horse and Groom in Groom Place. There, sitting at the bar, was Richard Longman, one of the cast in the Boxer Rebellion play. He was very friendly and bought me a beer. He also decided to give me some advice, which was to stop acting as I would never be any good at it. I met Richard again towards the end of his life and he reminded me of the incident. Apparently I had replied: 'We'll see.'

As we were leaving the pub, he suggested I should go and see his brother, Mark, at Longman Green, the publishers. He told me to meet him back at the Horse and Groom the next evening, after he had spoken to his brother.

I didn't want to bother Mother with my problems but she rang to tell me that the nursing home was finally going to close down. She already had another job lined up, working for a Mr Mufti in the City, selling furs and Bokhara rugs.

'But you know nothing about furs and rugs,' I said, worried that she was jumping from the frying pan into the fire.

'No, but Mr Mufti is very happy to teach me. I shall be working on commission. Then, of course, darling, there's the Bulgarian money,' replied my ever-optimistic mother.

That evening I went round to the Horse and Groom, not really thinking that Richard would be there or that he had remembered to talk to his brother. I was wrong: Mark Longman would see me the following Monday morning.

Why anybody should want to employ a dyslexic dunce in a publishing house was beyond me, but no stone could be left unturned. You never know, the guiding hand of fate might be giving a gentle shove.

Mark Longman was the epitome of an English gentleman, tall and slim, wondrously courteous and urbane. He gave me fifteen minutes of his time, and showed me a framed, hand-written copy of 'The Raven' by Edgar Allan Poe. Having appraised my potential (nil) in a very short time, I thought it good of him to be so kind.

Jack Evers also tried to help by getting me an interview with a friend of his at J. Walter Thompson. I went along and did an intelligence test. Putting square wooden bricks into square wooden holes wasn't that difficult, but the spelling test was a mite trickier.

Mother suggested that I ring Boris Christoff, head of the Bulgarian section of the BBC World Service. I had forgotten all my childhood Bulgarian so I didn't think that this avenue would be very fruitful but I was proved wrong. I was asked to read some poetry, in English, to be broadcast to Bulgaria. I recorded three programmes at two guineas a time. I also met a Bulgarian broadcaster, Liliana Brisby. She and her husband befriended me and often fed me during the struggling times.

I was desperately trying to find an agent. I knocked on Miriam Warner's door persistently. I was halfway up the stairs to Nora Nelson King's office when her door opened and a rather drunken, middle-aged man came hurtling down the stairs. 'Don't bloody come back either, you sot,' was screamed after him.

I wasn't drunk but I decided to follow him down the stairs and I didn't go back either.

I shall never know why I didn't return at once to Richmond, confess failure to Andy Melville and get my old job back. Pride, I suppose. Anyway, I had a few bob in my pocket.

There was only one thing to be done – straight into the Duke of Wellington in Chester Row for a quick half. While there, I decided that I had to ring Andy Melville; he said he'd get back to me in a day or two.

I didn't dare miss his call so hardly ventured out of the flat until the evening for three days. But there was Fay and there was Ginny so the days weren't all that dull.

True to his word, Andy Melville telephoned and said he would take me on for three productions as an acting/ASM. The productions were *The Shop at Sly Corner* by Edward Percy, *The School for Scandal* and *This Happy Breed*. There was nothing for me in *The Shop at Sly*

Corner, except to play a Brandenburg Concerto on the Panatrope and try and get the needle on to the right groove. I was to play Trip in *The School for Scandal* in which Leslie Crowther, a fellow ASM, was playing a servant – a funny man and wonderful company.

I got on pretty well with Trip until I came to: 'Why, nothing capital of my master's wardrobe has dropped lately; but I could give you a mortgage on some of his winter clothes, with equity of redemption before November. Or shall you have a reversion of the French velvet, or a post obit on the blue and silver? These, I should think, Moses, with a few pair of point ruffles, as collateral security.'

I could not get the hang of it at all, and our director, John Citrine, was not a great help. I shied like a startled horse whenever I reached the speech and stumbled over the equities and redemptions and reversions until the poor man was forced to come forward to the orchestra pit to give me his opinion.

'You know, trying to teach you to act is like flogging a dead horse.'

Leslie Sands, who was playing Sir Peter in the production, saved me. He called me into his dressing-room and showed me how to play the speech. I practised assiduously, and on the first night rewarded Leslie's kindness by getting some lovely laughs.

Playing Sam Leadbitter in *This Happy Breed* was much more up my street and I enjoyed playing the part of the Cockney communist.

Those few weeks back at Richmond were happy ones but, as I had not been given my old job back, when the plays finished so did I.

Money was running out again and things were looking bleak, but the sun was shining and the lido at the bottom of Roehampton Lane was packed with starlets, some of whom I knew and some of whom I was delighted to meet. Diana Dors and Lana Morris were frequently there. I had met Diana at an audition for, I think, *Tobacco Road* at the King's Theatre, Hammersmith. She got the part she went for, but I went empty handed.

Life took a sudden and unexpected turn for the worse. First, Ginny decided that she wanted to go to Mexico and join her mother and, secondly, whatever ministry it was that had originally requisitioned the Chester Square flats, now decided that they must be returned to their owners. So the flat at 38 Chester Square went, the cheap rent went with it and I had just one week to find myself somewhere else to live. Jack Evers had already decided that he would leave the Cheltenham job and work in Sussex. Fay was out of a job.

My only recourse was to have a quiet and confidential talk with the Lord in the calm of St Michael's in Chester Square. Feeling sustained and hoping that help was at hand, I walked round the corner to the newsagent. In the window there was a card advertising a small room in Lowndes Street. The rent was thirty shillings a week, which was dreadfully expensive, particularly if you had no job.

I went to see it. Cassie Kelly, a very large woman who, despite her comparatively young age, suffered from chronic rheumatoid arthritis, showed me the room. In a previous existence it must have been the imposing half-landing of this Georgian house. It had been converted into a small room and smaller bathroom. The bed folded back into the side wall and a cupboard held a two-ringed Belling cooker. There was a table and two chairs and another small cupboard for clothes. The terms were a week's rent in advance, which left me with fifteen shillings to my name.

The Salisbury, a pub in St Martin's Lane, was a great place for the exchange of information among actors.

'Beatie de Leon is casting at Kew.'

'Peter Saunders is sending out a number three tour of *Fly Away Peter*.'

'Frank Fortescue is casting for a twice weekly at Accrington.'

But all hopes and expectations of work faded when it was time to say a very sad farewell to Ginny who was ready to leave for Mexico. A lovely light went out of my life.

I did see her again, about ten years later, shopping in Sloane Square, and we went and had a drink in one of our old haunts, the Wellington. Now married to a chap in the consular service, she told me she'd seen some of my films and enjoyed them. While she talked, my mind was full of The Dolphin Hotel in Chichester, the top flat of 38 Chester Square, and the tiny room in 41 Lowndes Street. As we were saying goodbye on the corner of Sloane Square, she took my hand and, holding it, said, 'I always loved your hands' and kissed my palm. She turned and walked away briskly. As I watched her, I wondered if, while we were talking, her mind had been making the same journey as mine. I looked after her, knowing it would be the last time I would see her.

9

Feeling very low after Ginny's departure, I wanted to get out of London, away from happy memories, so decided to try my luck with the auditions for Accrington. I auditioned in London for Frank Fortescue and was engaged to play in Accrington twice nightly/twice weekly — that is when each play plays a matinée and evening performance, from Monday through Wednesday and Thursday through Saturday. I borrowed £5 from Fay, paid three weeks' rent and travelled north. I secured a part in two productions – *The Crystal Ball*, a splendid northern farce, and *The Red Barn* about somebody burning down a barn. I was dreadful in it. It was a drama and at one moment I had to stand at the bottom of a flight of stairs, lusting after the juvenile lead while at the same time accusing her of arson. 'Don't stand there breathing like a bull. Go and help them put out the fire,' said the juvenile lead. 'I'm on fire for you, Mary,' was my reply.

Arriving at my Accrington digs one Sunday evening after a long, hot journey I asked if I might have a bath. The Smithers family was made up of mum and dad, three girls and a boy. The eldest girl was eighteen; the boy sixteen and the other two girls must have been twelve and nine. When I made my request, the family was at tea but, as nothing was too much trouble, dad got the hip-bath out of the shed and started filling it with hot water from the copper.

'Right, there you are, lad. Take no notice of us, we're used to it.'

They may have been used to it, but I wasn't. I was loath to continue but more terrified of backing down. I 'screwed my courage to the sticking point', undressed and had my bath. Thank God, no one offered to scrub my back. Nubile Lizzie never returned the compliment of taking a bath in front of me while I guzzled a bacon buttie.

Eight weeks in Accrington and sixteen plays under my belt. I was doing my training. RADA could never be so good and the bad habits one picks up from quick and slipshod work could never be so bad. These would be sorted out in the years to come.

The Bedford Theatre in Camden Town had been refurbished, and restored to its Victorian music-hall colours. Pat Ney and John Penrose had persuaded Camden Council and some philanthropic organisations that the borough needed a theatre. When the theatre opened, they needed an ASM – unfortunately not an acting one, just your ordinary dogsbody. I heard about the job from *Spotlight* and applied. But I had to pay the rent, so it was dogsbody or nothing.

The first night of *Lady Audley's Secret* was lavish; it really was the buzz of the grease paint. West End managements were in the audience and we were told there were film producers out front. There was every possibility that we might transfer to the West End! The play continued to do well and one morning, three weeks later, some of the cast clambered into a stagecoach drawn by four black horses and were driven to the Phoenix Theatre, accompanied by fanfares from the post-horn. It was heady stuff. This was proper theatre.

Although the play transferred, I stayed at the Bedford Theatre to work on their next production. This was to be *Wind Across the Heath* by Campbell Singer, starring John Justin and Sheila Shand Gibbs. One day I noticed that John Justin was reading a book by Ouspensky, *Strange Life of Ivan Osokin* – not one I had heard of. After a while, I plucked up courage to talk to him about it.

Having committed suicide on Moscow station from unrequited love, Osokin finds himself in the cave of the Great Magician. He is furious and complains that if he had known what was going to happen in life he would have done it all differently. The Great Magician arms him with prescience and starts him on his second journey through life. As each event of his past life presents itself, he knowingly makes the same mistakes. A kind of spiritual bravado makes him decide that, as he has free will, he will follow his old path. We see him at the end standing on Moscow station with a gun to his head. Very Russian.

I have, on many occasions, had prescient moments, known the detrimental outcome of a certain choice and followed my free spirit with disastrous results. Everyone must know the feeling of 'If only I hadn't . . .' or 'Why did I say that?' Ah well. Free will!

The great excitement came in the next production, *The Guardsman's Cup of Tea*, because not only were Bessie Love, Duncan Lamont and Andrew Crawford in the cast but also Jane Baxter – there she was, my star of *Blossom Time*, the film she made when I was three and which I saw when I was seven on a moonlit night in Bulgaria. I'm happy to say my idol did not have feet of clay. And she was to be there again when I got my first part in the West End, in Frederick Lonsdale's *Aren't We All?* at the Theatre Royal, Haymarket. And very much there when I persuaded her to come to Bury St Edmunds to play Mrs Alving in *Ghosts*.

My job at the Bedford Theatre came to an end when *Wind Across the Heath*, the third production for which I had dogsbodied, finished. Bad times were just around the corner, but not quite yet.

I went to Richmond to see if there was anything doing there. They were going to do a production of Toni Block's *Flowers for the Living*, and offered me a small but showy part of a spiv. This was good news but, first, I had to get through the next four weeks. I went to the Labour Exchange but they could do nothing for me beyond franking my card. I didn't have enough stamps to warrant a pay-out. They suggested the National Assistance Office.

The nearest one to where I lived was situated on Knightsbridge Green. I reckon that the National Assistance Office was run in order to refuse money to even the most needy. I was prepared to do anything, but apparently there were no jobs. The small, bald man listened to my story with a withering little smile playing around the opening where his lips should have been. He made me sit there for most of the day. I was ostensibly waiting for someone on high to make up his mind. I sat for five hours. Finally the answer came. He was very sorry but there was nothing he could do. I can't blame him: a tall, young man with a public school voice and an actor to boot, asking for a hand-out. No way.

In the basement flat of 41 Lowndes Street lived the caretaker, Cassie Kelly. Poor girl, she was vastly overweight and spent a great deal of her time in bed. We sat and discussed my predicament. As I was already two weeks behind with the rent, she suggested that I should move out immediately, leaving my things in her box-room. She would have invited me to stay in her small spare room, but she had a friend staying there for another two days. I brought down my belongings and gave Cassie the keys. I assured her that I would be all right, that I could go and stay with my mother.

I wandered off into the evening to try and find Fay. No luck. I went to the Unity Restaurant and had a bowl of spaghetti for 1/9d. I walked round Chelsea and Victoria, had a half of bitter here and there, and finally went to sleep on the Embankment. I was utterly depressed and sorry for myself. I was also a great fool: I could have phoned my mother, but I was angry with her. She had forgotten it was my eighteenth birthday.

God knows, the poor woman had enough to do to keep a roof over her head and try to pay some school fees. Not only was the St Anne's Society helping towards these, but now also was the Thomas Walls Trust. She was still working in Upper Thames Street with Mr Mufti selling furs and carpets.

I rang her there. 'Come on down,' she said. 'There's a nice café in Thames Street and we'll have a sandwich and a cup of tea.'

I told her about my predicament. 'That's wonderful, darling. You have a job in three weeks' time, wonderful! Is it a good play? I'm glad it's at Richmond. By the way, did you know that George Villiers, Duke of Buckingham, had his palace in Thames Street?'

We had our sandwich and our cup of tea and looked at the site where the palace had stood. 'I've thought of something for you. Ring me at four when I'll have sorted things out. You can sleep at East Sheen tonight and then you can see if Cassie will fix you up after her friend has gone.'

'Four o'clock is teatime, Mother!'

We both collapsed in a fit of giggles thinking of the very proper Frank.

I rang at four. She had made friends with one of the directors of Gordon Russell Furnishings and had rung him up to ask if there were any odd jobs I could do for a week or two. Apparently, I would be the answer to their prayers. He needed someone to put his small London stock-room in order.

The stock-room was in Marylebone High Street and I was to start there the next day at a salary of £6 a week. I arranged with Cassie that I could rent her small room for £1 a week. But that night, I stayed with Mother in East Sheen. We sat in the kitchen, drinking endless cups of tea and talking – it was an evening I will always remember.

She talked to me about her novel. This is the same novel she was writing when four of her children arrived in Sussex, utterly dazed from the marathon journey from Yorkshire, and found she was too busy writing it to feed us. It was the novel that kept her sane. She would finish it and then lose it in the post, or leave it on the bus while taking it to a publisher. She frequently cited the fact that T.E. Lawrence had had to rewrite *The Seven Pillars of Wisdom* after losing it at a railway station. She always rewrote it. It was a romance of the Russian Revolution, taking a group of White Russian officers and their wives and sweethearts from 1912 to the Stalin purge of 1936. She enjoyed writing it – and rewriting it.

That night, she also talked to me about her progress with the Foreign Office and Papa's Bulgarian money. The Germans had paid a rent throughout the war for the house in Varna. She found it quite incomprehensible that a nation that could put millions of people to death should bother to put a minuscule rent into the account of the British Consul.

Yes, it was a truly memorable night with my mother. It was a milestone in our relationship; we were becoming friends and less and less mother and son.

The next day I went to Marylebone High Street and started pushing carpets around, trying to get some practical order into the Gordon Russell stock-room.

There was a block of flats opposite the stock-room and one day I became aware that I was being watched. She was very pretty and we conducted mutual seduction over the heads of the passing pedestrians. I found this very titillating – but that was nothing to when she indicated that I should open the door because she was coming over. We spent what turned out to be the first of several joyous afternoons on a pile of well-sprung mattresses.

She was Swedish, very blonde and very pretty and was working as an au pair. We confined our activities to the afternoons in the stock-room. We never met outside, nor went for coffee or a drink. If the curtains were drawn, her employer was in and she would not be over. If, on the other hand, the curtains were open, I was to leave the door on the latch. I worked like a fiend in the mornings to get ahead of my work and then if Inga couldn't come over, I read.

All good things come to an end. We said a fond farewell and I went off to Richmond.

Nearly thirty years later, in 1975, I was playing at Stratford; I can't remember now whether the play that evening had been *Hamlet* or one of the *Henry IV* parts, but I do know that I was having a drink after the show at the Arden Hotel. A very elegant blonde left her party and came over to me.

'George Baker?'

'Yes.'

'You don't remember me?'

How can you tell a beautiful woman who is standing in front of you that, no, you don't remember her. I stalled for time.

'Marylebone High Street.'

'Inga?!'

'Yes.'

She took me across to meet her husband and family, introducing me as a friend she had met in London when she was an au pair. We had a good evening.

I was happy to be back at Richmond. *Flowers for the Living* was a great success and transferred to the St James's Theatre. Was I at last to make my West End debut? Not a bit of it: I had had to tell the management that my National Service call-up papers were due and they couldn't take the chance of letting me play the part and then being called up in the middle of the run. I was deeply disappointed in missing out on the transfer, particularly as the play didn't have a long run and was off by the time I was called up.

Once more, I had to worry about where the next penny was coming from but thankfully something turned up quite soon. I ran into an actor friend who said he had a good job as a waiter at the Savoy. He told me to go to the Denmark Street Labour Exchange which specialised in catering. In no time at all, I presented myself there and asked for a job.

'Do you speak French?'

I wasn't going to let that deter me. 'A little,' I said.

I was told to get down to the Regent Palace Hotel and ask for Mr Sawyer, the kitchen clerk. Once there, the doorman directed me down the stairs and into the kitchens. The kitchens of the Regent Palace were vast. There were meat stores, vegetable stores, fish stores, all laid out like high street shops; in fact, it was like a small town. Everyone was dressed in check trousers, white coat, apron and tall white hat. There were very few women and those few were sitting round big barrels, peeling potatoes. The whole world, down there, seemed to be bustling about doing things. Eventually, I found someone to direct me to Mr Sawyer's office.

Mr Sawyer was going on holiday and needed someone to cover for him. I was to work with him for a week so I would get the hang of all my duties. I was to start the very next day at a salary of £5 a week.

There was a long hotplate that ran the width of the kitchen. The kitchen clerk – that was me – stood at one end of it, collecting the written orders from the waiters as they streamed in from the restaurant. Then I had to shout out the order to the appropriate chef – and this is where the French came in since the order had to be shouted in French – and the chef would shout back confirmation. The food, on its plate, was put on the serving hotplate and I then placed the waiter's order on top of it. I had to keep my eyes skinned to see that the right waiter picked up the right plate, and I then had to give him the other half of the order. Waiters would very happily poach each other's orders so as not to have to wait too long.

There was one particular waiter who was a dab hand at this particular ploy; he always managed to insinuate himself to the front of the queue. It wasn't an orderly queue. It was a seething, heaving mass of black-coated penguins lurching for their plates.

It was a wonderful job. Raucous banter, filthy innuendo and sexy *double entendres* flew about during the preparation. The head chef walked through the kitchens, tasting this, watching the preparation of that. He was a small, meticulous man with a clipped moustache and, immaculately dressed in his whites, he ruled his kingdom with the air of a man who knew he was Number One. If the Salmons or the Glucksteins were dining in their suite, he always prepared their food himself.

When at last my call-up papers arrived, I knew I didn't want to go into the army. The ethic of war was abhorrent to me. It still is. Perhaps I could be a conscientious objector?

Frank, my big brother soldier, was very scathing. 'Don't be so crass.'

My mother gave me the 'If you saw a soldier bayoneting your mother, sister or wife, what would you do? But don't let me influence you, Jora.'

In March 1949, I went in front of an army board which convened in a church hall just over Hammersmith Bridge. There were three men sitting behind a trestle table. One man had a patch over one eye, another had an arm missing. I don't know where the third had been wounded but a fourth man walked into the room on a tin leg.

They were all young men.

No contest.

I put Catering Corps, Catering Corps, and Catering Corps on the application form as my three preferred choices – but perhaps they couldn't read since I was sent to Winchester to do my training with the Rifle Brigade. The Rifle Brigade is a far cry from the Catering Corps but I decided that since I was in it I might as well try and enjoy it.

There were six weeks of primary training to get through at Bushfield Camp just outside Winchester. There were seventy-two people in the intake to get to know, people from all walks of life. Michael Crombe, whom I had met at Waterloo station on the way down, was my staunch friend and remained so for many years. And there was Joe Varley who had a motorbike which he was frightened to ride; he more or less gave me sole use of it.

During our initial six weeks, there was a unit selection board. In order to assess our skills, we had to put together various dismantled items lying on a bench – the inner workings of a lavatory cistern, a rusty bicycle pump and sundry other household artefacts. Having lived through such a dotty childhood, I had them all working in no time. It was deduced from this that I was mechanically minded. Nothing could have been further from the truth.

After we had done our initial training, we were stationed in Winchester Barracks and had more spare time. Michael Crombe and I went up to London in his smart 1939 MG whenever we could and on one bright June day, Joe and I went off on the motorbike to the Derby. From there, we went to London and at the Connaught Hotel met his parents. Joe's father, Colonel Varley, was chief executive of Colman, Prentice and Varley. Sitting with them was a tall, thin, almost effete young man; he had a long thin face and his hair was marmalade colour, his eyes were blue and danced a lot. His name was Peter Meyer. He was a great raconteur and enormously funny.

We all drank rather too many champagne cocktails and on the way back to the Varleys' house, we had an accident as we were driving past Hyde Park Barracks. I ended up in St George's Hospital with severe concussion and remained there for five days. Peter came to see me; he was very jokey and excellent company. He was an artist who earned his living by teaching art as a therapy at Harefield Hospital. When the regiment told me to take two weeks' sick leave, he suggested we should go to Paris. We each had just about enough money to get us there, and Peter thought he knew someone who could put us up in the Rue du Bac. Without having any spending money, I didn't think I could go but Mother came up trumps.

'A French firm owes me fifteen pounds,' she said. 'I shall ring them up now and tell them you're coming over to collect it.' And she did just that. The French company agreed and the deal was sealed. 'I never expected to see that money again,' she added. 'I've been trying to get it out of France for years.'

Nothing much had changed at the Hôtel Cambri since I had been there in 1940. The walls were painted the same colour and the antiquated lift was still grinding its way up and down.

The next morning we collected our £15 from the French company and then went to find Hank in the Rue du Bac – although Peter confessed to me that he was not even sure that Hank was still in Paris. Having been to Paris several times before, Peter took us on a wonderful circuitous route. My eyes were out on stalks.

As we walked, Peter gave me a thumbnail sketch of Hank. Even so, I was not prepared for what I met. Hank was a huge, bearded ex-GI and was in Paris on an army grant to study art. Since coming out of the artillery, he had let himself go to fat. We found him sitting in a sarong, stitching a garment of some sort. He had wrapped the sarong above his vast stomach on which his pendulous bosoms rested heavily; his shoulders and his arms hardly moved as his surprisingly small hands and fingers passed the needle in and out of the cloth.

'Hi, Pete!' It was as though Peter had never been away. 'And what have we here?'

'This is my friend, George.'

'Hi, friend George. You guys want to stay? You're welcome.'

His very Parisian apartment, with its large wooden doors, concierge's lodge and courtyard, had six rooms. The extraordinary living-room, with French windows leading out on to the courtyard, was where Hank held sway. There was a long refectory table spilling over with books, drawings, sewing, wine bottles and glasses, and an immensely tidy corner at one end with a blotting pad, writing paper and pens.

There was a kitchen, and I longed to wash, clean and scrub the dirt of ages from its surfaces. The other rooms were all bedrooms. Hank heaved his bulk out of his chair, walked over to a door and threw it open.

'There you go, guys, here's happiness. Goin' down the club around nine-thirty to hear Adelaide Hall. If you folks want to come, you're welcome.'

Adelaide Hall was an eye-opener to me. She stood quietly by the piano, with a red shawl draped over her black dress, and sang. She sang and I cried. I don't know why I cried: it wasn't real crying, just eyes so wet that moisture dropped down my cheeks. Edith Piaf, on the other hand, was never still. She had never had her voice trained properly and she was forcing it until the veins stood out on her neck. There was no comparison between the two singers: Edith Piaf was the darling of France and the world, and Adelaide Hall is forgotten except by a few who loved her.

Peter and I spent a glorious week in Paris: endless museums each morning, walking from one to another. The Luxembourg Gardens and Versailles in the afternoons. Hank cooked a sublime *bouillabaisse*. He prepared a stock from fish heads and bones, herbs and saffron, strained the stock into another pot, then cooked the fish – a mixture of cod, sardines, rockfish, sea bass – in it for about seven minutes. 'There are many ways of cooking *bouillabaisse*. I've decided to stick to the way I'm doing it now. I line a soup terrine with bread, pour the soup over it and serve the fish separately. Oh, my God, my God! You guys got some Muscadet? Let's have Muscadet!'

I went back to Winchester, where the drudgery of blancoing the belt and polishing the brass buttons soon brought me back to the realities of life.

I stayed out late one night and got myself six days' jankers (confined to barracks). On one of the evenings, I was set to scrub out a cell and, being a dab hand at scrubbing floors, I was making a good job of it when the corporal came to tell me that I could stop. I told him that I would finish it off, and the look on the corporal's face was a joy to see. He retired through the cell door as though escaping from a lunatic.

At ten o'clock that evening, we paraded again in full kit for final inspection. While standing to attention waiting for the orderly officer, the same corporal hesitated in front of me. I thought he was going to find something to pick on and add to my prison sentence. No, he was just looking at the madman who scrubbed floors for pleasure.

While I was in Winchester, I went to see a production by the Salisbury Arts Theatre in the town hall. I can't remember what it was but I do remember saying to myself that I would like to join the company as soon as the army had finished with me.

The army now excelled itself. It sent me off to Barton Stacey to a War Office selection board to assess what use I might be to it as an officer. An assault and initiative course was set and, by dint of using the help to hand – some very bright Royal Engineer cadets – the selection board decided that I had qualities of leadership. I also appear to have impressed them with a five-minute extempore speech on the subject of a box of matches. I was sent to the Mons Officer Cadet School at Aldershot to train for a life in tanks.

Michael Crombe came with me to Mons before joining the Royal Artillery. Joe Varley went to train for the infantry at Eaton Hall; he gave me his motorbike before he went – and what a bonus that turned out to be. Whenever I had a forty-eight-hour pass, I shot up to London on the bike, staying in Cassie's spare room. There were people to see, and Mother was first on the list. She was now living in part of a Queen Anne house on the Mortlake towpath, just by the brewery. A family whose last child had been born in the Roehampton nursing home had taken her in. The Wades were voluptuously kind. They were two large people with an abundance of love, enough to spill over to anyone who happened to be passing by; luckily for my mother, she was passing by.

From their generosity, Mummy had food to eat and Evie and the boys were able to come to Mortlake for the holidays. Eve, now aged fourteen, was growing into a beauty but was shy and retiring and always seemed rather timid. Pat had sorted himself out a job for the holidays; he had learned to string tennis, squash and badminton racquets and was employed by Mr Mufti's partner Yusef Dodhi. He earned a shilling for each tennis racquet, a bit less for squash and badminton. Not a princely sum but the going rate.

At least Mother was getting food and some of Pat's money helped to put it on the table. Terry was coming up to eleven and a more bewildered little boy there never was. My mother never found time to spend with him. Although she was still working for Mr Mufti, all her energy was spent on the 'Bulgarian money' problem.

She read me a letter she had written to the Foreign Office, giving them chapter and verse of the monies owed to her from my father's estate by various firms in Bulgaria which should, she said, be taken into consideration when her claim for compensation was settled by the Foreign Compensation Commission.

It was eating into her soul that she had money and could not get to it.

One evening, after I had had a drink with Peter Meyer in Chelsea, I offered to drop him off in Chiswick Mall where he was going to a party. Chiswick was on my way back to Aldershot and not out of my way at all. The house where the party was being held was on the corner of the Mall. A wooden balcony ran the length of the first floor and standing on it was a girl with close-cropped hair, a lovely figure and glasses. I only mention the glasses because I've always found glasses attractive. The host shouted down that I was more than welcome to join the party and, with the incentive of this pretty girl, I parked Joe Varley's motorbike and went up.

I sought out the girl who turned out to be Julia Squire, the daughter of Jack Squire to whom I had sent my poetry at Peter Glanville's suggestion six years before. Julia was a costume designer for films and, with a tenuous professional connection, we talked until the party finished and then went to the Black Lion pub at the other end of the Mall. By the time I said goodbye to her at the end of the evening, I was absolutely certain that she would be my wife.

The time had flown and I suddenly realised that I had exactly thirty-five minutes to get back to Aldershot by midnight. There was nothing on the road and where there were corners I straightened them out. A guardian angel must have been riding pillion: I reported in at five to twelve.

Having passed out of Mons Officer Cadet School into the 3rd Royal Tank Regiment, which was stationed in Hong Kong, I had to be fitted for my uniforms at Flights in Bond Street. I had to have luggage. It was a crowded few weeks. After Julia got back from the studios each evening, we would meet and have a drink at The Antelope pub off Sloane Square.

Before I left for Hong Kong, the most important thing I had to do was to ask Julia Squire to marry me.

She said, 'Yes.'

10

MY MOTHER WAS THRILLED WITH THE NEWS THAT I WAS GOING TO GET MARRIED. I suppose she felt she could now fully shed any responsibility for me. Julia's mother, on the other hand, suggested that her daughter should take me to Paris and 'get him out of your system'. Julia was deeply shocked.

Julia was working on *The Magic Box*, the film industry's contribution to the Festival of Britain, which starred Robert Donat and every star in the firmament playing a cameo role. It was an exceptional opportunity for a twenty-four-year-old designer and Julia was working very hard. On the day of our wedding, 22 December 1950, she attended a full day's fittings with Robert Donat. He was difficult to fit because, when he had an attack of asthma, his neck would enlarge and go from size fifteen to eighteen, so he had to have three sizes of collar. His asthma didn't diminish his sense of fun. He knew that Julia was on tenterhooks to be gone, and teasingly delayed her.

We were supposed to be married at St Barnabas' church in Pimlico at 6 o'clock but, owing to Robert Donat's 'sense of fun', we were not married until 7 o'clock. The congregation consisted of Julia's mother and brother Rag, my mother and Mr Wade from Roehampton; Peter Meyer was my best man and there were one or two other friends on either side. Pat, Terry and Evie were not there; I can only think they were still at school.

After the service, Rag gave us a reception at his home in Chester Row. Julia and I then went to dine at the Society, Helen Cordet's nightclub in Jermyn Street. I had taken a one-bedroom apartment in Chesham Place where we spent our wedding night.

The day after the wedding, there was no lingering in bed: Julia had to be up early to go to the studios. However, Ronnie Neame, producer of *The Magic Box*, gave her four days off over Christmas and we borrowed a cottage in the Cotswolds from one of Julia's friends, and this was our honeymoon. Michael Wade lent us one of his old cars. I think it was a Singer but whatever make it was, it broke down at Hyde Park Corner. We continued our journey by train, which is what we should have done in the first place.

The cottage was the old village school at Aston Subedge near Chipping Campden in Gloucestershire. The schoolroom was the sitting-room. It was vast and not easy to heat, but it had a big open fire which I lit. It smoked; it smoked for four days.

Julia had brought some costume charts with her that had to be finished before she went back to work. What with her working and me opening this door or that window to create a draught, we hardly saw each other at all. But we were happy.

We got to know the Organ family: old Mr and Mrs Organ at Manor Farm, and their son and daughter-in-law, Bill and Dolly, whose farm was in the middle of the village. We bought milk, eggs and a plump chicken from them and started a friendship that continues, with their children, to this day. We listened to the carols from King's on Christmas Eve, and we had roast chicken for Christmas lunch, which we ate at three o'clock while listening to the King's speech. On Boxing Day we went to see the hounds which were meeting at Manor Farm.

After our return to London from Gloucestershire, Julia worked every day at the studios, and I revisited some old haunts, said goodbye to old friends. We continued to live in the little flat in Chesham Place until I sailed for Hong Kong.

Departure day, 5 January, came all too soon. We said goodbye at Waterloo station, desperate in the knowledge that we would not be seeing each other for a year.

I embarked on the SS *Fowey*, flagship of the Bibby Line; the journey was scheduled to take twenty-five days. Crossing the Bay of Biscay was ghastly: almost everyone on the ship was sick, bodies lay in groaning heaps everywhere and the lower decks were awash. I spent the second day in the Bay as orderly officer trudging through the ship. The time-honoured question, 'Everything all right, Private?' seemed a touch inadequate.

Port Said, at the head of the Suez Canal, must be as stinking a city as any in the world. The gully-gully men with their three fez hat trick: which fez is the marble under? There was always somebody to take them on and lose their money. The bumboats hawking bananas, the boys diving for pennies when they weren't hawking their sisters, the horse-drawn carriages that took you sightseeing. I sat with a friend from the Northumberland Fusiliers and got legless on ouzo. We called in at Aden, which was comparable in its awfulness with Port Said. However, two days in Colombo and then a stop in Singapore restored our equilibrium – both very civilised places, especially Raffles Hotel.

I was, however, looking forward to Hong Kong. Brother Frank was stationed there and I thought it was incredibly decent of the army to pay for me to go and see him. Frank left for Singapore two days after we arrived.

I was the only National Service officer in the 3rd Royal Tank Regiment; however, everybody was very kind and they did their best to make allowances for the shortcomings of the amateur.

We were stationed at Sek Kong in the north of the New Territories, about twenty miles from Kowloon. The camp consisted of a barrack square surrounded by Nissen huts and hard standings for the tanks. At the far end was an RAF squadron of jets. Noisy. Sandwiched between us and the runway was the mule train, presided over by a captain in the Vet Corps. He was quite elderly and I think he probably felt he hadn't achieved all his early ambitions because he took it out on the whisky bottle. Beyond these military installations lay the paddy fields and, beyond them, the foothills and the mountains leading into China. And, very often, leading out of China. There were daily sightings of straggling bands of what we now know as asylum seekers.

A couple of days after my arrival, my squadron leader, Major

Bowling-Smith — known as 'Bolo' — took me out in a jeep to show me where my troop position would be in the event of invasion. It was in the foothills, just off the road to China. I remarked that there didn't seem to be much of a way out.

'There isn't. You stay put,' he replied with a smile.

Was it cowardly of me to hope the Chinese wouldn't invade for a year or two? Julia and I exchanged letters of love almost every day and the separation was almost intolerable so the thought of 'staying put' highlighted my cowardice.

The regiment wanted a saddle club, and I was appointed equitation officer. My troop sergeant, Sergeant Mitchell, who had been in the cavalry and had done a course at Weedon Remount School, became my equitation NCO. We took delivery of six Australian brumbies which had, according to their documentation, been 'saddle broken'. We soon found that this ominous phrase meant that some intrepid man had managed to hold each beast still long enough to slap a saddle on its back. I certainly don't think that anyone had gone as far as trying to sit on the saddle.

We spent hours reigning, lunging and finally backing these ponies. On one memorable day, I flew into the air twenty-eight times in as many minutes. The pony's name was James Pig. In fact, the saddle club didn't really take off, but the ponies had to be exercised. We would take them, three at a time, up to the stream and swim with them.

There was nowhere really to ride. We had to negotiate the paddy fields with their narrow walkways and steep banks before we got to the foothills and even then the terrain was tortuous, stony and unwelcoming. However, there was a Buddhist monastery up in the hills where the children and chickens ran amongst the cats and dogs, the women did the washing in the stream and the monks were silent but welcoming in the cool corridors of their home. I would ride up there on James Pig and take my copy of Shelley with me. I was busy working on an idea that 'Prometheus Unbound' could be put on the stage. Well, if you're a young English soldier sitting in a garden of a Buddhist monastery with the golden Chinese pheasants rubbing shoulders with the common speckled hen, you are liable to believe that anything is possible.

It was a wonderful and solitary place to write letters home. It is such a pity the world no longer writes the *belles-lettres*. The quick email doesn't serve half as well as considered information, imaginative thought and flights of fancy and of love. It was a special love.

We did, in fact, a fair amount of serious soldiering – manoeuvres on top of the hills and showing other regiments on their way to Korea how they could use the tank for cover. It brought it home to us that there was a war going on and that British troops were very much involved. My brother Frank had been posted to Intelligence, IS9 Korea, on account of his Russian and Cantonese Chinese, so there was a personal involvement in the war, too.

When the rainy season arrived, and the tanks could not move from the hard standings, the troops had to practise 'interior economy': in other words, scrub the barrack room floor yet again. I decided it was my duty to find an alternative amusement so I told my troop that I would be reading them a story. The NCOs looked at me as if I were mad but said nothing; the troopers, on the other hand, were quite vocal in their pleas to return to routine and interior economy.

I chose Paul Gallico's *The Snow Goose*. I knew Sergeant Mitchell had been at Dunkirk; I also knew that three NCOs and two troopers had been in Normandy on D Day. The period of internal economy sped past: the rapt attention to Gallico's story would have done the author's heart good. I swear I saw some fingers wiping moisture from the eyes.

The humidity was quite dreadful and I began to feel ill. I could hardly drag myself around. My mouth became ulcerated – I think the doctor thought I was swinging the lead. I lost about a stone in weight, and then the dysentery arrived. I was sent to the 36th General Hospital for a check-up in the Tropical Diseases ward; here I was diagnosed as having contracted something called sprue. The dictionary definition is 'chronic disease, especially of tropical climes, characterised by diarrhoea and emaciation'. They thought I might have contracted the bug swimming in the streams with the ponies. Whatever, I continued to lose weight rapidly and spent a greater part of each day sitting on the loo.

I was wonderfully looked after. I had a comfortable bed, I had all the medicines I needed, and the best medical attention and, finally, I began to get better and was able to visit other wards. In the surgical wards there was a Major Paddy Morton who was in the army's legal section. He had been a junior at the Nuremberg trials. One day when I went to see him, he produced a big brown folder which had been sent over to him from his office.

'You'd better have this,' he said. 'They are some of the affidavits used at the trials. You should read them. I don't need them. I shall never forget them.'

I was extremely moved by them and when I came to compile *The Hungry Tigers* fifteen years later, I drew heavily on them. When I read them in hospital they made horrific reading; when I read them fifteen years later I was so distressed I could barely read them through. I was eternally grateful to Paddy Morton for letting me see them and to listen to the spirit of those who survived.

When I had put back a stone and a half and was just over nine stone, they reckoned I was well enough to be repatriated. There was a ship leaving in two weeks' time and six weeks after that I was sitting half the world away, in a flat in Eaton Mews South. Julia's brother Rag's secretary had lent her the flat until we knew where I was to be posted.

I had arrived in Liverpool and had gone to the military hospital in Chester to be checked and 'processed'. I was passed as P7 – P8 was chronic and pensionable – which was still quite ill. I was given a seventy-two-hour pass and then I was to report to the Hospital for Tropical Diseases in Millbank, London.

When I arrived in London, I telephoned Julia at the studios and learned she would not be back until about 7 o'clock that evening. It was midday and the obvious thing to do was to call round to see Bridie and May at the Horse and Groom. Things didn't seem to have changed one little bit while I was away: Elspeth Grant, film critic for the magazine *She*, was sipping her third gin and tonic. 'You were very good in that play at Richmond,' she quavered.

'That was nearly two years ago, Elspeth!'

'I know, but you haven't been in or I would have told you sooner. Where have you been?' She sounded quite cross.

'In the army. In Hong Kong.'

'Oh, you poor darling! Have a drink.'

Elspeth was one of the few critics who championed me in my early movies. Ours was a pub acquaintance: we drank in many of the same watering holes around Chelsea. When I lived in Hasker Street, I drank in the Shuckburgh. Elspeth lived in Chelsea Cloisters and also used the Shuck. She was a very unhappy woman: after thirty years she had been sacked from the magazine. The film preview and getting her review written before she went to the pub was her only reason for living. In the early sixties, she swallowed a tin of liquid Brasso and was found by the porter some days later. I mourned her going and remember her with much affection.

I had some lunch at the pub and then went back to the flat. It was going to be at least four hours before Julia got home. I found some innocuous reading and soon got bored with that. There was a writing-case of Julia's sitting on the table with a letter from Peter Meyer sitting on top of the pile. Stupidly I read it. Peter had written it from Sardinia, saying that he wished she were lying on the beach beside him. It was a nudist beach, he told her. The sun was shining, the weather was marvellous and the world the right way up.

I had several hours to brood on the letter before Julia returned from the studios, and brood I did. If my school days and early childhood had left me with anything, they had certainly left me with a bad case of low self-esteem, lack of confidence and an appalling persecution complex. Why does jealousy assume that, since the letter was written at all, the receiver must, naturally, share the feelings of the sender?

Poor Julia, she walked in on a bear with a sore head. She was shocked by my appearance and utterly distressed by my accusations. Her young husband was not only a bag of bones but spitting acid. She burst into tears and chokingly told me that Peter had been extremely nice to her all the time I had been away, but had never so much as laid a finger on her nor made any suggestion of love. Having been working for thirteen hours, she was tired and she was hungry, and said she might just as well go back to her mother. I said I was sorry, and burst into tears too. We stood there in a tight embrace and kissed away the hurt. We went to dinner at the Unity restaurant and by the time we got home the world was a better place.

The next day, I walked her to Victoria where she got a bus to Elstree, and I went to see my mother in Upper Thames Street. She looked thin and tired, and was her usual unmotherly self. We sat in a café in Queen Street while she gave me the latest news on her Bulgarian affairs.

She had been trying to get a visa to return to Bulgaria and open up the Varna office with Papa's old clerk, Mr Jacov, running it. The Board of Trade had made her sign an undertaking not to trade if she returned to Bulgaria. 'They promised me that if I signed it, they would give me a visa and the moment I signed they told me no visas could be granted for private visits.' She had taken her protest to the Foreign Office who told her that there must have been some misunderstanding as nobody had any objection to her continuing her business. But, they couldn't issue a visa either.

Now she was hoping to get a power of attorney for Mr Jacov so that he could get some money out of the F. P. Baker account to buy postage stamps, which she would sell here. She maintained that there was a hungry market of philatelists baying for Bulgarian stamps. The joy of this plan was that Mr Jacov did not need a licence to export stamps nor did he need a licence to export rose oil. Attar of roses was used in every perfume and my mother thought it could be one of Bulgaria's biggest exports.

Lady Reid-Dick had befriended Mother once more and again given her a lease on the flat adjoining her husband's studio which she had shared with Gene McQuatters. She lived there with Evie who had left her school in Petworth and was now going to the local school.

I was waiting for her to ask me how I was but she forgot to. I told her I was going into the Hospital for Tropical Diseases for a few days to be checked out.

'That'll be great,' she said. 'It'll be good to know exactly how you are. By the way, how's Julia? It went completely out of my mind to ask you.'

Thank God there were some real constants in this world. Something to cling to while you're drowning.

At the hospital, they confirmed everything I had been told in Chester. I was given two weeks' leave and told to wait for my next posting. Julia's mother found us a flat in Walton Street. It was furnished and cost £4 a week inclusive. I moved us in while Julia continued to work at Elstree.

The doctors decided that I was not ill enough to be invalided out and not well enough to go back to active service. My posting came: the army was sending me down to Pembroke where I was to be the range officer on the Castle Martin ranges.

There was no officers' mess nor quarters so I was billeted to a small cottage a couple of miles from the camp. There was an RSM, another sergeant and ten troopers on the establishment. The ranges were not used during the winter so it was really a question of making sure the hard standings for the tanks were in good repair and that the targets were clean and painted. There were seventy Ukrainian men who were billeted there as displaced persons, or DPs as we called them. Their job was to walk in a long line across the ranges looking for unexploded shells with metal detectors. They were glum, silent and far away from home. They lived in three huts at the edge of the camp where they had their own kitchen and shower hut. Some evenings you could hear them singing. They had food and shelter and I suppose that compensates for a lot, but they were not free.

The reason for my posting to Pembroke was to shunt me out of the way until the end of my National Service – about four months. Definitely out of sight and out of mind. I did the few duties I was given as diligently as paralysing boredom would allow me, and spent the rest of the time riding, drinking and making friends in the area.

I was given Christmas leave and went home to London where, temporarily, Julia was out of work so we could actually spend some time together. Although we had not seen much of each other during our first year of marriage, our lives were coming together and our love was growing. We were laying plans and thinking of our future. It was to be very bright! I was to become a great movie or theatre star, we were to have a Georgian house in the country. We were to have children, horses and ponies. Hey diddly dee, an actor's life for me.

During my week's leave, I got to know Julia's family a little better. It was not a straightforward family. Her father, Sir John Squire (Jack, to friend and foe) was a poet and editor. As well as being literary editor of the *New Statesman* and chief literary critic for the *Observer*, he founded the *London Mercury*. He was highly influential in literary circles but was not well liked by the Sitwells or the Bloomsbury Group. He and his friends were christened The Squirearchy. Jack was also a comprehensive drunk. As his father and grandfather had both died of alcohol, Jack was a teetotaller until his was forty, then he made up for it. He was a beer and cheese man, a no-nonsense Englishman whose cricket team, The Invalids, played on village greens on glorious summer days and then drank the pub dry. Jack's drinking finally did for his career. However, he was retained by the *Illustrated London News* as a monthly contributor.

He and his wife, Eileen, had long been separated and, in order that she should have some money from him, his sons persuaded him to authorise the *Illustrated London News* to pay his salary direct to Eileen. He was a skilful and brilliant essayist. Eileen was a woman whose intellectual capacity was considerable but she was not as talented a writer as Jack. I christened her 'the old 'un' and we got on very well. She had not had a happy sex life and told Julia that if she wanted children she would have to 'bite the sheet and bear it'.

There were three brothers: Raglan (Rag) was an architect of considerable reputation; Anthony (Ant) was a film director, and Maurice. Maurice was Julia's favourite brother and she told me she had suffered dreadfully when he was killed in the war.

Julia and I went out to Surbiton, where Jack was living with a Miss Osborne – she had always to be referred to as Miss Osborne. Although Julia then had very little time for her father, she did feel it was important that he should meet his son-in-law. Miss Osborne directed Julia and me to a pub where we found Jack sitting with his half-empty pint of beer. He was very civil and allowed me to buy him a drink, a large scotch. It was a very pleasant two hours and Jack was welcoming to us both.

I summoned up the courage to tell him that I had once sent him some of my poetry.

'What did I say about it?'

'You told me I needed a broader vocabulary of adjectives and that I should read Swinburne.'

'That was good advice. And did you?'

'Yes.'

'You'd better send them to me again. Do you play cricket? Better come and play for The Invalids in the summer.'

By the time we left him, he was drinking half a pint of neat scotch in a pint mug and a glass of bitter chaser.

On 22 December 1951, it was our first wedding anniversary. We spent Christmas Eve at 1 Chester Row with Julia's brother, Rag; Christmas Day at home in our Walton Street flat, and Boxing Day with Mother and the children.

Mother was determined to get herself to Bulgaria; the stumbling block of the visa had to be overcome somehow or other. She was very broke and very desperate. Her job with Mr Mufti had more or less come to an end and she was trying to get a job with her friend at Gordon Russell Furnishings. The offices were in Wigmore Street, no more than a stone's throw from Maida Vale. She could walk to work and would be quite near the family if needed.

The tension in the flat was palpable, the spirit abroad was the spirit of survival. Every man for himself. Evie had been flying into ungovernable rages; she had thrown a teapot at her mother, only narrowly missing her. I think the same tendency to obsession that drove her to a nervous breakdown while she was at the BBC was now taking hold again in her determination to get back her Bulgarian money.

The next day I retreated to the comparative numbing duties of a range officer in Pembroke. I was sad to be parting from Julia and was relieved to hear soon after that she had got a job as a costume supervisor/designer and assistant to Vertez whose conceptions she had to interpret for the film *Moulin Rouge*. Before she started, however, she came down to Pembroke to be with me for two weeks in the middle of February.

Jones the chemist was wonderfully kind and lent me his Standard 8 so I could drive Julia round Pembrokeshire. The coastline there must be one of the most beautiful in Britain. St David's was our first port of call, visiting the small cathedral which is set in a hollow below the main street of the small town. We sheltered in the ruins of the great hall of the monastery and kissed against a granite pillar. We were falling more and more in love. We went to Whitesands Bay and walked on the beach in a fierce February wind. I wiped away the sea spray from Ju's glasses with a spare hanky, and kissed away her tears of happiness.

I took her to the lily ponds at Bosherston, not that there were any lilies out. We drove across the ranges to the tiny St Govan's chapel which hangs halfway down a cliff, built into the rock. It was full of sheep hiding from the weather and we sat with them and watched the Atlantic beating on the rocks below and the rain sheeting across the opening to the chapel.

We decided to make a run for it – but the car was gloriously stuck, the wheels spinning in the mud. Julia had never driven before and now was her moment of truth. I gathered branches and sticks to put under the back wheels. Julia sat petrified in the driving seat. I started the engine and put the car into second. Julia was firmly pressing down the clutch. 'When I shout "Go!", press your right foot on the accelerator and take your left foot off the clutch.' I heard her muttering the instructions as I walked to the back of the car. I started to push and shouted 'Go!' The engine roared, the car leapt forward. Through the shower of muddy sticks and branches which hit me, I saw my wife disappearing in a series of fits and starts across the headland towards the Atlantic. I ran after her, screaming into the wind, 'Take your foot off the accelerator! Take your right foot off, your right foot off the pedal!'

The car spluttered, shook, stalled and stopped. Julia was trembling all over, and I was wet, dirty and bleeding. I got into the driving seat, put the car into reverse and went gently backwards. Thank goodness the car didn't stick again. When we were at a safe distance from the edge, I put the car into first gear and drove quietly off the ranges.

While Julia was with me in Pembrokeshire, we heard the announcement on the wireless of the death of King George VI. We were both immensely sad, and I remember we cried. I don't know why we were so affected: I suppose it was because he had been such a strength during the war, staying in London and visiting the bombed areas. We had seen this on the Pathé or Movietone News when we went to the cinema.

It was 6 February 1952 and there was to be a new Elizabethan era. Amen.

Just a month later, I was out of the army and back in London. I was not yet twenty-one.

11

JULIA WAS BUSY WITH THE PREPARATIONS FOR *MOULIN ROUGE*. She commuted to Paris at least twice a week for meetings with John Huston, Vertez and Schiaparelli – the latter was designing and making Zsa Zsa Gabor's dresses – so I saw precious little of her.

One of Julia's school friends, Lynette Furse, had come to share the Walton Street flat with us, which helped with the expenses. 'Birdie', as she was known, was a tall girl with auburn hair, long, thin hands, and long, thin feet. Magically it worked with the three of us sharing. I think Birdie was very patient. She had a great deal to put up with, what with Julia backwards and forwards to Paris and me mooching about at a loose end, trying to find work.

On 30 March, Rag Squire rang me to say that he needed some plans delivering to a client in Paris and would I be prepared to fly over with them immediately. He was very businesslike about it. He pretended to be surprised to hear that it would mean I could be with Julia for my twenty-first birthday.

It seemed a world away to sit outside a café on the Champs Elysées, the *Moulin Rouge* offices being above the café. I drank coffee, sipped a small brandy and waited for Julia. After some time and after three or four people had come out of the building and passed by my table surreptitiously glancing at me, I realised I was being scrutinised. A little before lunch, Jack Clayton, the associate producer on the film, and John Huston who, incredibly, was wearing cavalry twill trousers, hacking jacket and a flat cap, stood by my table talking about God knows what and making me feel very embarrassed for about three minutes before moving on about their business. Finally, Julia appeared with Leigh Aman, the production manager, with whom we were destined to become great friends.

Julia told me we had to wait for the French production manager, Louis Fleury. Louis was a big man, at least six foot five; he had a good French nose on him and a fine belly. He was a superb gourmet, a wine connoisseur, and a man who knew all the good restaurants in France. He loved his country and knew France intimately. He was able to find the right locations at the right price for any film. His lineage was aristocratic, his bearing imposing, and this gave him entrée to all sorts of locations which might otherwise not have been open to film companies. Louis was not a man of great culture, but he knew his food.

Having arrived, he took my hand and told me how lucky I was to be married to his 'deah Juulia'. As we got to know him better, we formed a society for the preservation of Louis's English. He took us to Chez Jacques just off the Boulevard St Germain. It was a small and impeccable restaurant, wooden tables with blue check cloths and a warm welcome, especially warm for Louis. We were to have the *poularde à l'estragon*, the speciality of the house.

I had walked into an unfamiliar world, full of epicurean delights and puzzlements. I was allowed to hang around while everyone went to a restaurant in the Bois de Boulogne where one of the scenes in the film was to be shot. Then we all went on to Longchamp. I was introduced to Huston as Julia's husband and he assured me that I was a 'lucky guy'.

I was a lucky guy, but it seemed that my coming of age heralded an even more bizarre future than my past had been. I returned dazed and disbelieving to London and a sharp reminder that I had no work.

Rag Squire asked me to come into his office in Eaton Square for a chat. He had just signed the contract to build Brize Norton, Upper Heyford and Mildenhall American air bases. He had taken on hundreds of extra architects and draughtsmen and they needed feeding. Would I be prepared to come in and make sandwiches for the night shift? This was an excellent solution to my problems as it gave me the day free to look for work.

I renewed my acquaintance with agents like Miriam Warner and

Nora Nelson King, I spoke to Andy Melville at Richmond, wrote to Frank Fortescue in Accrington. I had my photograph taken by Anthony Buckley, from which I got a batch of small repros to send off to casting directors. When I popped into the *Spotlight* offices to tell them I was out of the army and available for work, I left two photos with them.

I bought loaves and loaves of bread. I don't think there was such a thing as sliced bread in 1952; if there was I had certainly not come across it. I had to hand-slice the bread for about three hundred sandwiches of varied thickness and different fillings.

Urns of tea and coffee were always on the go. This job lasted for about six weeks, then I got a call from Rodney Millington at *Spotlight*. The Salisbury Arts Theatre was holding auditions in London for a summer season in Carlisle.

The first audition was a general audition rather than a specific test, and I appeared to pass because I could walk and talk. I was told to go and see Guy Verney, the company's artistic director, that evening. Guy was a slight man with blond hair and blue eyes and great charm. I rang the bell of his flat in Cleveland Square and waited in some trepidation. I remembered my intuitive feeling while I was stationed in Winchester that I would be part of the Salisbury Arts Theatre.

A book was open on the table. Guy picked it up and gave it to me.

My heart sank – he was going to ask me to read. Should I tell him about my dyslexia? What was the play? It was *Man and Superman*.

Guy read me a cue line. 'Well, well, Octavius, it's the common lot. We must all face it some day.'

I heard myself answering. 'Yes: we must face it, Mr Ramsden. But I owed him a great deal. He did everything for me that my father could have done if he had lived.'

By some quirk of fate, I had read the play sometime earlier and remembered it well. The words were coming out in the right order; they weren't jumping about on the page. It was miraculous.

I walked home across Hyde Park, called in at The Enterprise for half a bitter and went home to Julia. She was waiting for me at the top of the stairs.

'Guy Verney wants you to ring him.'

Rehearsals would start on 7 June, he told me, in just two weeks' time. Leslie Phillips would be directing two of the plays, *Black Chiffon* by Lesley Storm, in which I would play the son, Roy, and *Harvey*. I had seen Sid Field play Elwood P. Dowd in London and the great James Stewart in the film. A wonderful story. I was cast as a thug-like male nurse in the asylum. I was to receive £8 a week and play as cast. I would be playing Octavius in *Man and Superman*. The stage director would let me know the time and place of the rehearsal, he told me.

Julia and I stood hugging each other. I was an actor in work. We went to the Unity restaurant to celebrate.

Rehearsals were held in the function room of a pub on the corner of Broadwick Street in Soho. The season was to open with *Man and Superman* and close with *Harvey* and the other plays were *To Dorothy, A Son* by Roger MacDougall, in which I was to play the second taxi driver, *Charley's Aunt* (Leslie Phillips had just had a great success playing Fancourt Babberley at the Savoy Theatre in London), *Ring Round the Moon* and *Black Chiffon*. The season would last two months. I would be in Carlisle for that time and Julia and I reconciled ourselves that we would have to communicate by telephone or by letter. Separation and touring are part of an actor's life.

Guy Verney directed and played Jack Tanner in *Man and Superman*. It was a splendid company; working for it had a feeling of being on summer hols. When there was racing at Carlisle on a Saturday, Guy very sensibly put on a 5.30 performance rather than the usual 2.30 p.m. matinée.

I thoroughly enjoyed playing Octavius (affectionately known as Ricky-Ticky Tavey) in *Man and Superman*; Guy was a splendid director but, poor man, I think he soon realised he had an uphill job with me.

The army had done me some good and some bad. I had had proper food for two years, I had taken plenty of exercise and, although I had been ill, I was incredibly fit. It had given me a straight back, square shoulders but it had also given me a tight neck and 'peggity' legs on which to stamp stiffly about. Before going into the army I had moved fluently without self-consciousness, but now ... Things improved gradually but the parade ground did not disappear until

I began to attend Philip and Betty Bushel's dance studio in Flood Street. The trouble with dance studios is that they have mirrors all round the walls and the bum of a man of six foot four is not a small item, particularly when compared to the shapely buttocks of diminutive dancers. It seemed to me that my bum filled up all the mirror space as I circled the studio.

Michael Ingrams, who was to take a very colourful part in my life for years to come, played Roebuck Ramsden in *Man and Superman*. He was a big man. George Devine described him as a cross between Edmund Kean and Chaliapin. Certainly his performance as Messerschmann in Anouilh's *Ring Round the Moon* made a lasting impression on me; it was huge and powerful, he tore up his money and tore out his heart and gave the audience of Her Majesty's Theatre, Carlisle, a display of barnstorming acting that left them dazed and applauding. He was far too clever to remain an actor for long. He was to become an ATV newscaster, a documentary film-maker and a parliamentary candidate for the Liberal Party. But here he was playing Roebuck Ramsden in Carlisle.

Leslie Phillips taught me a great deal about acting and the theatre, but I thank him most for teaching me how to do a 'double take'. During the action of *Charley's Aunt*, Jack Chesney and Charley Wykeham send Fancourt Babberley to slip into the 'Aunt's' costume off-stage. Charley goes upstage to look off and see that all is going well. He must satisfy himself that it is and only when he turns back to face the audience must he realise that all is far from well, the realisation being the double take and the laugh. I couldn't get it. One evening Leslie got the electrician to fix a flashing red light under his skirt and when I went to see if all was well, I was confronted by Leslie with his skirt over his head, pointing his bum at me, merrily flashing red. I could not believe what I had seen, I turned away to continue the scene and then, disbelieving, turned back to make sure that what I had seen was real. A 'double take' is a look for the expected and an affirmation in your mind and then another look to verify that you didn't see what you thought you saw. Dazed by the unexpected turn of events you tried to press on with the scene. I got the idea and the laugh.

Rachel Roberts, a Welsh clergyman's daughter, full of wit and bubbling over with laughter, joined us to play in *Harvey*. She came to share my digs, and the little house in Howe Street shook with laughter. She was an explosion of talent. She was with us for the last week in Carlisle and then transferred with the rest of the company to Salisbury for two more productions before taking on the film industry – *Our Man in Havana*, *Saturday Night and Sunday Morning*, *Picnic at Hanging Rock* and many other great films. I last saw her when she came to see me in *The Glass Menagerie*; she was then with her second husband, Rex Harrison. In a horrible echo of Elspeth Grant's suicide, she took her own life by drinking a tin of liquid Brasso. She is one of the souls I often recall with great joy; souls who slip into the mind from wherever they are and cheer up a drab day.

They were good days at Salisbury where we were a three-weekly rep – each production played for three weeks and each rehearsed for three weeks. The first week was in the little theatre in Fisherton Street and then we toured towns round about – Frome, Castle Carey, Chippenham, Weymouth, Winchester, as well as a couple of RAF bases and some local village halls.

Frank Hauser came to join the company as associate artistic director, and we were to see less of Guy Verney as the season progressed. Frank brought academic intellect and a great love of music with him. The tone of the plays changed: we played *The Hollow* and *Murder at the Vicarage* by Agatha Christie, Benn Levy's drama *Return to Tyassi*, and John Whiting's *Penny for a Song*. Prunella Scales joined the company, as did Gwen Watford. Gwen and I were friends until she died. I was terrified of Pru Scales, she was so clever, but I loved acting with her and remember our playing *While the Sun Shines* with the deepest affection. *Home and Beauty* with Gwen Watford and Prunella Scales; the cup runneth over. And certainly I number Pru Scales and Tim West among my dearest friends.

The paucity of my education was beginning to play havoc with my self-esteem and I was developing a regrettable chip. Frank Hauser had the unkind ability of finding an Achilles heel and making me cringe. I don't really think it was malicious but it was certainly effective. We liked each other for all that and he was a good mentor and guide. It was on his recommendation that I read not the plays but the short stories of Ivan Turgenev, Anton Chekhov and Gogol. From these stories, most particularly from Turgenev, I learned that things are as they are and writers should refrain from moral judgement. Ouspensky was right, Ivan Osokin, even with prescience, would knowingly make the wrong choice. I'm afraid that in the course of my career I have deliberately and wilfully made the wrong choice over and over again.

During the time I was in Salisbury, Julia was toing and froing from Paris. Sometimes brother Anthony would drive her down to see a Saturday performance and we would all drive back after the show. Sometimes I would hitchhike back to London on a Saturday night, arriving home in the small hours; I would return to Salisbury by coach on Sunday evening.

Location filming had started in Paris: they were filming all night and Julia was having to do costume fittings all day. I was offered a small part, a guard's officer escort to Suzanne Flon, but Frank Hauser wouldn't release me from my contract with Salisbury. I ploughed on and finally left Salisbury at the end of November 1952. I was miffed that Frank didn't let me off my contract. God knows there were enough young juveniles to take my place.

Mummy was, as ever, in a desperate state for cash but was putting a brave face on it. Everything was apparently going well in the negotiations with the Foreign Office to procure a visa to travel to Sofia in order to have conversations with the Bulgarian Minister of Commerce and Finance. She planned to arrange trading transactions so that sums of money could be released in settlement of 'blocked balances' in Bulgaria. She may well have been told she could not trade but she would take little notice of the telling.

She had taken in a lodger, an actor called Keith Banks, and was busily throwing her daughter at his head. Julia and I did what we could to help her with money.

Michael Ingrams kindly spoke to Doris York of the Grand Theatre, Croydon, about me and she offered me the part of the Rev Lionel Toop in *See How They Run*. It is a masterpiece of farce and greatly enjoyable to play and, best of all, I was able to return home every night after the show. Edward Woodward and Geoffrey Palmer were both in the company. Our paths were to cross again a number of times in the future.

There was nothing in the Christmas panto for me but I was asked to return to Croydon in the New Year to rehearse *Our Family*, the play written by Ken Butler for Coronation year. A young woman, thinly disguised as Princess Elizabeth, falls in love with a dashing but impecunious naval officer, thinly disguised as Prince Philip, who is supported by his great friend and confidant, another young naval officer, thinly disguised as the Marquis of Milford-Haven, and then there's mum and dad and younger sis, all thinly disguised. Rosemary Dunham played Elizabeth, I played Philip and Geoffrey Palmer, Milford-Haven.

The *Daily Telegraph*'s critic came to see the play and was pretty rough with it but very nice to me ... 'George Baker should be seen in Shaftesbury Avenue very soon.'

Moy Charles asked me to go to Bromley and appear in a new play called *Hat Hung on Cupid*. Moy was a splendidly forthright woman and ran the theatre with great zest and flair. It was a coveted place to appear. They obviously liked me at Bromley since I stayed for three productions.

After Bromley, I returned to Croydon. When the whole world was looking for job security, it seems strange that the actor is better served by flexibility. To finish a play at Croydon and then have a couple of weeks out before going back to Bromley was heaven sent. It meant that I could go around the agents and casting directors. Sometimes you made an appointment, sometimes you heard of a casting session and just turned up. You couldn't stand on ceremony if you wanted to work.

Ronnie Curtis was a casting director for 'B' pictures at Merton Park Studios. I went to see him. There were about five of us in the waiting-room. Nobody had warned me that Curtis had the mother and father of a squint and that you took your cue from where his nose was pointing and not where his eyes were looking. He came out of his office door and stared at the chap at the end of the line who did not move. Somebody nudged me.

'Me?'

'Yes, you! Don't be so dozy.'

I went in and met the director, Ken Hughes, and read the designated part for him. I was booked for two days at £15 a day. This would be my first film. I knew nothing of filming and was terrified. We were to start work the very next day. Due to my dyslexia, I needed time to learn my lines, and I was horrified when I saw that I had a page-long speech tying up the forgotten clues in this ridiculous murder. It was even more depressing when I found it was the first scene of the day.

The next morning dawned and I didn't know my words.

We were taken by car to a location just outside Merton. The camera was set. The action was that a police car with me in it drew up at the pavement where another policeman was waiting to speak to me. I got out of the car and, having spoken three lines, dried stone dead. Nothing came to me.

It was expected that one take would be sufficient. I got another chance at it and failed again. On my third failure, I was sacked and I heard the producer saying that they should get somebody down to play the part who could learn it.

Ken Hughes sacked me very kindly and said many people had trouble with their lines. The production manager apologised that he had no spare cars to take me back but if I took the bus across the road going to Merton it would drop me at the studios. In normal circumstances, I wouldn't have minded about this at all but I was covered in make-up and very embarrassed by having to travel on public transport in such a state. Having got back to the studios and changed, I went to Merton station to go home. Coming up the steps was the actor who had been asked to replace me. I knew him from Bromley and I also knew that we were shortly to play *Dial 'M' for Murder* at Bromley. He was very kind and conciliatory about what had happened, then with a wave said, 'See you next week', and was gone.

I went home, sat on the dining table, my legs swinging, and burst into tears.

Michael Ingrams, now turned actor/manager, came to my rescue and I joined him for an eight-week season at the Palace Theatre, Walthamstow. However, the plays were dreadful, the theatre three-quarters empty, and the whole affair nearly bankrupted Michael.

What was nice, though, was that my sister Eve joined us for some ASMing. Things were still not good for her at home, and Julia and I found her a room near us in Cadogan Square. Keith Banks was much in evidence which didn't please the landlady.

Ronnie Curtis seemed to have forgiven me since he cast me in a sad little second feature, whose name I can't even remember, for the Danziger Brothers at the Riverside Studios. Frances Rowe and I were the leading villains and Victor Maddern, our henchman. The first assistant director was the same as on the Merton Park picture, but this time all went well.

I had a deathless line to speak: 'Tell Maisie, it's all right for tonight.'

The sound department wanted me to do a wild track of the line – speaking the line for sound only and not on picture. I stood in the middle of the stage under the microphone and repeated the line. There was some technical reason why it was never quite right and I had to repeat it again and again. The electricians in the lighting gantry, the technicians on the floor and the camera crew were in stitches of delight. I managed to keep a straight face and gave the line a myriad of meanings and inflections. For years to come I was to have the fun of walking on to a stage at Ealing or Pinewood, Shepperton or Elstree and hearing 'Tell Maisie, it's all right for tonight.'

Julia was now working on *The Heart of the Matter*, directed by George More O'Ferrall. Trevor Howard, Maria Schell, Denholm Elliott, Peter Finch, Elizabeth Allen and Michael Hordern were all in the cast. Oh yes, quite a cast! Guy Hamilton was the first assistant director and was to play a considerable part in my future.

One Sunday during the shooting of the film, we gave a small party to which Peter Finch came with his wife, Tamara. I had bought a firkin of beer from The Enterprise, our local pub, and set it up in the kitchen. The party was not of the size to drink seventy-two pints so there was plenty left. Peter knew this and a few days later, at about two in the morning, there was a loud banging on the door and a ringing of the bell. I thought it must be some idiot from the Jacaranda Club in the mews opposite. But the banging persisted so I went downstairs to see who it was.

Standing in front of me, looking very jolly and swaying slightly, were Trevor, Peter and George More O'Ferrall, who had stupidly decided that if he went out with them he would be able to control them.

'Peter tells me you've got some beer, old cock. We'll just pop in to have a little drink,' said Trevor. He stepped past me, closely followed by Peter.

'Sho shorry about this,' said George. Not being a hardened soak, he was truly drunk and ricocheted off the walls as he went upstairs to the sitting-room.

I poured them all a beer.

'You got any scotch, old darling?' asked Peter. He said it in a voice which told me that if I couldn't produce it he would burst into tears. He enjoyed his chaser and then one or two more.

Julia came down and made herself a cup of tea. Birdie very sensibly stayed in her room. Next morning she confessed she would have loved to have met Peter Finch, but not under those circumstances. They finally left at four in the morning.

We saw Peter and Tamara Finch quite often. Peter was a wonderful raconteur, and I remember the story that he told us about the time he was playing Iago to Orson Welles's Othello. Late on dress rehearsal night, Orson was padding up and down the stalls with a glass of brandy in his hand. Peter was playing a scene with Maxine Audley, Desdemona. Suddenly Orson stopped and in a loud voice shouted, 'I am suffering. Christ on the cross did not suffer as I am suffering.'

Without a pause, a matter-of-fact voice came from the gantry and shouted to the stage: 'Charlie, got a couple of six-inch nails?'

I had no agent so I can only suppose that the bush telegraph was working well and in my favour. In the spring of 1953, I was called by Daphne Rey, the casting director of H. M. Tennant, to audition for a new production of Freddie Lonsdale's *Aren't We All?* I did my audition for Roland Culver who was to direct the play, and I got a very small part plus understudying the leading man, Ronald Howard.

We were to rehearse on the stage of the Haymarket Theatre during May and go out on tour in June. I arrived at the first rehearsal not knowing what to expect; after all, this was the West End. There was to be no read-through. We started at the beginning and Roland Culver stood on the apron of the stage, just behind the footlights, and told us where to move. Rolly told me that he had written some extra lines for my part but warned me I should have 'a pencil poised for cuts' because Freddie had not seen the rewrites and, being rather a peppery author, it was conceivable he might object to them.

The first scene was a short exchange between the butler, played by Vincent Holman, and Ronald Howard, the romantic juvenile lead. Then I came on, escorting Marie Löhr on my arm. From the opposite side of the stage came David Geary, playing another small part and, like me, understudying, escorting Annie Robinson, our beautiful stage manager. There was a quick exchange and I got three laughs. We then all go off stage to a party, leaving Ronnie Squire – the great 'high comedy' actor in the tradition of Hawtrey and Wyndham – to have a scene with the heroine, Jane Baxter.

Jane quite stole my heart away once more by remembering me from the Bedford Theatre, Camden Town, and being what Jane Austen would call 'pleasantly condescending towards me'. Freddie Lonsdale was pleasantly condescending too, thank God. I kept my lines and my laughs.

Those rehearsals were wonderful: here were some of the finest comedy actors of our time working together on the play. Marie Löhr had started her career at Daly's Music-Hall and been Herbert Beerbohm Tree's leading lady at the age of sixteen; she had become an actor/manager in the twenties and had run the Globe Theatre in Shaftesbury Avenue. Marie had a straightforward approach to comedy. She reckoned that if you said your line clearly and loudly, and if the author had done his work, you got your laugh.

While Marie was on for this scene, I was standing with Ronnie Squire in the wings. 'Listen to her, booming away, booming away,' he said. He took a pinch of snuff from his box and sniffed some gently up his nostrils.

After I had said my few lines with Ronnie, I went off and stood with Marie, waiting to escort her back on stage. 'Beats me how they hear him, chucking the lines into the footlights as he does.' She would take out a tiny, exquisite, silver shovel, and putting a little snuff in it would delicately offer it to her nostrils. She became my adopted stage grandmother, and one of the dearest friends I ever had. Their scenes together were a joy to watch, two very different styles of comedy, each masterly in its own way and both players considerate to the play, the audience and each other.

Also in the play was Marjorie Fielding, whose comedy timing was so deft she seemed to be doing nothing. I would watch her carefully. She sat knitting and listening to every word that was being said, without appearing to, so that when she dropped a remark into the conversation the audience was surprised and delighted. She taught me as much about the serious business of playing comedy as anybody I have ever met, except, perhaps, Morecambe and Wise.

We were to open at the Opera House, Manchester. I asked Annie if she had a list of digs; the stage manager usually did.

'I have the best digs in the world in Manchester, my dear. I'm staying with Mrs Leach. They have a funeral parlour and a hardware shop and she's a marvellous cook. Where else can you get a bed, a bag of nails, a coffin and a steak and kidney pie? I'm staying there. Shall I book you in?'

The train call was on Sunday and the company travelled up en masse. When we arrived, the sun was shining and the theatre looked splendid. I was standing in front of it, looking at the photographs, when our scenery arrived from the station. It was loaded on two drays pulled by massive bay shires with white-feathered fetlocks.

Ronnie took Annie and me to lunch at the Prince's Grill. He talked of Gerald du Maurier and Charles Hawtrey. 'Hawtrey knew the character he was playing inside out, even to the colour of the socks he would wear. Young fellows like Michael Redgrave go on about Stanislavsky and the Method, but it's as old as the hills. We just didn't go on about it, that's all.' Then he said: 'Playing comedy is like going fishing, you know. You put out your bait and listen. If they try to take it and begin to laugh, stop them. Then give them another chance, let them smile. Another and let the smile broaden and when you know they'll swallow the bait, let them have their laugh and they're yours for the night.'

A critic once described Ronnie Squire's voice as 'biscuit and cheese with fine port wine'.

We played in Golders Green, Streatham Hill, Brighton. On 6 August, we opened at the Theatre Royal, Haymarket. Although there was a feeling of great excitement, the first night was only a prelude to the Royal Charity Gala we were to have in October.

Walking home through Green Park every night, I was more often than not on cloud nine. I loved my wife and she loved me. 'God's in his heaven, all's right with the world.'

A character actor called Hugh Dempsy regularly drank at the Royal Oak in Elizabeth Street, a haunt of mine since the early Belgravia days. Hugh had become concerned that I had signed a contract for my first West End play without the advice of either an agent or solicitor. He had just joined a new agency which had been started by a tall, camp Scottish chorus boy and a plump, small-part English actor who had private means. Jimmy Fraser and Peter Dunlop were destined to become one of the most powerful agencies in the country. Hugh gave me an introduction to Jimmy and I became client number fourteen.

On 3 October, we were to play a Royal Gala for the new Queen Elizabeth II. I can't remember which charity it was for, but it was a spectacular occasion with an audience of celebrities, and glamorous young actresses selling programmes. The sense of occasion was palpable, the atmosphere in the theatre electric. Personally, I was full of a feeling of 'the world at my feet'. I was appearing in the West End four months after my twenty-second birthday. I hoped Papa would have been proud of me.

Julia came with her brother Anthony and after the show we went to the Café de Paris to see Marlene Dietrich. It was a hypnotising show, but it sadly confirmed what I had always known: Marlene could not sing. Put a number across like no one else, but sing, no.

Aren't We All? completed its limited season and closed just before Christmas. Marie Löhr wrote to Laurence Olivier and asked him to audition me for his forthcoming season at St James's Theatre. I didn't know anything about general auditions. I had always done auditions for a specific part. I should have prepared two or three pieces, one of which would have shown off the secret actor hiding down below. Instead, I did a couple of pieces of Shakespeare which I didn't know how to play properly. Olivier turned me down very gently and wrote a kind letter to Marie saying he thought I had a bright future ahead of me.

During the run of *Aren't We All?* I had begun to make a little extra money from modelling for a photographer, Geoffrey Morris. I posed for various advertising campaigns and he was always kind enough to make sure my full face did not appear. There was and, up to a point, there still is a taboo that serious actors did not model. Later, this was to spill over into appearing in television commercials. My sister Evie became one of his star models; she had grown up to be very beautiful.

On 26 September, my mother rang me from Victoria station to say that she was on her way to Belgrade where she planned to sit in the Bulgarian legation until she got her visa to take her into Bulgaria. I tried to argue with her. 'Sorry, darling, the train's just going.' The line went dead.

As far as we knew, she had no money. She had left us no address. However, we spoke to Lady Reid-Dick and learned that Mother had set up a company to trade with Bulgaria, persuading a number of friends to become board members and buy shares while some of the firms she was to represent chipped in a few hundred pounds; this is how she had financed her trip.

Lady Dick was most concerned because she had, in fact, sold her house in which Mother had a flat and which was full of her belongings. She told us that Mother was very much in arrears with the rent and appeared to be in debt to most of the shops. We paid the debts and Julia and I held a council of war. Not only did Mother have no home to come back to, but the boys had nowhere to go for the holidays. I packed up her few belongings and put them into store.

We decided we had to find a flat big enough to have the boys with us in the holidays. I went down to Ardingly and told Pat what was happening. With all the vicissitudes of his life, I think that this latest news was simply par for the course. I also went to see Terence at Lord Wandsworth College. He hated it there, which, from my brief visit, didn't surprise me at all. He was learning nothing and his hopes of becoming a farmer were more than remote. I decided that something had to be done about him, but first: the flat.

I found a suitable flat in Lower Belgrave Street for £7 per week inclusive. It had a master bedroom, an enormous sitting-room and two more rooms at basement level. One of them could be partitioned to make two bedrooms. The only problem was the 'key' money of £600. We took Julia's brother, Rag, into our confidence and he lent me the money.

Opposite the stage door of the Haymarket Theatre was the Buckstone Club which was run by Gerry Campion, famous for his television portrayal of Billy Bunter. He ran the club with great flair and it was the meeting place for young actors and directors in theatre and film. I used to go into the club after the show and would very often meet Ronan O'Casey and his fiancée Louie Ramsay. In fact, most of the chorus of *South Pacific* met there before and after the show which was playing at the Theatre Royal, Drury Lane. Louie was very attractive and obviously going places. I was delighted for her when, some time later, I saw her name in lights over the title at the Hippodrome. Little did I think we were going to get to know each other a whole lot better many years later.

The Buckstone had a congenial restaurant where actors met for supper after the show. Stanley Baker was often to be found there, growling away that there was only one Baker in the film industry.

Guy Hamilton, who had been the first assistant director on *The Heart of the Matter*, was about to direct a film of his own, *The Intruder*. He had been to see *Aren't We All?* and we'd had a drink in the Buckstone afterwards. He had a small part in the film for which he thought I would be very good. My agent, Jimmy Fraser, arranged everything so that I could do the film without working on matinée days.

I was playing a young officer who had to walk into the officers' mess and over to the CO, played by Jack Hawkins, and say, 'Group Headquarters would like you to call them, sir.'

Jack was standing by the bar surrounded by a group which included Richard Wattis, Patrick Barr, Hugh Williams, Dennis Price and Nicholas Phipps – quite a formidable array of senior talent on your first day's shooting.

I had a long walk from the door to the bar. We rehearsed and everything went well. When we were about to film, the doors were closed, the bell rang out, the red light went on, and silence was called. Turn over. Action. Off I went. Half way through my walk I realised I had not the faintest idea of the words I had to say. I didn't dare stop, so I just walked on. As I approached, I saw Jack looking at me. He turned to Guy Hamilton and said, 'I'm so sorry, Guy, I'm not quite sure what you said . . .' I can't remember the rest of the question, my relief was indescribable. Jack had realised my plight and thrown me a lifeline. We were to sct up from the top. As I turned to leave Jack gave me a wink. The next take was fine.

There was a dinner scene in which George Cole, an officer newly made up from the ranks, was about to commit a social solecism. I was to shake my head and will him not to do it. Guy gave me an enormous close-up.

Jimmy Fraser got permission to show the clip from *The Intruder* to Bob Lennard, casting director of ABPC – Associated British Picture Corporation – and that changed the course of my life for the next few years.

12

JULIA HAD BECOME FRIENDLY WITH THE DESIGNER, SOPHIE HARRIS, WHO WAS MARRIED TO GEORGE DEVINE. They were about to sell their flat in Addison Avenue and Sophie wondered if we would like it. It was quite impossible to even consider it because of the price but we went round to see it anyway. It was a fortuitous day since I met George who was then one of the directors of the Royal Shakespeare Theatre. They were holding general auditions and I was asked to go along.

I asked Peter Finch what he thought I might do and he suggested Mercutio's Queen Mab speech. He came over one Sunday and coached me. I cooked lunch and we got nicely pissed. A few days later, I went to the Shaftesbury Theatre and spoke my speech which tripped off the tongue so Peter's help had been invaluable.

Then came the offer from the Royal Shakespeare Company of small parts and understudying and this is what I should have done. But the money was small and there was the problem of the boys' schooling. There was still no word from Mother. I had committed to the flat in Lower Belgrave Street. I had taken Terry out of Lord Wandsworth College and persuaded the Reverend Snow, headmaster of Ardingly, to let Terry go there the following term. I wrote to all the societies that were helping with Pat's fees and asked them to help with Terence's. I went to see them all and they were kind enough to make further contributions. Chris Hilyard, Canon at Westminster Abbey, persuaded the Pilgrim Trust and the Army Officers' Association to help. We weren't doing badly but there was still a great deal to find. Julia wrote to Frank in Korea and told him what we were doing. He replied, giving both verbal and financial support. He had made an allotment from his pay of £10 a month to Mother; he now transferred this to help with the boys.

Jimmy Fraser rang up in a state of high camp excitement, his best Scottish Morningside accent was squealing with pleasure down the wires. ABPC was offering me a seven-year contract. Alleluia, God was good! I was to start at £25 a week.

Perhaps we could find the money for the boys after all. The price was having to turn down the RSC. Shakespeare was to come later, but had I been able to go to Stratford at that point ... who knows?

At last, we received a telegram from Mother. She was fine. She was in Belgrade and gave us her number there. She would contact us from Sofia. I called her and told her what we had done about her flat and the boys. I gave her our new address and telephone number. I also told her, in case she had forgotten, that the school holidays were starting in three days' time.

I was still painting the vast space of wall in the sitting-room of Lower Belgrave Street when Pat arrived. His face fell: this was not a new and permanent home, this was the usual muddle. However, Julia's forethought and caring in having the boys' bedrooms ready calmed him. All was going to be well.

Terence arrived, tiptoeing round the situation, watchfully.

Julia and I had become parents to two teenage boys. I was twenty-two, she was twenty-seven. In four short months, my mother had irrevocably transformed our lives.

I found a memoir in the papers she left me when she died which give a clue to the progress of my brave, mad, eccentric, caring mother through the Eastern Communist Bloc for those four months. She did care, she cared for us deeply. The whole journey had been undertaken in order to retrieve our father's money, so that life would be for us as he would have wanted it to be. Ah!

Every day she went to the Bulgarian legation to see if her visa had arrived. Every day she was disappointed and went on her round of sightseeing. After seven weeks she gave up and blagged her way across the border with no visa by charming a Russian Tartar officer. They even arranged a car to meet her and a hotel for her to stay in.

She had finally got to Sofia. She was allowed to use money from her bank to pay her expenses and the Chamber of Commerce gave lip service to her trading ambitions but made it clear that there was no question of her taking money out of the country. She was defeated. She asked for a visa to return to Yugoslavia and was refused. 'You came in without one, go out without one,' they said and advised her to use another border.

She arrived at Victoria station with 1/9d to her name. I went to fetch her and took her back to Lower Belgrave Street.

She continued the fight and three years later she was paid £1,500 in compensatory settlement. A fraction of the £12,000 she calculated she was owed.

I signed my contract with ABPC and immediately wrote to Frank telling him that he could reinstate his standing order to Mother, but that I would be grateful if we could continue to enjoy £3 of it. So Mama got £7 a month and we got £3 towards the boys.

Next door to Lincoln Cathedral is the Saracen's Head and that is where we were to live while we were filming *The Dam Busters* at Scampton airfield, from where the Lancasters for the real raid had flown. It was the spring of 1954 and the sun shone intermittently between the clouds. We seemed to spend a great deal of time lying around on the grass while Erwin Hillier, the cameraman, stared into the sky to see if we could shoot film. The first assistant would give the call and suddenly all the actors and crews rushed towards the waiting planes, only to be stopped because the sun had gone behind a cloud. It was my initiation into the extreme boredom of filming on location.

Now, with fast film, digital cameras and technical advance, we can shoot in cloud, rain and sun; just roll the cameras and tweak later. But then we had to wait for the weather. There was time to talk, to make friends, and to encounter the imbecilic class system of Her Majesty's Forces.

We had been invited to use the officers' mess, but when Robert Shaw and Brian Nissen walked in wearing their sergeant's uniforms, they were politely asked to leave. The taciturn Bob Shaw was fit to be tied. The production manager calmed him down and came to a compromise with the mess. Those actors who were playing NCOs were to take off their uniform jackets and put on 'civilian' jackets when in the officers' mess. Bob, however, was still not satisfied and he boycotted the place for at least a week.

Intelligent, aggressive, competitive Bob Shaw found out that there were squash courts on the camp. Nothing would do but I must teach him how to play squash. I was not a great squash player but capable enough. I taught him to play. Bob had a great eye for ball games and was soon good, but still not beating me. After the film was over he joined the Hampstead Squash Club and took lessons from a professional. Very soon he was playing for the club and not long after for the county.

We played futile games of squash at the Chelsea Cloisters. Once you have achieved the dizzy heights of playing for the county, a player of my meagre skills couldn't hope to get a point. I simply couldn't think why Bob wanted to play me. We were in the court one day when he had taken a love game and, turning on me with a face full of malign fury, he shouted, 'When are you going to lose your bloody temper?'

So that was it. It wasn't a game of squash at all.

On her return from Eastern Europe, Mother had moved into a room around the corner, in Ebury Street. My sister Eve came to live with us for a while. Julia was working from film to film and I had my seven-year film contract. This was the beginning of the years of pretension and self-delusion.

It was a time when everybody smoked and drank. My corner cupboard was full of every imaginable spirit and liqueur. Thanks to Julia's location in Burgundy on *Father Brown*, and Leigh Aman and Louis Fleury's advice, we had a cellar of Premier Cru 1945 and 1947. It became *de rigueur* to have the first gin and tonic at six thirty. I was twenty-three and playing at grown-ups with silver cigarette boxes and Ronson lighters dotted about the room. One had to be seen around, and Julia and I spent far too much money on what we thought were the 'in' places.

We lived just up the road from the Plumbers Arms, which I had known well when I had a room in Chester Square and which I now visited daily. Its greatest claim to fame was that Lady Lucan raised the alarm there on the night of the nanny's murder and the disappearance of her husband. I drank daily and I drank plenty, sometimes too much.

Then I got a call from Bob Lennard, the casting director at ABPC. I was to do a test for John Huston for the part of Ishmael in *Moby Dick*: Denholm Elliott, Don Taylor and Robert Urquhart were also testing.

I was first on in the morning. The stage was set as the deck and midships of the *Pequod*, an enormous mast reaching up into the gantry. On the deck squatted Queequeg. God knows how long he had been in make-up: the formidable tattoos and native carvings on his face and body must have taken for ever. They were testing not only us but doing a make-up test on him as well.

Ossie Morris was busy lighting the set, Queequeg and me. I stood waiting for John Huston to tell me what to do. He sat in his director's chair, reading a racing paper. Just as when I had first met him in Paris two years before, he was dressed in tweed trousers and a hacking jacket and sported a flat cap.

He looked over the top of his paper, 'Just take your time and show me what you'd like to do.' He went back to his paper. I realised I was on my own.

I started to rehearse, but certainly came up with nothing very interesting. I leaned against the ship's rail and started my speech to camera.

When Huston saw that he was going to get nothing more from me than that, he wound himself out of his chair and came across to me. 'Would you consider leaning on the rail looking out to sea, then turn around as if you had been interrupted in your reverie. Someone has spoken to you. Who are you? You turn around. You look at them. You don't want to disclose your identity. You tell them, "Call me –" What name will you give them? Oh yes. "Call me . . . Ishmael." It was wonderful, it informed the rest of my lines. The wanting to remain anonymous, the defensive approach to Ahab (whose lines were being read by Huston) and the whole scene lifted. It was such a pleasure working with him that I thoroughly enjoyed the film test even though I knew I hadn't got the part. I was still not sufficiently experienced to know how to prepare for an audition.

None of us was going to get the part. I learned later that Huston was testing us in order to scare Richard Basehart into accepting it. Which he did.

My test was good, and Jeanie Sims, Jack Clayton's secretary, suggested to Huston that he should make me a present of it. Bob Lennard, Jimmy Fraser and I viewed the test. Jimmy was sure he knew what to do with it.

While Ju and I were down in Gloucestershire, at Jo Baird's cottage for a week, a script arrived from Jimmy. It was a script from a Monsarrat story, *The Ship that Died of Shame*. I was to read the part of Bill Randall. If I liked it they were going to test me.

If I liked it? It was the leading part.

This time, I prepared myself for the audition, thank God, because I was to meet an extraordinary antagonist. Basil Dearden, the director, did not want me for the part. He wanted Terence Alexander who had been the leading man at Richmond when I was an ASM there. Basil decided to ask Terry to stooge test with me, playing the part opposite me when I tested. He then chose a scene in which Terry had the dominant role.

We lined up the scene, planning the moves, so that the cinematographer could get on with lighting the set while we went to make up and sorted out our wardrobe. When we started to rehearse I realised what Basil had done. He was testing Terry and I was the stooge.

I didn't go to the canteen at lunchtime; I went to the pub and had a think. I decided that I must play for the value and truth of the scene. The scene belonged to George Hoskins, the character that Dickie Attenborough was to play and which Terry was playing in the test. In the afternoon, we shot the scene and I played my part with honesty and for all its worth.

I rang Jimmy Fraser and told him what had happened. He was very camp and Morningside about it. There were a lot of Aahs and Oohs, but he was also very supportive. Imagine my incredulity when I got the part. Michael Balcon, on seeing the test, said that I had played the scene impeccably and had rerun the Huston test for Basil. He told him he wanted me for the part and, being the head of the studio, his word was final. Basil was not happy at being overruled and, being a bit of a sadist, he was going to have a field day.

Dickie Attenborough tried very hard to befriend me. He saw that the potential was there but the experience wasn't. Obviously the Huston test had made me look to have star quality and the film industry loves a new face. He was wonderfully kind and supportive to me as an actor, helping me with the formidable job I had been given. I knew nothing of film acting and Basil's sighs, groans and 'Let's try and do it better' were not the most encouraging directions. I listened to everything Dickie said and tried to act on it. It was on the personal level, however, that I rejected his help because I didn't know how to accept it. Knowing I was only twenty-three, Dickie was avuncular and concerned that I was not spending my money wisely. He tried to tell me what investments to make, that I should be buying shares. 'Make it a rule to buy a picture, preferably by a young artist you think has a gift, from the proceeds of every film you do.'

Too late, Dickie, we were already overreaching ourselves, not only because we were having to look after the boys but were trying to put a middle-aged, middle-class home around us. We felt we had to take on the gravitas of parenting. I think Julia and I both believed that if we had the right trappings, we would have the permanency. Because of spending large sums in Peter Jones, Harvey Nichols and Harrods on her film budgets, Julia was able to open personal accounts there, and these apparently had no credit limit. Every now and then, we would settle down in a panic and try to make some sense of our debts. With the best of intentions, we would pay small amounts on account to the most clamouring.

I was learning how to rob Peter to pay Paul.

Dear Dickie, if only I had been in a position to take your advice.

I was as green as anything and didn't know what to do in front of the camera but I did know I was driving our cinematographer, Gordon Dines, mad. We were in Poole by this time, staying at the Sandbanks Hotel. One evening, I was sitting at the bar, staring into my drink in abject dejection. I remember thinking that since I was obviously going to be sacked, I wished it would happen sooner rather than later.

Gordon Dines came into the bar and studiously avoided me.

To hell with it all, I thought. 'Look, Gordon, I know I don't know what I'm doing, but rather than throwing up your hands in despair, couldn't you just tell me. I've done three days on one film, not much more on *The Dam Busters*, a test for Huston and a test for this film – and that is my entire film experience and this is a very large part. Just tell me what to do.'

Gordon took me at my word and there and then he gave me a lesson on the theory of film. He discussed the difference in the size of the lenses and their functions. We went on talking over dinner. I listened and began to learn.

On the set the next morning, he told me where my key light was and a simple way of making sure I was on my mark in front of the camera without having to look down to check. It made me feel slightly better to know that, apparently, Spencer Tracy had never learned the trick of it. If you watch one of his films you will see him looking down just before he stops walking. He always cleverly incorporated the look down into the performance.

We had reports of the 'rushes' from the studio. We were told they were good in most respects but that my eyes appeared to be sunk in dark caverns.

Gordon told me about the eyes. 'I just find the sun too difficult to look into,' was my reply.

'OK, I'll put a pup under the camera.' I looked at him in amazement. 'It's a small light,' he explained. 'It will shine up into your eyes and help counteract the glare. And we'll get you a piece of black velvet.'

'Why?'

'Just before the camera is ready to turn, you put the velvet in front of your eyes and look at it. It will dilate your pupils and you'll be able to look into the sun much more easily.'

How right you were, Gordon, and how often I've used your advice.

The crew had begun to like me and were more than happy to help, advise and befriend. But there was still Basil and that was bad news. Much as Michael Relph, our producer, told me that the rushes were good and that the performance was there, it didn't really help. I thought he was just being kind.

Bernard Lee was also in the film and his advice on acting is the best I have ever had. I had gone to him for help. 'I don't know how to play this scene, Bernie.'

'What do you mean?'

'I don't know what to do with it.'

'There is nothing to do with it. Just tell the story. That's what acting is about. Telling the story.'

The difference, of course, is that some people are better storytellers than others, or find better stories to tell.

It was while we were on location that Julia telephoned to tell me she was pregnant. I worked out the moment of conception. When we were having our week in Jo's cottage at Aston Subedge, we celebrated the arrival of the script of *The Ship that Died of Shame* at the Lygon Arms in Broadway. Returning home, we had a nightcap and went to bed. A moth flew in through the window, no doubt attracted by the light. I had no idea that Julia was terrified of moths. She threw herself into my arms but I extracted myself in order to catch the moth and put it back out of the window, drawing the curtains behind it. I returned to bed, determined to comfort my wife out of her fear. Candy was certainly born within nine months give a day or two of the flight of the moth.

The location had moved to Weymouth, and here we had our own MTB, a refitted torpedo boat left over from the war. We had a Lt Commander, Ken Peace, as our advisor. He would squat, out of sight on the bridge, and give me instructions as I brought the boat alongside the harbour.

It was an important scene in the film. I bring the boat alongside and switch off. Birdie, played by Bill Owen, ties off for'ard, and George Hoskins, played by Dickie, ties off aft. Birdie is becoming suspicious that we are carrying contraband goods. Guns, he suspects. I go for'ard to placate him; here we are joined by Hoskins and a good healthy row ensues. Basil was at his worst. Nothing I could do was right. He was having a field day and the more he bullied, the worse I got. Suddenly, in the middle of the scene, Bill walked down the gangplank and away up the quay.

This is the conversation as I remember it.

'Where're you going, Bill?' called Basil after the retreating figure.

'Home.'

'What?'

'I'm not staying on this picture, Basil, if you're going to continue to treat George like that.'

'What have I done?' Basil appealed, his arms stretched out in front of him, his guiltless hands and palms open to proclaim his innocence.

'You know perfectly well what you're doing.' Bill turned on his heel and walked away.

Basil ran after him and, after a while, they returned, Basil with his arm round Bill's shoulder – the time-honoured embrace of the director who has quelled the rebellious child.

But, God bless you, Bill Owen. I was never bullied again.

By the time filming had moved into the studio, Basil and I had a good working relationship and he was more than generous in his praise in interviews.

It was a good film, had decent notices and did quite well at the box office. Jack Warrow, the great publicist, made sure that my photograph was in every film magazine, in the tabloids, in trade papers and that I was interviewed by them all. I was an up-and-coming film star.

If the studio to which you were contracted rented you out to another for a film, you received a bonus on your salary. Not a big bonus but sufficient to make you silly enough to go gadding about 'being seen'. The Mirabelle, Pastoria's, the Caprice – they all saw us for dinner. There were clothes to buy for premieres. Yes, we were very stupid.

The war in Korea was over and brother Frank was back on leave and staying with us. Eve decided to marry Keith Banks. Frank did not think him good enough for his sister, at all, at all. He said so loudly and clearly. They were married from our house. I was working and couldn't get to the ceremony, but had laid on a grand reception which I was able to attend. Frank had dressed in his Number Ones and looked resplendent in his uniform. He gave Eve away.

After their wedding, Eve and Keith set up home in a garden flat in Abbey Road. Mother, round the corner from us in Ebury Street, was still pursuing the Foreign Office, the Board of Trade and the Compensation Board. She popped in to see us all the time, especially when Pat and Terry were at home. She was relieved that the boys were being looked after, with one weight taken off her shoulders. She was her buoyant, bubbling self, full of plans for the future.

Pat was very happy at Ardingly and doing well. Terry, not so happy, wasn't going to be there much longer. Both the boys worshipped Julia and she was a wonderful surrogate mother to them.

Frank was having troubles with the army. Having learned Cantonese Chinese, become fluent in Russian and spent two years as an intelligence officer debriefing Korean prisoners of war, he wanted to do something useful. He had been given the rank of brevet major and felt that a good career move would be to go to university and put some time in on his languages. However, the army department that dealt with the Artillery had other plans.

'You've had your fun, Baker. It's back to proper soldiering for you.'

His substantive rank was lieutenant and to that he was to return. He was to be sent to Larkhill to learn about what one does in warfare – as if he hadn't learned all about war during his service in Korea.

Anthony Squire was friendly with the managing director of Pinchin and Johnston Paints. He suggested Frank might like to have an interview with him. The MD was a fluent Russian speaker and conducted the whole interview in Russian. The upshot was that if Frank wanted to leave the army, he had a job. He would be trained at the company's factory in Ripon and then take over as their sales representative in Singapore. The incumbent was retiring and they needed a replacement. Frank jumped at the opportunity.

Julia herself was still working flat out. By this time she was designing the clothes for *The Man Who Loved Redheads* with John Justin and Moira Shearer.

I was going from film to film. Bill Fairchild's *The Extra Day* was a bit of a joke. Simone Simon complained bitterly that I was too young so I found myself, at the age of twenty-four, wearing grey pieces in my hair but not before the make-up department had dropped a bottle of peroxide on my hair. Half my head went blond and a lot of my hair fell out. I rang up my hairdresser, Ivan's of Jermyn Street. You see the self-deception? I desperately wanted to belong to the established idea of being an English gent, whilst hanging on to my socialist principles.

Ivan dyed the ginger hair given me by the make-up department back again to black and cut it so that it would not show how much had fallen out. I was given white wings to my hair and looked just like a twenty-four-year-old actor wearing white hairpieces.

It was the most wonderful and supportive cast. It included Richard Basehart, who tried so hard to get me to go to Hollywood and take my chance; he would introduce me to his agent, he said. There was Sidney James who became a lifelong friend, as did Joan Hickson, John Humphry and Beryl Reid. Joan and I were destined to work together many times, culminating in my playing a West Country detective to her Miss Marple.

The only exception was, perhaps, Simone Simon who was a past master of the art of putting another actor out of countenance. Just as the director said 'Action', she'd come in with, 'Oh, my darling, your tie.' She would step forward and adjust the tie, saying, 'There, that's better, *chéri*. Forgive me. So continue.'

Some years later I was sitting in a cinema in New York watching a 'B' movie and thinking there was something familiar about it. Then I recognised the coat the leading man was wearing: it was my brown check hacking jacket. Then it dawned on me – I was the leading man. That's how good the film was! God, I was acting badly, acting to save my life, I'd say.

From an early age I had hated myself. I could see in myself nothing but a failure. It must be said that my schooldays bore out this assessment of myself. When in one of these self-deprecating moods, I would flail about, shouting that I might as well be dead and why couldn't anybody understand me. I would often storm off into the night, only to reach the first corner on the street and return. This self-loathing was growing with the belief that the film industry did not understand that I was not a juvenile lead but a CHARACTER ACTOR, AND FUNNY.

I didn't know how to play the young romantic leading man. I was the wrong actor in the wrong body. And sitting in that New York cinema watching myself proved it.

My first daughter, Candy, was born on 15 May 1955 in 42 Lower Belgrave Street. Dr Mary Adams was the gynaecologist who delivered her. She was a straightforward, punchy woman who had no time for squeamish fathers. 'If you're going to stay here, you're going to help,' she told me.

I did. I was on the bed with Ju, rubbing her back and mopping her brow. It was not an easy birth as Candy weighed nearly thirteen pounds and Ju tore badly and was in great pain. 'Put her leg over your shoulders. That's right.' Ju pushed once more and the child slid out, Mary gently supporting the head. From my position, kneeling on the bed with Ju's leg over my shoulder, I had the clearest sight of my first-born.

The kettles were waiting ready on the kitchen stove. 'Go and get the boiling water,' instructed Mary Adams. I disentangled myself, gave Ju a kiss on the forehead and ran down to the kitchen. When I got back with the water, I was told to take the child while Ju was cleaned up.

Even though it was May, I had a fire going in the sitting-room. I put a cushion on the floor and put the baby on it. I poured myself a large brandy and lit a cigarette, because that is what fathers are supposed to do.

I sat down and looked at my tiny daughter and experienced a miracle. She had a flat little nose with no bridge. But as we sat there together, her head grew, and her face opened. We seemed to be there for hours and by the end of that time she had a bridge to her nose.

Being under contract meant that I had to accept whatever dropped on my desk. There was no consultation. The money situation was parlous and I was always getting a loan from my studios against the next bonus. I really hadn't a leg to stand on about picking and choosing my scripts.

My bank manager was becoming desperate. The situation was obviously not helped by our not having Ju's salary; in addition, we had to pay Eileen, the monthly nurse we had engaged to look after Ju and baby Candy. I just managed to keep one step ahead by robbing Peter to pay Paul. What I could not do was to stop us spending money, despite really wanting to do something about our finances that would put us on the path to solvency. Ju paid lip service to the intent as we sat doing sums far into the night but it was not going to work – we had different ideas about what was essential and what wasn't.

On the other hand, we were very happy with each other and, as a family, never more so than when we returned to the cottage at Aston Subedge which we did as often as possible.

I always went back to the theatre between films; luckily either Richmond or Croydon seemed happy to have me, and I to be there.

The studio sent me to the Cannes Film Festival. Julia came with me and we managed to get Eileen to come back and look after Candy for the week. We were unprepared for the elegance of the Italians, the chic of the French, the swagger of the Americans and the dowdy English. Except for Diana Dors: she arrived in her powder-blue Cadillac and wearing our bathroom curtains. Our bathroom curtains were made from tastefully flowered grey-and-yellow chintz with a splash of green here and there. Di carried off the material beautifully, but then she had a silver fox draped round her shoulders.

The actress Muriel Pavlow, sitting on the terrace and writing postcards home, looked up for a moment to see why so many photographers were whooping and shouting 'Over here, Di!' and 'This way, Di!' Muriel went back to the urgent business of writing home.

Diana Dors was on the front page of every paper. By the way, she was a prude. We were dancing on a tabletop in a harbour café, as one does, when I put my leg inside hers to add pressure and stability to the turn we were about to execute. Di was very shocked. 'That's a bit rude!' she whispered.

I swore that if I ever went to Cannes again, I would be as elegant as any of the Italians.

Peter Noble interviewed me for his magazine. I was quite widely photographed. The studio publicity team were highly satisfied. I had a chance encounter with Lindsay Anderson and made a pig's ear of it. The Ivan Osokin syndrome: I've been here before, I've messed it up before. This man could be of enormous help to me. He is of the new movement in film and in the theatre. I had just seen *Waiting for Godot* at the Arts Theatre and been bowled over by it. Why couldn't I do theatre like that?

What did I do? I got pissed and talked a lot of self-indulgent rubbish about how badly the film industry was treating me. Lindsay was writing for a paper at the time and was kind enough not to publish. However, he never employed me.

Waiting for Godot made me long to be part of this new theatre. No such luck – wrong actor in wrong body and the exterior is so much easier to see than what lurks inside.

In November of that year, 1955, Neil Paterson offered me a smashing script – *The Woman for Joe* which was a circus fairground story. I couldn't help thinking that the fairground boss, Joe, whom I was to play, should have been played by Peter Finch. But I was determined to make as good a job of it as I could. Also in the cast were Diane Cilento, David Kossoff, Violet Farebrother (known as Fairy) and Joan Hickson again; Jimmy Karoubi played the smallest man and A. J. Dean the strong man.

Jimmy Karoubi was four foot seven inches in his socks. A. J. Dean was six foot nine in his. Fairy, a large woman but pretty, sat in the make-up chair for hours and hours while they made her even bigger with jowls and flaps to her chin and hair on her face. Then into wardrobe for layers and layers of plastic foam. The beautiful Miriam Karlin played a wonderfully vampy part. Denis Rossaire brought his circus and flying ballet. The circus gathered on the back lot at Pinewood; the animals were well looked after but nobody will ever convince me that keeping lions, tigers, panthers and pumas in cages is anything other than cruel.

There was an enormous amount to do. Our first assistant was magic as were his second and third, but we had a problem. George More O'Ferrall was our director. George was a nice enough man, but he really had no idea what he was doing. He knew nothing about the camera, he did not know what lens to use or why. He needed all the help he could get and, when given it, he almost always refused to take it.

Jimmy Karoubi and I had a very tense and difficult scene to play. It was set in Joe's caravan. There is a great explosive row which culminates in my picking Jimmy up and throwing him into the corner of the banquette. Jimmy was not primarily an actor; he was an interpreter, speaking flawless English, French and German.

He had interpreted for the world middleweight boxing champion, Randolph Turpin, and at the United Nations. He had been cast in this film because he was so perfectly formed. His parents, his brothers and his sister were all of average height. Being picked up and hurled into a corner was not easy for him.

Jimmy and I had talked about the big scene and knew exactly what we were going to do and how we were going to do it. We rehearsed it for camera, the set was lit and we were ready to go. At the time of the final rehearsal, there was a fair amount of noise on the set. George leapt up from his director's chair, and jumping up and down on the spot, he shouted, 'I will have quiet! I will have quiet! This is a very difficult scene. Isn't it enough that the little man's deformed?' He sat down again.

I picked Jimmy up and he sat on my knee like a small child, crying.

'Right,' bawled George, 'let's do it.' He had no idea that his insensitivity had almost destroyed another human being.

I looked at Jimmy. He nodded. 'Yeah, let's do it.'

It was a magic moment when he looked up from the corner where he had been thrown: his tears were genuine.

There were some good times during the making of *The Woman for Joe*. I had a small Morris Minor convertible and every evening, Man Mountain Dean, all six foot nine of him, tiny Jimmy Karoubi and my stand-in, Roy Everson, would pack into the car and I would drive them to Shepherds Bush, where passers-by would stop and stare as the little car disgorged its load.

But then those convivial evenings stopped. This was because, one day, I wandered back to my dressing-room and, standing in the open doorway of the dressing-room opposite, was Brigitte Bardot over here to film *Doctor in the House*. I shall never know how it came about that Brigitte was in my dressing-room and in my arms, or how it came about that I was in her bedroom in her arms. It just happened. I was completely dazzled and hopelessly in lust. It was not a love affair. As far as Brigitte was concerned, I felt I was there to provide a dalliance while she was filming. As far as I was concerned I was mesmerised and followed on wherever she led.

Of course I lied, telling Julia I was going to be delayed at the studio with photo calls, evening interviews, meetings, anything. Shabby and deeply hurtful to both Julia and to me. I did try to get away to go home, but found it almost impossible. Brigitte was in London for six weeks and then it was over.

In due course, Julia knew and I knew she knew. There was a tacit agreement not to mention it. For Julia, there was nothing but pain. The emotions were not quite so easy for me. Although I knew I had behaved badly towards her, unfairly, without cause or justification, I had a tingling feeling of satisfaction that I had attracted one of the most beautiful women in the world. My career seemed to be destined for shallow waters so any fillip to my ego was welcome.

While I am in the dock I must ask for other crimes against my wife and family to be taken into consideration. Some were love affairs and some were not, but all of them caused pain. I was finding the constant pressure for money – no! I cannot make feeble excuses; there was no justification. In three or four cases, I certainly lost what would have been good family friends by my crassness. As Emmie Shepherd said all those years ago in Quentin Road, Blackheath: 'George, it takes two to make a bargain.'

With Dickie Attenborough in *The Ship that Died of Shame*

Being presented to the Queen with Kenneth More and Tommy Steele in 1957

Opposite main Sally Home:
'Won't you buy my pretty
flowers?'
KENNETH RIMELL

Top inset The company:
the Music-hall at
Bury St Edmunds

Middle inset Your chairman,
Mr John Moffatt
KENNETH RIMELL

Right Susan Hampshire in
The Sleeping Prince

Below Matrimonial fury in
The Fourposter: Sarah Badel
applying the cure for love...

Private Lives: 'Very flat, Norfolk'...

The author enjoying his joke

MICHAEL WARD

Above The Theatre Royal, Bury St Edmunds: directing Jane Baxter as Mrs Alving and John Gulliver as Oswald in *Ghosts*

Right Sally Home with baby Sarah

The Lady's Not for Burning by
Christopher Fry: Thomas
Mendip 'nodding in' (*above*)
and (*right*) with Jennifer Hilary
as Jennet – love conquers all

13

The Ship that Died of Shame was about to be released. It was to have a premiere at the Odeon, Leicester Square. Here's the rub: I was at Bovington Camp doing my two weeks of Territorial Army training. The army had not relinquished its grip on me entirely since, after National Service, we had to serve for four years in the Territorial Army. I was with the 3rd/4th County of London Yeomanry. I was supposed to go to camp for two weeks every summer and to St John's Wood Barracks to play soldiers every fortnight. The fortnightly sessions that I did attend took me back into the mad world of pretend enemies, commies and the Russkies are coming. As I could not go to camp with my own regiment I was seconded to the Staffordshire Yeomanry, which is why I was stuck down in Dorset. I did, however, get permission to go to London to attend the premiere. It was a good premiere and the film was well received.

Having finished filming *The Woman for Joe*, it was back to Ealing for *The Feminine Touch* and the gorgeous Belinda Lee. The film was directed by Pat Jackson and produced by Jack Rix. Pat Jackson was a superb wartime documentary director, *Western Approaches* being probably his best film.

Halliwell's Film Guide gives *The Feminine Touch* an appropriate rating, calling it a 'portmanteau soap opera of no absorbing interest'. I think I must agree and certainly the press did. It held other interests for me. There were some wonderful actors in the cast including Diana Wynyard whom I had just seen in *Much Ado About Nothing* in which she was wonderfully funny. To work with her and have some good scenes with her was the utmost pleasure. Then there was Richard Leech who was to become a great friend.

We were filming in Guy's Hospital at one point and a ward sister asked me if I would go up to the children's ward one morning and say hello to them all. It was the brightest, happiest of wards but some of the children had sustained such horrendous burns that, if they lived, even with the expertise of plastic surgery they would be disfigured for life. I soon realised that I was visiting a terminal ward. All these little people were going to die.

'Is there no hope?' I asked.

'Miracles don't come that often,' I was told.

There was a boy called Edward, a little blond chap of seven. He took to me and I took to him. I would visit him and read to him as often as I could. His parents never gave up hope. His room at home was waiting for him, newly decorated. They asked me for an autographed photograph to hang on his wall. I gave it to Edward, who kept it on his bedside table. Some weeks after we had finished filming, the ward sister rang me at home and told me that Edward had died.

Fifteen years later, I was doing a radio play in Broadcasting House when a man with a broad smile and extended hand approached me. 'You won't remember me, it was all such a long time ago, but I'm Edward's father.'

The penny didn't drop.

'You were making *The Feminine Touch* at Guy's Hospital.'

'Of course! I remember Edward.'

'We had another Edward. He's twelve now. I always told my wife I'd bump into you one day. I work here, you see, on maintenance. Just wanted to say thank you. Your photograph still hangs in Edward's room. Thank you!' And he was gone.

It was soon after *The Feminine Touch* that my agent, Jimmy Fraser, put me up for a part and received this answer from Michael Balcon. 'He has never fulfilled his early promise.' Jimmy was kind enough to tell me. As you can imagine, it did a great deal for my morale.

My next film was *A Hill in Korea*: Ian Dalrymple was the executive producer of the film and wrote the screenplay with my brother-in-law, Anthony Squire, who also produced it. Julian Amyes was the director. It had a strong cast: Stanley Baker, Harry Andrews, Michael Medwin, Ronald Lewis, Stephen Boyd, Victor Maddern, Harry Landis, Robert Brown, Barry Lowe, Robert Shaw, Charles Laurence, Percy Herbert, Eric Corrie, David Morrell and, in his first film, Michael Caine.

My brother, Frank, recently back from Korea where he had served with British Army Intelligence, was able to give a first-hand account of the fighting and much of his advice was incorporated into the script.

This was at the beginning of Bob Shaw's ambitious career. He was a powerful actor and had just begun to develop that sneer at death that was to serve him so well in *Jaws*. His bright intellect and wide reading made him a charming companion – when he wanted to be or thought you might be useful to him. Later he was to show what a wonderful writer he was. If he had a character flaw, it was that he couldn't bear to lose. This trait in him got worse and worse and some years later he had his wrist broken while arm-wrestling with a sailor in a New York bar.

We were to make the film in Portugal and the whole cast had been signed for eleven weeks; we were then to come home and finish the film in Shepperton. It was cheaper to keep us all there rather than pay air fares back and forth to England. The actual location was miserable; miles from anywhere, in the middle of sand dunes. The heat by midday was almost unbearable. We were based in Lisbon and had a two-hour drive to work every morning and, of course, two hours home at night.

I was on location every day as I had a colossal part but many of the cast had a wonderful holiday. Bob was among those who had a rather easier life on the shoot; in all, he had about four weeks' filming and the rest of the time he spent with Stanley Baker and Michael Medwin on the golf course at Estoril. By the time Bob began his first two weeks of work, some of us were already tired and jaded. However, we had a wonderful crew and Julian Amyes was a good and sympathetic director. Freddie Francis was our distinguished cinematographer and Arthur Ibbetson our camera operator.

The location was a mound of desert sand where the encircled platoon had dug in to live or die. The platoon consisted of Harry

Andrews, myself, Bob Brown, Stephen Boyd and Bob Shaw. Bouncy Bob was fresh from his golfing triumphs in Estoril. He was full of sleep and wellbeing, while the rest of us had been exposed to temperatures of between 95°F and 105°F for some weeks. I have to admit that, after a day or two, we could not wait for L/Cpl Hodge to be killed off by the advancing enemy.

Bob set about winding everybody up, suggesting all sorts of improbable bets with the odds all stacked in his favour. We were speechless when Arthur Ibbetson asked Bob if he would like to race him over a hundred yards. Bob couldn't believe his ears. His gimlet eyes bored into Arthur's fat stomach.

'A fiver! You're on!'

'Hold hard, Bob. Hold hard. I've put a little weight on since I last ran the hundred yards. I shall need a handicap.'

'What handicap?'

We realised that Arthur had hooked him anyway: Bob would run whatever.

'When the starter gives the "Go", I'll start running but you'll be handed a glass of water which you have to drink before you come after me.'

Bob laughed his cackle of delighted anticipation of a sure win and agreed the terms.

We measured out the course and appointed Harry Andrews the starter.

The runners went to the start. We all stood in happy anticipation at the prospect of this unlikely race. Harry was holding a Very light gun, which he was to fire for the start. 'On your marks, get ready,' and the gun blasted a Very light into the sun. The focus puller approached Bob with a glass of water which he was holding in thick leather gloves – it was boiling water.

Arthur walked quietly down the course whistling 'Roll out the Barrel'. End of contest. I really thought that Bob would die of apoplexy. He swore he had been cheated and that he had no intention of paying up the money. We all explained the bet to him. It was to drink a glass of water before setting off. The heat of the water had never been mentioned and, as far as we were concerned, it didn't figure in the equation. Bob paid up with very little charm, but it did keep him quiet for the next week or so. Sadly, it didn't serve to curb his aggressively competitive spirit. I reckon he died of a self-inflicted heart attack brought on by his nature.

One of the pluses of this time on location was that I struck up a great friendship with Harry Andrews who was to become my friend for life, and godfather to one of my daughters. Along with three other actors, neither Harry nor I had a day off in the schedule so we were thrown together naturally. There wasn't really anywhere to sit that could be described as comfortable – camp-stools sank into the sand. Where we did find to perch was inadequately shaded from the burning sun.

Julian Amyes had cast Michael Caine, with whom he had done a television play in which he had given a wonderful performance; but now here he was without a single line to speak. I tackled Julian and Anthony about the sense of bringing a good actor over from England for eleven weeks and not giving him a line to speak or a scene to play. The upshot was that we devised a scene which included him and I have always been a little pleased that I suggested the scene and wrote the first lines Sir Michael spoke on film.

We returned to England and Shepperton to complete the film. The art department had built a replica of the temple. The monsoon lashed down from water hoses above our heads. The mud was muddy. The film had been hard work but rewarding.

However hard we tried, we could not escape from the debts. The income tax people said they would be most interested to have some payments and I had a number of awkward discussions with the local inspector. Julia had run up some substantial bills, mainly at Harvey Nichols and Peter Jones. Somehow or other, I had managed to stay abreast with the boys' school fees, but all in all it was a bleak outlook.

Work formed some escape. Peter Saunders offered me Agatha Christie's *Towards Zero*. It was billed 'her latest and greatest' but it was a dog of a play. So bad, in fact, that Milton Shulman wrote in the *Evening Standard* of 5 September 1956:

George Baker and Gwen Cherrell, as two of the chief suspects, try stoutly to give credence to their parts, but even their bold efforts could not restrain the gallery from guffawing at some of Miss Christie's more melodramatic flourishes. A recent cartoon showed a disgruntled figure picketing a theatre with a sign that read: 'The butler did it.' I know exactly how he felt. 'Well, Neville did it.'

So bad was it that we experimented with fourteen endings on tour and finally got it somewhere near right after we had been running for two weeks at the St James's Theatre in the West End. I needed the money so when I was offered less than I should have accepted, I took the job because I was frightened not to. The body language of insolvency and fear are great communicators. Employers see through the hapless, cringing, unconfident, cap-in-hand fellow and it sometimes feels as though they might have the nerve to ask the poor unfortunate to pay them for the privilege of being allowed to work. I knew it was a bad play, but all Agatha Christie's plays ran, I told myself. It ran for six months which, for an Agatha Christie, was a great failure.

Besides Gwen Cherrell, Mary Law and Cyril Raymond, Frederick Leister was in the cast. Freddie taught me many lessons but two I remember with joy. The first was 'be brave'; the second was 'never stop working on your performance'.

He had been a song and dance act in the 'folderols' at the end of seaside piers around the turn of the century. Aged twenty, he left the seaside for the bright lights of London and got a job at the Lyceum Theatre with Fred Melville. His first part was that of a marine lieutenant who, landing with a handful of troops on a South African island, is surrounded and outnumbered by Hottentots.

He spreads the Union Jack across his chest and delivers the immortal line: 'Fire on that, if you dare.' He got a great laugh from the gallery.

Fred came to his dressing-room and explained how the line should be delivered. 'You spread the Union Jack across your chest. You turn and face the audience. You pause. You look at the gallery as though they are the enemy. You pause and only then do you deliver.'

Freddie went on the next night and followed the precise instructions. The gallery rose to its feet and cheered.

Herbert Wilcox offered me a part in his film *The Dangerous Years* with Frankie Vaughan at the same time as the ABPC studios told me I was to appear in their film, *No Time for Tears*. I was in the theatre, how could I possibly do the work?

This is how they worked it out. As both films were being made at Elstree, I was to make one film in the morning, another in the afternoon and do the play at night.

The Suez crisis was on and so was petrol rationing. I bought a 1936 Austin Seven for £60. Its low petrol consumption got me to the studio in the morning and to the theatre at night. I found the routine a great strain. My temper was very near the surface although I managed to suppress it. I drank too much.

My self-esteem took a further knock when *A Hill in Korea* was shown. It coincided with a national newspaper strike and, although Dilys Powell put it in her top ten films for 1958 at the end of the year, we didn't get a single review at the time of its release.

Even with two films and a play, the money was not enough. In fact, I was broke. We had an au pair, Ina Vermeer, from Holland, and a daily, Mrs Griggs, both of whom had to be paid. We couldn't afford any of it. Our great friend and accountant, Justin Daly, said to us, 'You two will never be solvent while you're together.' Sadly, they were prophetic words.

Television was beckoning. I did a play for the extraordinary Dennis Vance at ABC; I can't remember the name of the play but I think it was the first to be broadcast on ABC's newly formed 'Armchair Theatre'. It was set in a French château at the turn of the century. A wandering lover returns to find his loved one blind; will he–won't he stay? Isabel Dean played the blind woman and I the wandering lover.

The rehearsals were the most bizarre I have ever known. Vance was, at that time, head of drama at ABC. He attended the first read-through and then disappeared back to his office or the pub or wherever. His secretary, Janice Willis, stayed with us that day, gave out the rehearsal schedule for the week and also disappeared. We were a cast of four, the other two playing servants. They were not called for the rest of the week. Isabel and I came to rehearsals the next morning to find the room above the pub in Windmill Street empty. We sat and waited. After a while I rang the ABC office and they were very surprised that Vance and his secretary weren't with us. They certainly weren't in the office, the voice told me.

As the play was, to all intents and purposes, a two-hander, Isabel and I fell to rehearsing and learning our lines. The week went by with no sign of the great Vance. We had the weekend off and when we returned to our room above the pub on Monday morning, we found the other two actors had now joined us. The moves given us by the author, Michael Nightingale, in the script were perfectly functional and were incorporated into the play. Michael was an actor who had appeared in *Towards Zero* and was now playing the butler.

On Friday we were to have a run-through and in the afternoon the camera crews were to come in and see the play. When we arrived at the pub that Friday morning, Dennis and Janice were there. There was not a single word of apology or explanation.

'Let's just run through the play,' Dennis said. And so we did.

We had a lunch break in the bar downstairs. The camera crews joined us, all very convivial and normal.

The astounding performance that followed from Vance that afternoon was the most consummate piece of braggadocio I have ever seen. As we were running the scene, Vance walked about with his viewfinder to his eye, the crews following him, while he explained to them what the shots would be. Janice followed closely, making notes; after all, she had to translate this entire imaginative splurge into a cohesive camera script for the studio.

We brought the run-through to a triumphant end. Dennis thanked us and dismissed us. He would, he said, stay behind and talk it through with the camera crews.

I went home bursting to tell Julia about the bizarre events, but all of it paled into insignificance when she told me she was pregnant again. It was wonderful news and made working with the mad Vance tolerable.

The following Monday the crew was to travel to Manchester in readiness for filming the play two days later. All performances in those days were, of course, live. At eight o'clock on Wednesday evening, ABC's Armchair Theatre, directed by Dennis Vance, was presented to the British viewing public.

The morning after the broadcast I drove back to Ealing to start rehearsing *The Last Troubadour*, a play for television about Percy French, the Irish poet, songwriter and entertainer. I had originally refused the part because I cannot sing and I was adamant that I would not try. There is something malign and quite inexplicable about people who simply will not believe you when you say you cannot sing. Hal Burton, the producer and director, promised me that I would not have to sing a single song. I was no sooner into rehearsals than the pressure was on for me to do just that.

'The Mountains of Mourne' is a 'speak song'. Rex Harrison did it to perfection in *My Fair Lady*, I was told.

'Rex Harrison is musical.'

'Not at all! Anybody can do it,' they said.

I let myself be persuaded, allowed them to let me make a fool of myself. I ended up with four numbers. I don't think I've ever been so frightened in my whole life. I tried desperately to learn the tunes and I suppose I got near some of them. Every other member of the cast could sing but they were all Irish and knew the songs. Oh, Mother of God, did I suffer!

Jack MacGowran was in the cast: now there was a genius actor and mime. He was a great stalwart and persuaded me that all was not as bad as it seemed. Joan Hickson, dear friend, was spectacularly supportive. Paddy Joyce could not have been a better pal. He took me through the songs again and again.

The play was great fun and I enjoyed every moment of it. Where there was recitation or sketches, there was joy, but where there was song, there was sorrow. The sorrow was compounded because instead of finding the Percy French music, they gave me the Houston Collison settings as sung by John MacCormack. These were all tarted up with an octave jump and a 'shut eye' note at the end of the song. I wandered about in a daze of fear. I didn't sleep. I just repeated lines of song or lines of verse, or lines from scenes.

The day of transmission came. The BBC had acquired the Riverside

Studios and it was from here that we would broadcast *The Last Troubadour* – live, of course.

During the rehearsals, Stephen Mitchell had approached Jimmy Fraser, my agent. Stephen was producing *The Restless Heart* at the St James's Theatre with Mai Zetterling and Donald Pleasence. Robert Urquhart, who had been due to be in the play, was to be replaced and Mitchell wanted me to rehearse and open almost immediately.

Jimmy Fraser was desperate for me to do it, so was Stephen Mitchell. I pointed out that I was in the middle of rehearsing a play for television which had suddenly turned itself into a musical and, because I couldn't sing, I needed every bit of rehearsal available. Their suggestion was that, after finishing rehearsals for *The Last Troubadour*, I should dash along to the St James's Theatre and rehearse *The Restless Heart*, giving me four evening rehearsals. I would be allowed the weekend off to do the final rehearsal and transmission of *Troubadour*, then we would have the dress rehearsal of *The Restless Heart* on the Monday and open on the Tuesday.

I resolutely refused.

Stephen Mitchell rang me and put the pressure on. 'If you don't do it, you'll be putting all those actors out of work. We'll just have to close the show.'

I agreed to do it on condition that nobody came to the Monday dress rehearsal.

Rehearsals for *Troubadour* continued. We had a run-through on the Friday and moved into the Riverside Studios on Saturday. Now came my worst nightmare. Percy French accompanied himself on a banjo. I had not only been trying to learn the songs, but also the fingering on the banjo. Hal Burton had a mobile crane set up in the studio carrying the camera and as it pulled away and up, so my banjo accompanist had to move back with it. I could not hear a single note.

This state of affairs was, I was promised, going to be improved by the time of transmission. Well, they weren't, but once we had started, there was no going back. I thundered from set to set, from costume to costume, usually changing as I ran across the studio floor. I went from note to note and key to key. I can change key four times in a bar. I had just finished 'The Mountains of Mourne' with a grand shut-eye note and had raced over to the courtroom scene. As I galloped across the stage, I hissed at Paddy Joyce, 'Did I hit it?' Meaning the shut-eye note at the end of 'The Mountains of Mourne'.

'You didn't kill it, George, but let's say you wounded it.'

Everybody was very kind. After the performance, we went over to The Chancellor and I very quickly got very drunk. I took the glass out of the door with my head as I left the pub. Jackie MacGowran came with me to St George's Hospital where they put a couple of stitches in my head.

When I got home, I could see on Julia's face that she had not liked *The Last Troubadour*. The notices weren't all derogatory. The *Irish Times* praised my acting and was kind enough not to mention the singing.

The next morning a billboard in Victoria station carried the headline: ACTOR INJURED IN PUB BRAWL.

Explanations were needed swiftly. Peter Bull was wonderfully sympathetic. About my performance in *Troubadour*, he simply said to me, 'Oh, my dear. On to the next.' He became, and remained, a dear friend. He laughed at affectation, a wonderful hissing laugh between closed teeth, full of disbelief. He punctured pomposity: 'an actor in my position couldn't be seen to . . .' became 'an actor in my awkward attitude'.

The Monday morning rehearsals of *The Restless Heart*, following the traumatic transmission of *The Last Troubadour*, went well. In the afternoon, Anthony Armstrong-Jones took photographs. All too soon I was due at the St James's Theatre for the dress rehearsal. There would, as arranged, be nobody in the auditorium for the dress rehearsal except the director and producer, Billy Chappell and Stephen Mitchell, and I felt confident that I could iron out any creases. I had little to do in the first act and so enjoyed it. As I was returning to my dressing-room, however, I saw a procession of people coming through the pass door from the auditorium. I could hardly believe my eyes. Apart from Billy and Stephen were the playwright Jean Anouilh and his agent; Lucienne Hill, the translator; the playwright Terence Rattigan, and a representative of the Theater Guild of America. Billy must have seen the look of pure terror on my face because he followed me into my dressing-room. 'Going wonderfully. They're loving it.'

'Billy, you promised that there would be no one there!'

'Well, they're the management. I can't keep them out.' Regrettably, I had to see the truth of this.

Fear pumped me into an adrenalin-charged performance. Anouilh and Lucienne were happy bunnies. They felt the part was being properly played. Mai Zetterling had arranged a dinner for the cast and, at the last minute, asked me to join them. She was never one to do anything without deliberate calculation. All was coming up roses compared to *The Troubadour*. The next day, Terence Rattigan sent me a telegram, thanking me.

Unfortunately, the same surge of adrenalin did not take place on the first night. I gave a flat and disappearing performance, typical of second nights. It earned me an affectionate rebuke from Kenneth Tynan. 'We know the part was underwritten but was there any necessity for it to be undercast?'

On Sunday I had the double whammy of notices for *The Restless Heart* and *The Last Troubadour*. I decided I would never read a notice again unless I had been previously assured that it was either very kind or very good. I tucked my head under the bedclothes and slept until whisky and water time. The play was off in two weeks.

The ABPC studio next tested me for the part of Lord Dawlish in *The Moonraker*, a swashbuckling adventure set in the stirring times of the Civil War. The film also starred Sylvia Syms, Peter Arne and Marius Goring. The whole experience was great fun. David MacDonald, our director, had been in Hollywood directing second features and acquiring a taste for alcohol. Our producer, Hamilton Ingles, decreed that there was to be no drink anywhere near the set, but David got the prop man to put a great deal of vodka and a little Lucozade into a Lucozade bottle. The afternoons weren't too good. However, he brought a splendid Western film axiom to the movie. If it's an action picture, let there be action. Don't speak if you can grunt, don't walk if you can swing from a branch or beam, keep your rapier always at the ready.

David MacDonald and I were having a drink at the end of a day's filming and I told him I didn't rate the love scene which was played between Lord Dawlish, me, and the character played by Sylvia Syms. I suggested how the dialogue could run.

'Well, write it,' he said. The scene was scheduled for the next day. I got home to find that Julia was about to go into labour. I rang Dr Mary Adams who said it was far too early and to let her know how things developed. Iris Pitt, the monthly nurse we had arranged to come for the birth, was at hand and we felt safe.

I read her *The Young Visitors*, thinking it appropriate in the circumstances. The nine-year-old author must have been formidable. The problem was that it made us laugh so much that Julia's waters broke – and Mary Adams arrived to considerable pandemonium. Tessa was born soon after. It was 7 September 1957.

It was two o'clock in the morning when I sat down to write *The Moonraker* love scene for Sylvia and me. I had a couple of hours' sleep, a bath and by eight o'clock we were setting up the scene ready to shoot. Acting is an incomprehensible life except to those who do it and even to us it seems more like good luck than good management.

The Moonraker worked because the film is still shown all over the world. Unfortunately, in those days actors didn't have a share of the film but I have a great affection for it, nonetheless.

I was next asked to do a play for television, *The Guinea Pig* by Warren Chetham Strode. Cliff Owen directed but the other pluses were a reacquaintance with Michael Hordern and Nora Swinburne and a meeting with Wensley Pithey. Wensley was to give a hilarious performance of the love-lorn Spettigue with an eye to Auntie's money in my later revival of *Charley's Aunt*. Ann Firbank was also in the cast; she was to become a great family friend, not only to us, but also to my daughter Candy.

The Guinea Pig was broadcast live on 30 October 1957, on *Play of the Week*. The great significance of this television play was that Mrs Silvio Narizzano watched the broadcast and when Silvio was looking for someone to play Biff in *Death of a Salesman* by Arthur Miller she suggested me. Silvio had also seen *The Guinea Pig* and was delighted by the suggestion. He spoke to John Murphy, head of casting, and all seemed to be well.

Sidney Bernstein, head of Granada, would allow nothing to happen without his ratification. He now objected to the casting on the grounds that I was a film actor and wouldn't be able to play the part of Biff. Silvio stuck to his guns that I was the right man for the job and a compromise was reached: I was to rehearse for two weeks on approval. Henry Oscar was playing Uncle Ben. 'We are all salesmen, and what life does to us depends on what we've got in the bag and the way we sell it.' He was outraged that anyone should be made to rehearse on approval and took every opportunity to guide and support me. Albert Dekker had played Willy Loman on Broadway and he too was a wonderful help. He had worked closely on the play with Arthur Miller so was able to advise straight from the author's mouth. Silvio was an inspired director and, anyway, had stuck his neck out for me.

On decision day, we were rehearsing in the old North Kensington swimming pool, a lacklustre place if ever there was one. We met at 10.30 a.m. and talked through a few scenes. The men in suits were due to arrive at 11.30 when we were to go through all the Biff scenes. At precisely 11.30, Sidney Bernstein walked in with his entourage. There was John Murphy, the casting director; there was Stanley Mann; there were production managers, assistants, secretaries, and a never-ending stream of hostile eyes. Bernstein had his secretary beside him with her notebook open and her pencil poised.

'Take no notice of anybody or anything. Just go for it. Remember you're good,' said Albert and squeezed my shoulder.

I went for it and at quarter to one we had done all the Biff scenes.

Silvio told us to go to the pub where we usually had lunch and that he would join us as soon as he could. We got some drinks and sat down to wait for the verdict. We had to wait for nearly forty minutes before he came in. I had already made up my mind that enormous fortitude would be needed to take the bad news well.

'You made it! Now we can start work, thank God.' Jubilation!

On 27 November 1957, the play was broadcast live from the Didsbury Studios. It went out in two one-hour segments with a fifteen-minute interval. This had never been done before and I don't think it has ever been done since.

There were some memorable unrehearsed moments in the play. Before Willy goes into the garden to commit suicide, he has a scene with Biff in the kitchen. It is the renunciation of his father; he can no longer listen to the gospel according to Willy Loman. At the end of the scene, Biff turns to his mother and says, 'Take him away, will you? Take him away.' I stood in front of Albert and it seemed absolutely right that the son should kiss the father before consigning him to suicide. Albert and I kissed each other on the mouth and held each other for quite a moment before I said the line. In 1957, this was shocking and had never been seen on television before. After the show, Silvio said he was waiting for the storm to break. It never did, nobody noticed. I believe that the reaction had been so natural that it caused no comment.

The cemetery scene was played on a tall rostrum with the camera on a high crane zooming in from the roof of the studio. Linda, Happy and Biff stood by the graveside. As the camera approached us, I heard Albert saying, 'Look up . . . look up.' I looked up from Willy's grave and out beyond the camera. The critic in the *Observer* wrote that Biff's look outwards and upwards had transformed the play from the darkness of the present into the hope and light of the future.

Sidney Bernstein rang Silvio and congratulated him and asked him to pass his congratulations to the cast.

I did not work for Granada again for seventeen years. I met John Murphy at a party soon after he had retired and asked him why I had not been cast in anything for so long. He replied that Sidney had put me on the black list.

Many years later I often used to see Sidney at the Garrick Club where we would frequently lunch together. One day I decided to ask him why he had given orders that I should not work for Granada. His reply was typical of the man I had come to know and like. 'I hate being proved wrong.' The subject was never referred to again.

In fairness, very soon after Sidney retired, I was employed by Granada and did many plays in Manchester.

A week after *Death of a Salesman* was shown – to wonderful notices – I was filming on location in Sheffield with *Tread Softly, Stranger*. We were working in Steel, Peach and Tozer's steel works – there was still a steel industry in England in those days. It was a good film, with a wonderful performance by Wilfrid Lawson. Also in the cast was Di Dors: although I'd known her for several years, *Tread Softly, Stranger* was the first time we'd worked together. She was a no-nonsense professional and I already knew she had a smashing sense of humour.

While we were in Sheffield, I went to see Jane Baxter who was playing at the Playhouse in a light, frothy comedy on its way to the West End. I didn't know if she would remember me from *Aren't We All?*, so I didn't go backstage. Instead, I went to the nearest pub by the stage door and hoped she'd come in after the performance. Sure enough, after a while, the cast came in for a well-deserved drink, including my heroine from *Blossom Time*. She saw me and walked, smiling, across the room towards me. Certainly, she said, she remembered the Bedford Theatre and the Theatre Royal, Haymarket. We had a drink and then supper at a local Chinese with the cast. Restaurants that were still open after the show were hard to find in those bleak and far-off days.

I wasn't on call to film the next day and suggested we might drive to Haddon Hall, only about half an hour from Sheffield. I had been to this magical house before, when on tour nearby. For me, the particular joy of Haddon Hall is the roses, a passion I inherited from my father. I don't know how many varieties grow there but there seem to be roses all the year round.

Jane had never been to Haddon and was delighted at the prospect of an outing. On the way, this mild-mannered comedienne enthralled me with stories of racing at Brooklands before the war. I can't quite remember if she had actually driven round the track in a proper race or if she had just taken a car round on her own. Whatever, it sounded very glamorous.

She was delighted that I remembered *Blossom Time* so well. Well, I couldn't really explain it away by telling her she was my first sexual fantasy when I was seven . . .

It was a delightful day and I saw in Jane Baxter a woman whose demeanour belied her inner strength. Our paths did not cross again until I asked her to play Mrs Alving for me in Ibsen's *Ghosts*.

There was to be a royal film premiere and I was to be presented to the Queen. I can't remember what the film was or which charity benefited. The publicity department sent a limo; the usual photographers were there to take the pictures and there was a vast outside broadcast camera from the BBC. We walked upstairs to the circle foyer where we were to stand in a long line to be presented. As I was walking up the stairs, I saw my mother standing in the crowd. I went over to her, delighted to see her, but ashamed that I hadn't asked her to come with us. She had never shown any interest in coming to other first nights.

The glitz and glamour of a royal film premiere. The craning of necks and turning of heads. The hand waving from dahling to dahling. The fanfare for the royal party. The lining-up of those to meet the Queen. It was wonderfully exciting and I felt honoured to be selected to be there. Others waiting to be presented were Kenny More, Tommy Steele, Sophia Loren, Michael Craig, Heather Sears, Jack Hawkins, Stanley Baker, William Holden and many others but for the purposes of my story this list will do.

After being presented to the Queen we were shepherded to a hospitality room where we waited patiently for the moment when we would all file out on to the stage, take our bow and then disappear into the wings on the other side of the stage. I was to lead on Heather Sears so we were standing together, waiting our turn. Suddenly a look of great consternation came over her face. 'My zip's gone!' she said. It was a side zip and a long one so a lot of her showed, small as she was.

Jack Hawkins was standing close behind me with Sophia Loren. 'Jack, we need a wardrobe mistress or a needle and thread,' I whispered, urgently. Jack passed on the message. The wardrobe mistress could not get through the crowd but a needle and thread was passed along to us. Sophia Loren took charge. She threaded the needle and advanced on Heather. 'Hold the opening together,' she commanded and then, looking me straight in the eye, 'Are you married?' she asked.

'I am.'

'Good, hold it together then.'

Sophia Loren was wearing a classic Empire, pleated white gown, the pleats falling from just below her bosom. She looked gorgeous. She sank on to her knees so as to be nearer to her work and expertly sewed

The Way to Wexford – 187

up Heather's zip. Sophia Loren must have been all of twenty-two, a star in the ascent. She stood up, smiled at Heather, and dusted off her knees without even looking down at her dress. My heroine! We all paraded across the stage and bowed and curtsied and went our ways; the big night was soon over.

I don't know what I expected from life; possibly to be in prestige movies, a respected actor, I don't know. My general feeling of inadequacy was not helped by gossip column writers printing a profile picture of me and asking how on earth this actor could be given camera space when all he had to show for himself was his profile? Those are not the precise words of Margaret Hinxman's column in *The Picture Goer* but near enough. Peter Noble presented a programme from the BBC Birmingham studios, Pebble Mill, called 'Answer Your Critics'. He invited me on the show to meet Margaret Hinxman.

We met for rehearsal before lunch and Margaret Hinxman had a happy hour insulting me about my acting, my looks and my general demeanour and there was no stone she didn't leave unturned. I defended myself as best I could. However, when the time came to go on air, live, Margaret dried stone dead. Suffering, I suppose, from some old-fashioned maxim that the show must go on, I gave her prompts out of the corner of my mouth, and she dutifully repeated insult after insult. Peter Noble declared it a good show; he had not noticed anything untoward.

Margaret was seriously grateful, and so she should have been. If I'd been bright enough, I might have had a real go at her. She asked Julia and me to lunch with her and, in turn, I asked her to come to the Grand Theatre, Croydon to see me in *The Tender Trap*. Margaret came and saw and was conquered. In her column she wrote an open letter to film producers. 'The man is a comedian,' she headed it.

However, if the producers had any ideas for me, they certainly weren't in comedy.

14

My mother, who had moved from rooms to flats to rooms again, had finally found safe harbour in Tachbrook Street near Victoria station. Best of all, she had found a job in the press office of the Electrical Development Association. She got on extremely well with her boss, whom she respected and who respected her. She took on the campaign for electric under-floor heating, electric cookers, heaters, kettles (nothing to beat a Russell Hobbs), with the same ardour that she espoused the cause of the untouchable Bulgarian money, injustice, Trubie King babies and, new to the list, the desirability of traffic lights at the corner of Tachbrook Street.

When Eve gave birth to her first child, Mother became seriously angular. Evie had chosen to have the baby in the St John and St Elizabeth Hospital in St John's Wood. It was a Roman Catholic hospital run by nuns.

Mother came over to Lower Belgrave Street to wait for the news. The time passed, the night spilled into early morning.

'Whatever possessed him to put her in there? Shows a terrible lack of religious knowledge.' Another cup of tea and another cigarette.

'Mummy, it's a first-class hospital and they know what they're doing.'

'You don't know what you're talking about.' Now she started pacing. It was a big room and she had ample opportunity to get the hips moving. 'The mother is the last consideration. With them, it's save the baby.' Another turn across the room. She marched out into the hall and got her coat and hat.

'Where do you think you're going?' I asked her.

'Over there, to stand over them. I know something about delivering babies. I might remind you that I am a senior midwife.'

'I know it, Mummy, I know it.'

'Don't take that tone of voice with me. I've delivered more babies than you've had hot dinners.'

'Amen.'

'She's only been in labour for six hours,' pointed out Julia.

'That's true, darling, that's true.' And she put down her hat and coat.

Another cup of coffee and another cigarette.

'If I had a gun, I'd be dug out of that chap. How dare he put a Protestant girl in the hands of nuns!'

'You once told me there was no finer nursing in the world.'

'God, if anything happens to my beautiful girl I'll go in and shoot them. So help me, I will.'

Now she had the coat on again.

Another cup of coffee and another cigarette.

'Now get me a taxi because I'm going up there.'

'Mummy, come on. Give it another few minutes. At least Keith knows where you are.'

'Damned Papists!'

The telephone rang. 'It's a boy!'

Mother broke into 'Unto us a child is born. Unto us a son is given.'

More coffee, another cigarette and a flood of tears.

And this was the mother who had always taught me that the only way to world peace was through religious tolerance.

We went to stay in Josie Baird's cottage at Aston Subedge for eight weeks during the summer of 1958 while I was working at ABC's Birmingham studios in a television serial. From Gloucestershire, I had to go up to London to talk about a television play and, while I was there, Richard Leech invited me to dinner. It was here that I met an enormously wealthy American lady, Edna Chappell, bright, intelligent and fun to be with. It was not she but her daughter and son-in-law who were to be friends for life.

The next day I had arranged to pick up Tessa's godmother and take her down to the country. Anna Walmsley had just been dumped, and Julia and I felt that the country air would do her the world of good. I booked a table at the Lygon Arms in Broadway for Saturday night as part of the recuperative treatment.

We were walking in through the front door when I saw Edna Chappell coming down the stairs. We greeted each other with delight and surprise and agreed to join up for dinner. Joan, her daughter, had been a victim of polio when in her early twenties and was paralysed from the waist up, her arms hanging limply by her sides. She would lean them on her knees and kick them up on to the table; then by dint of push and shove, she would manoeuvre her fork to spear her pre-cut food and eat with gusto. Joan's husband, Covington Hardee – known as Cuz – was a senior partner in a New York law firm. He had spent a great deal of the war in London and was a thoroughgoing Anglophile.

Edna was leaving the next morning so I suggested that Joan and Cuz should come and see some of the sights of Gloucestershire: Dover's Hill from where you can see so many counties; The Fleece at Bretforton, one of the oldest pubs in England with a wonderful collection of medieval pewter; Chipping Campden and Cow Honeybourne. The sun shone and the day was full of laughter. Before they left, we were told to be sure to look them up when we came to New York. We exchanged addresses, me thinking it was much more likely that they would come to us than that we would go to them.

Shortly after this, I got a call from the studio to meet Robert Clark for lunch at the Mirabelle. While we were lunching, Ian Fleming came over to the table.

'There you are, Robert, there's your James Bond sitting there. You should turn those books of mine into films for him.'

'Aye, they're good readable books, Ian, but they'll never make pictures, never.'

When Cubby Broccoli and Harry Saltzman finally bought the rights, Ian rang me up and said he was going to suggest me for Bond. Obviously, Broccoli and Saltzman had ideas of their own. Pity.

The Way to Wexford – 191

Whenever I felt down, I knew that I could go back to Richmond and do a play. At the suggestion of Toni Wyatt, I did *The Sleeping Prince*. My brother Terry had left school and he was now an ASM at Richmond. He played one of the footmen. It was a splendid production and I believe I was good in it. In fact, I was so pleased with myself I asked my agent to come and see it. Jimmy Fraser couldn't come himself so he asked his partner, Peter Dunlop, to cover for him.

Peter came to the dressing-room after the show. 'Let's face it, George, you can't act on stage. Stick to the movies. You can get away with it there.'

Absolutely furious, I rang Jimmy the next morning and told him I was leaving the agency and told him why. He said he would sue me for breach of contract. Jimmy got Arnold Goodman and I got a young solicitor from Denton Hall and Burgin. Jimmy was going for the kill and my solicitor was no match for Arnold who then did a rather extraordinary thing: seeing that my solicitor was no match for him, Arnold decided to act on my behalf as well as his own client.

'Mr Fraser, I know that agents are predators but perhaps in this case we should not be too wolfish.'

He then set the sum and wound up the meeting. I had to pay £750 to get out of my contract. It would be unheard of today. It wasn't usual practice, even then.

Some years later, after a performance of *Saint Joan* at the Old Vic, there was knocking on my dressing-room door. It was Peter Dunlop. 'Just thought I'd say I'm sorry. I was wrong.'

We had a drink and let bygones be bygones.

After leaving Fraser and Dunlop, I joined MCA and was looked after by Kenneth Carton. Kenneth knew that Noël Coward was looking for someone to play in *Look After Lulu* and arranged an interview and three weeks later I stood outside the door of Noël Coward's suite at the Dorchester. On my knock, Noël opened the door to me himself. He stood and looked at me for a moment.

'I'm George Baker.'

'Of course you are. Coley, pour Mr Baker a drink.'

Noël disappeared into the bedroom. Cole introduced me to Hamish Hamilton, Noël's publisher, and poured me a whisky. Whilst trying to look intelligent as I talked to Hamish Hamilton, I was listening with one ear to Noël who was talking on the telephone in the bedroom. 'I've just cast him, Cyril. His name's George Baker. I'll talk to his agent in the morning.'

He came bustling back into the room, shoulders straight and high, and head a little forward. 'I've based a new play on a Feydeau farce, *Occupe-toi d'Amélie*. I've called it *Look After Lulu*. Cyril Ritchard's producing for the first three weeks then I take over. Cyril's in a very silly play at the moment so he needs something to sharpen his mind on.'

The next morning, the deal was done. I spent the afternoon in the American Embassy getting a visa. Somehow the American management got me a work permit in double-quick time and two days later I was on an aeroplane to New York. It was all so sudden and so unexpected I hardly had time to say goodbye to Julia and the children, or deal with an offer of a play from the Henry Sherrik Management. Henry kept on ringing me up throughout my packing and farewells, telling me how much better his play was and how it would be so much more worthwhile doing. I kept telling him that the deal was done with Coward and there was no going back. He was really quite angry with me.

It was my first trans-Atlantic flight and my first visit to New York. On arrival, I was put up in a hotel on 56th Street and almost immediately summoned to tea with Cyril Ritchard. He greeted me coldly and I was to find out later that, at a party earlier, he had spoken to Tony Richardson. 'Noël's cast a George Baker for the part. Do you know him?'

'He's the worst actor in England,' Tony Richardson had replied. It was not a very auspicious beginning to my American début.

Cyril treated me with suspicion. He was obviously waiting for me to be the worst actor in England. His idea of farce was to swish your way through the play, overacting, winking broadly at the audience and tripping over the furniture and your own feet.

There were some wonderful people in the cast whom I was meeting for the first time: Roddy McDowall, Tammy Grimes, Ellis Rabb, Jack Gilford, and Polly Rowles. Jack Gilford was a victim of the McCarthy era and had not worked for five years. He was a deliciously funny man, an understated actor and full of invention. Roddy McDowall was extremely supportive. It was he who told me of Richardson's flip remark.

'We'll all be better off when the Master takes over.' And we were.

After a week or so, I rang the Hardees and got a very cross Cuz on the phone. 'What are you doing in a hotel? We said to come and stay with us.'

They sent a car and I was installed in 14 Remsen Street in Brooklyn Heights. The brownstone house was at the end of the street overlooking the Hudson River. The sitting-room was on the first floor and through the picture window you could see the Statue of Liberty, downtown New York and the Brooklyn Bridge.

Joan had been married before and had three children from her first marriage and two with Cuz. Lizzie was the youngest at the time. If she didn't want to do what Joan told her to, she would lie down on the floor, knowing that her disabled mother couldn't pick her up.

Joan put a stop to this in a very characteristic way. 'I may not have arms, Lizzie, but I have got feet.' She gave Lizzie a sharp tap with her foot and that was the end of winding Mother up. Cuz had converted the kitchen so that everything was foot controlled. By dint of her dexterous use of hip and elbow, Joan was able to do all the cooking. The family was a tonic and safe haven for me.

I found myself a very nice French restaurant on 55th Street where I ate whenever I could. One evening after rehearsals, I went to the theatre to see Eric Portman and Helen Hayes in *A Touch of the Poet* by Eugene O'Neill. Not the greatest play but a memorable performance by Helen Hayes. Portman was very powerful but the Irish accent was very often from Salford.

After the show that evening, I went to my restaurant and found John Gielgud sitting there. I knew him slightly, having met him with Harry Andrews. He was in New York playing *The Ages of Man*. He invited me to join him and we saw each other quite often there over the next few weeks.

One evening he told me that he was going to a rather grand party the next night so wouldn't be going to the restaurant. I had not been there long before he walked in.

'I thought you were going to a party and wouldn't be in?'

'My dear, they had invited so many dazzling young things. My heart was like a humming bird it didn't know where to settle. So I came away.'

With Helen Hayes' wonderful performance in the O'Neill play still in my mind, I went to see her give a master class one Sunday and at the end of two hours, she said, 'You may have noticed that I have not used a gesture. Gestures should only be used when they are big enough to be significant.' Then, lifting her arms high above her head and in a gesture embracing her audience, she said, 'Good night. God bless you all.' She had made her point.

Noël arrived and rehearsals for *Look After Lulu* took a spectacular turn for the better but not before Cyril had called us all together and formally handed us over to the 'authorette'. Noël was an incisive director and soon the worst excesses of overplayed farce were being ironed out. Before we left for Newport where we were to open, Noël invited me to a party at the Colony Club. The Duke and Duchess of Windsor were there and graciously allowed Noël to introduce me.

They looked ghastly, she old and bored and he old and boring. The protocol of royalty seemed to me to be archaic, even then. However, at least they didn't spit in my face like Tallulah Bankhead. This, she assured me, would bring me enduring luck throughout the run. Claudette Colbert, on the other hand, was calm and very like her film image. But as far as I was concerned it was Celeste Holm who was full of life and sparkle. I can't remember what the charity was, but she was a splendid auctioneer and people paid fortunes for unwanted *objets d'art*.

An incident that was to haunt me for many years happened on the evening of the dress rehearsal. I was wearing a splendid uniform designed by Cecil Beaton, the centre doors were thrown open and I marched in to say goodbye to Lulu, played by Tammy Grimes. At the interval, Noël came to my dressing-room.

'I can't see your eyes.' He looked at my face. 'No wonder! You're not wearing mascara.'

'I don't have any mascara.'

Noël turned to his assistant. 'Go and buy some mascara, Charles. There's a pharmacy in the hotel.'

Charles trotted off to the hotel.

Noël was now set to do some finger-wagging. It was always the index finger of the right hand. It pointed at me now and started wagging.

'Look, dear, I've given you a centre entrance anyone would die for. And what happens? We can't see your peepers. Do you know what a centre entrance is for?' The wagging accelerated. 'It is to make sure that every man, woman and dog in the audience falls head over heels in love with you. And what do you do? You come on with no eyes! How can anyone fall in love with piss holes in the snow?'

Charles came bustling back and handed a gold Revlon mascara stick to Noël who handed it to me. 'There you are.'

I am not used to mascara. I have never used it and have only seen girls, wives, mothers (but certainly not mine) and actresses apply it. Also, I am almost dysfunctional about objects near my eyes. I put the mascara brush tentatively to my lashes, blinking a lot.

'Oh, for God's sake, don't be so fucking dainty. Here, give it to me!'

Before I knew what was happening, the mascara was on.

'There you are,' he said, surveying his work, 'that's better.'

On I came, through the centre doors, for the second act.

'That's better, dainty darling,' Noël shouted from the stalls and into the tannoy system to be heard in every dressing-room and from that moment on, I was 'dainty darling' to the company for the run of the play.

Many years later, I was in New York for the private showing of an art exhibition. I was surprised to be greeted by a voice behind my back saying, 'Hello, dainty darling!' It was Roddy McDowall whom I had not seen since the play had closed, some thirty-four years before.

We opened in Newport to mediocre notices. I began to see why Noël Coward was such a great theatrical master. The notices didn't faze him at all. He simply set about cutting some scenes, rewriting others and rehearsing every morning to make sure that the show was as tight as it could be.

The American experience was a dazzling round of eye-opening

pleasure. *Don Carlos* at the Met, Radio City, the Metropolitan Museum of Modern Art, the Frick. Oh, the Frick! That calm, bewitching place; I would sit by the side of the fountain, listening to Mozart, looking at the Bellini hanging in the corner and writing letters home.

The curator of the Frick, James Fosburgh, was a friend of Noël's. I didn't meet him and his wife, Minnie, until quite late into the run of the play. One evening, after the show, Noël knocked on the dressing-room door. I wasn't expecting anyone and assumed it must be a member of the cast. I had a vest on and was busy cleaning the make-up off my face.

'Come in,' I shouted.

'I've brought Myrna Loy to meet you,' said Noël.

There, standing in my dressing-room, looking ravishing, was one of my favourite actresses. *The Thin Man* and all her gorgeous comedies flashed in front of my eyes. I looked at her, my face a smudge of make-up, my hands full of tissue.

'Oh, not like this, Miss Loy,' was all I could manage.

She smiled and the world lit up.

'We're going to a party at the Fosburghs' and you're to come along,' announced Noël.

'I'm wearing grey flannels and a sports coat. I can't possibly—'

'Don't be so silly, Dainty. They're all just friends.'

Off we went in a cab to Fifty-first and Fifth. As we walked up the stairs to the sitting-room, I looked at the pictures hanging on the wall. It seemed to me to be odd that anyone should want to cover his staircase walls with reproductions of small paintings and sketches by Van Gogh, Pissarro, Monet, Manet, Degas, and then I realised they were originals. That was the second time my heart had stopped in the evening. The third time was when Noël opened the sitting-room door and the first person we saw was Marlene. Now for a spat of name-dropping which could get me into *The Guinness Book of Records*. Marlene, Annabella, Anatole Litvak, Garbo, Douglas Fairbanks Jnr, Hume Cronin, Jessica Tandy, Duncan MacIntyre, Hope Williams, Claudette Colbert, Ronald Colman and Myrna Loy. But, thank God, no Tallulah Bankhead. Then there were some 'civilians', such as Jock Whitney and his wife. His father was the man who brought the family mansion up from the South and rebuilt it, stone by stone, on Long

Island. Rich or what? The wonderful thing about the party was that they were all there as just 'old friends'.

Unfortunately, *Look After Lulu* was a flawed play and my American idyll was soon over.

I got home to a wonderful welcome. I hardly recognised Tessa as she ran towards me down the hall. The change from thirteen months to seventeen months is extraordinary. I thought for a moment that a little girl had come to tea. She took me to a chair, sat me down and then sat herself on my knee from where she didn't stir for an age.

I learned that while I had been away, there had been a worrying financial development. The flat had ceased to be part of a requisitioned house and had been returned to the head lessee who rented it from the Grosvenor Estate. The rent was immediately put up from £375 to £1,000 and since our lease was up for renewal, £1,000 key money was also required. Julia solved the problem by borrowing £1,000 from her brother Rag. She had written to me in New York and told me that all was well.

When I had had a chance to talk to Julia about the loan from Rag, I asked why we couldn't have put his money towards a down payment on one of the newly converted houses in Cambridge Street, Victoria.

Julia's reply stunned me. 'Well, it's the other side of the tracks, darling. I can't live there.'

Where were we to find the £1,000 a year for rent plus the repayments to Rag, I wondered? As usual, I said, 'Never mind, something will turn up.'

Mr Wilkins Micawber never despaired and always felt certain that something would 'turn up'. I didn't have any 'bubble schemes'; I just prayed for a well-paid film. As I had got myself out of my contract in order to do the theatre, there was little chance of my prayers being answered. What was interesting was that I was the one who shouldered the blame for profligacy.

ATV sent me a script for *The Square Ring*, the director, Bill Hitchcock, wanting me to play 'Docker' Strakie. I was very surprised when I read it. The part was of a famous boxer making a comeback against everyone's advice. I was delighted, a character part at last.

Bill didn't want to meet me or talk about it; he just offered me the part. When I walked into the rehearsal room for the read-through and saw the look on his face, I realised immediately that he knew he had made a mistake. He thought he had offered the part to Stanley Baker, which would have made a great deal more sense.

'Let's go out and have a cup of coffee, Bill.'

When we were sitting comfortably, I said, 'You've cast the wrong Baker, haven't you? Why don't I just slip away and you can put the mistake right?'

'No, no! I didn't want Stanley. That would have been too obvious. No, no, I wanted you.' In which case he was stuck with me because I really wanted to play the part.

The cast list of *The Square Ring* was pretty impressive: apart from myself in the main role, the other boxers were played by Sean Connery, Alan Bates and David Davies; others in the cast were Alfred Burke, Thomas Heathcote and Percy Herbert. Sean Connery arrived on a scooter wearing jeans and a very tight T-shirt. I'm not sure it wasn't his first television, but you could see where he was going. Alan Bates gave a thoughtful, sensitive performance and you could see where he, too, was heading.

The play got good reviews and many congratulatory telephone calls. What with that and *Death of a Salesman*, I began to think I was getting somewhere. Nonetheless, I was very startled when my agent said Michael Benthall wanted me to join the Old Vic company to play Henry Bolingbroke in *Richard II* and the Earl of Warwick in Shaw's *Saint Joan*, Master Page in *The Merry Wives of Windsor* and David Wylie in Barrie's *What Every Woman Knows*. The money was terrible and wouldn't in any way help towards the mounting debts. But I took it because I needed to establish myself as an actor and not a film starlet.

Julia had developed psoriasis on her elbows and on her scalp. It is a dreadful itching disease which made her life extremely uncomfortable. She went to see a skin specialist in Harley Street and he prescribed some cream but he also asked her about her family life. Was she looking after her own children or did she have a nanny? On hearing that she had help with the children, he advised her to give up work or only do a minimal amount and look after her own children. Julia virtually gave up working. The psoriasis didn't get much better and the film industry lost a talented designer.

Josie Baird had had to give up the lease on the Aston Subedge cottage but had found another on the Rousham estate near Oxford. There was no running water and a communal pump served the whole village. William Kent created Rousham's garden in the early 1740s. The house itself is a hundred years older than that and the small family church even older still.

We went to stay with Jo at cottage no. 7 and fell in love with the place. Tom Cottrell-Dormer let us have nos. 1 and 2 at a rent of ten shillings a week each and gave us permission to knock them together. Logic was no longer applied to anything to do with money. What was a pound a week when put against what you would have to pay if you took the family on holiday? The fact that the cottages were unfurnished and tables and chairs would have to be bought wasn't even considered. We made a deal.

The indigenous population were the Walshes, the Tuckeys, the Wickersons and the Kings. The weekenders comprised Michael Campbell, author of *Lord Dismiss Us*, and his partner Bill Holden, publicity director of Heinemann, the publishers; they had one side of the semi-detached cottage, while Ian and Jennifer Smith (she was the author Jennifer Johnston) had the other. We were befriended by Kerr and Bea Elliot; Kerr was a neighbouring farmer and a fine hunting man. He was happy for me to exercise his hunters and I was happy to do so. A great friendship grew between us.

We had three weeks to settle in at Rousham before I started rehearsals at the Old Vic. There was a great deal of clearing and cleaning to be done in the house and, having made one room habitable as a living-room, I set about knocking out the big open fireplace in the other room. This room was designated the rubble room. Whenever I had a spare morning or afternoon, I would shut myself in there with a heavy sledge hammer and some sturdy chisels and beat the hell out of the incredibly tough filling they had poured into the gap behind the old stove. They had thrown bits of old iron into the cement to make it stronger. It did my muscles a power of good.

The glorious English summer stretched on into autumn. I had horses to exercise in the early morning; I can think of nothing more beautiful than riding through the woods and watching the leaves turn to their autumn colour. Julia pored over gardening books and we worked in the garden together. Candy and Tessa had their friends down the lane. The lane was safe and children could play without fear of cars or molestation.

I knew I had a job to go to. It was a joyous holiday.

But what was studiously avoided was how everything was to be paid for and our debts reduced. A pair of ostriches in the Oxfordshire countryside.

15

AFTER MY WONDERFUL HOLIDAY AT THE COTTAGE, I WAS LOOKING FORWARD TO WORKING AT THE OLD VIC. I was fit, I was well and the disappointment of losing James Bond had worn off.

The first play was *Richard II*, directed by Val May. We opened on 17 November 1959, a date fixed graphically in my memory. I was standing in the prompt side assembly, waiting to be called to the presence of the King. I was wearing long black tights and a very fetching tabard over my armour. On the other side of the stage, John Woodvine was waiting to be called to kneel to the King.

'Then call them to our presence: face to face'

It was at this point that I bent over to straighten the seam of my tights and felt the seam split up my bum. I sent an exploratory hand to assess the damage and, sure enough, there was a gaping hole in my tights. There was nothing to be done. The fanfare for our entrance was sounding. I marched on to the stage, tuned my back on the audience, and knelt upstage to the King.

'Many years of happy days befall
My gracious sovereign, my most loving liege!'

Merciful God, nobody laughed. Nobody had noticed the shining beacon my whiter-than-white Daz-washed underpants must have been signalling. I had time to change the tights between scenes and reckoned I had got away with it. Afterwards, however, Julia told me I hadn't got away with it – a bright patch of white knicker had flashed through my black tights. The next day I went to Marks and Spencer and bought myself some black underpants.

There was a gathering on stage after the show and Peter Potter – a frequent director at the Old Vic and who would be directing me in *The Merchant of Venice* in our next season – introduced me to Tyron Guthrie. He was very complimentary about my performance, which made me feel good since I had thought my performance very average. It had taken me a long time to realise that I didn't have to invest the part with anything; Shakespeare had done everything necessary for me.

Kenneth Tynan joined the group and was introduced to Guthrie. He stammered his 'How d'ye do?'

'Ah,' said Guthrie in his high voice, 'a stutter. You mustn't take it out on the actors.'

Tynan was critic for the *Evening Standard* at this time and was well known for writing some stinging criticisms.

There were new friends to be made in the company and old acquaintances renewed, such as John Justin from the Bedford Theatre days, still steeped in his Ouspensky. New friends were Robert Harris and Walter Hudd, known as 'Dickie', who was one of my heroes from when I went to the outdoor cinema in Bulgaria and I had seen him in *Sabu, the Elephant Boy*. He was twenty years older now and playing the Duke of York. Two actors starting out on their careers were John Stride and Jeremy Kemp. Joss Ackland was a friend in the making. John Moffatt, with whom I was to work closely later, was also in the cast; he is a 'hoops of steel' friend. There was also Jeffry Wickham who was later to appear as Dr Brock in my play *The Fatal Spring* for the BBC Playhouse.

It was after the notices for *Richard II* that Jack Rix, producer of *The Feminine Touch*, said to Julia, 'It's so good to see George making a comeback.' I was twenty-eight years old.

I would go down to the assembly one scene early to hear and watch

Maggie Smith play King Richard's Queen. It was a most beautiful performance.

After *Richard II* came *Saint Joan* in which I loved playing the Earl of Warwick. Leslie Hurry had designed me a super costume – a long green frock with side-splits to the hips, a rust-coloured, fur-trimmed cloak with a fifteen-foot train; I had to take lessons from Barbara Jefford about how to make it swing behind me when I turned. A big brown hat, which had a long liripipe attached to the end, topped this little number. Wonderful costume in which to make an entrance, swinging the cloak behind me, and say that, whatever the result of their deliberations, the Maid must burn.

The great joy of *Saint Joan* was the tent scene with Robert Harris as Peter Cauchon, Bishop of Beauvais, and John Moffatt as Chaplin de Stogumber. Shaw gave Warwick some wonderfully funny lines, as much in aristocratic attitude as in the lines themselves. There is nothing more heart-warming than an audience laughing and clapping joyously at superlative wit.

When, later, we took the play to Poland, I found the epilogue tremendously satisfying to play. Warwick enters with the line: 'Madam, my congratulations on your rehabilitation. The burning was purely political. There was no personal animosity, I assure you.' On the first night in Warsaw, I had only just got out 'The burning was purely political' when the house erupted with laughter. On 'There was no personal animosity, I assure you', they stood up and clapped. The Poles have a wonderful sense of humour and they certainly knew all about political burnings executed from the very purest political motives with not a sliver of personal animosity.

Some weeks into the London run, two of my dearest friends, Peter Bull and Jean Simmons, came to see the show. We were some way into the tent scene, and Warwick was at his most placatory, explaining that Master de Stogumber did not mean what he said when he calls the Right Reverend the Bishop of Beauvais a 'traitor', when my chair collapsed under me and authority was sitting on the ground. There was a gasp from the audience and from the fourth row of the stalls I could hear the sharp hissing noise that was Bully's embarrassed laugh. I did not falter. I started my speech as I stood up. 'My lord: I apologise to you for the word used by Messire John de Stogumber.

It does not mean in England what it does in France.' I continued speaking as I picked up the chair and handed it to an ASM in the prompt corner. 'In your language, traitor means betrayer: one who is perfidious, treacherous, unfaithful, disloyal. In our country it means simply one who is not wholly devoted to our English interests.' At the end of my speech I received a round of applause.

I only mention the incident because I am extremely proud of the way I dealt with it and, anyway, I don't have many such in my life. Thank God.

Douglas Seale's production was splendid. Looking back on it, there was no weak link in the cast. Barbara Jefford's Joan was a triumph and Alec McCowen's Dauphin moving, funny, frail and strong.

After the last performance of *The Merry Wives of Windsor*, in which Judi Dench made her first appearance on the Old Vic stage as Anne Page, Michael Benthall popped his head into the dressing-room I shared with Alec. 'Well, have you two learned anything from the experience?'

'Not much,' was our sullen answer.

'Well, you should have. Never be talked into playing Master Ford or Master Page again.'

I did another season at the Old Vic, playing both in London and on a national tour. This took up the whole of 1960. The triumph of the season was Franco Zeffirelli's *Romeo and Juliet* with Judi Dench and John Stride. I played Antonio in *The Merchant of Venice* and when our London season was over we took these two plays on the national tour. I had a very gentlemanly tour as I only played for the first three days of the week in *The Merchant* and while *Romeo and Juliet* was playing, I either drove home or took three days to drive to the next date. Liverpool to Glasgow and Edinburgh to Aberdeen on the B roads were particularly beautiful drives. Then there was time off to rehearse *Macbeth* and *The Importance of Being Earnest* and re-rehearsing *Saint Joan* before we went on a twelve-week national tour. After that, we were to take the plays to Russia and Poland.

The Old Vic Company flew into Moscow on 3 January 1961 to open with their production of *Macbeth* at the Filial Theatre of the Moscow Arts two days later. We were held up for hours at Moscow airport. At last I was called in to answer why I was born in Bulgaria and yet had a British passport.

'Heaven knows, once there was a free world,' I thought. I don't know what I answered, but whatever it was seemed to satisfy the authorities because my passport was stamped and handed back to our diminutive and redoubtable company manager, Julia Wootten.

As we stood on the steps of the Ukrainia Hotel, a sort of wood-panelled mausoleum, many storeys high, we saw three lorries drive past carrying our scenery. We knew it was our scenery because the lorries were open to the sky and we could see it. It was as wet and bedraggled and as tired as we were. How on earth could we open in two days' time?

Later in the evening, I came down from my room to find a despondent stage management crew. They were a small but mighty bunch: Oliver Neville, Annie Lee, Jonathan Webb and Peter Smith. They had gone down to the Filial Theatre to assess the extent of the damage to scenery and costumes after their disastrous open-air journey, but the theatre staff had taken one look at their tired faces and told them to go back to the hotel. Oliver Neville had made a good stab at fighting for the right to oversee the putting up of the set, the positioning of the props and the lighting, but the Russians had looked at the blueprints, decided there was nothing they couldn't handle and had sent our redoubtable team to get a good night's sleep.

When we went to the theatre the next day, a miracle had occurred. Not only was the set up but it had been repainted, our costumes had been cleaned, even our boots and shoes had been soled and heeled. Our mightily relieved stage management crew could smile again.

Moscow appeared to love our performance of *Macbeth*. Prolonged, rhythmic applause during eleven curtain calls turned a polished and sometimes spectacular performance into a scene of warm emotion. Showers of bouquets, including a huge lilac bush in full bloom, were presented to Barbara Jefford in tribute to her performance of Lady Macbeth. Sharing the curtain calls were Paul Rogers, playing Macbeth, William Russell as Macduff and Joss Ackland as Banquo. My contribution to that evening was a double of Third Witch and Porter; Rosalind Atkinson and John Moffatt were my sisters in sorcery.

Moscow is a forbidding city, even the snow on the golden minarets of the Kremlin couldn't dispel the feeling of repressed humanity. Queues in the shops, little to buy and sullen faces everywhere. John Moffatt and I shared a dressing-room and, in order to keep up the failing, homesick spirits, John would sing old music-hall songs. In fact, the idea of a doing a music-hall with John as chairman was born in that Moscow dressing-room and was to have reverberations throughout our lives.

The *Daily Telegraph* of 10 January 1961 reported that 'A Moscow audience gave a rousing ovation tonight to the touring Old Vic Players in their opening night performance of *Macbeth*.' A few days later, after the first night of *Saint Joan*, a number of embassies rang up our commercial attaché to find out what sort of trade deal Britain had done with Russia in order for the play's notices to appear on the front page of *Pravda*. Barbara Jefford had a personal triumph as the Maid. She was greeted as England's greatest actress. Not only had most of the cast come to stand in the wings to watch, but the Russian stage crew, wearing felt overshoes so as not to make a noise, were standing at any vantage point, mesmerised by the performance. After each performance there would be a reception: Barbara Jefford was the heroine of these parties which, after a time, we all found rather dull and tiring.

There were one or two hilarious episodes while we were in Moscow. One evening, when most of the company had gone to bed, there was a considerable commotion in the corridor. Bedroom doors flew open in time to see a very drunk Valerie Taylor slide out of the arms of John Bay and down the wall to the floor. Finding his support had left him, John pitched forward and lay down beside her. I think that had been the intention in the first place. They had no sooner settled than Dickie Hudd stepped out of his bedroom, immaculately dressed in white polka-dot dressing gown with scarf to match, and spoke for England.

'We are our country's representatives,' he reminded them. In the style of Coward, he actually wagged his finger at them. The prone figures had not only let down the Old Vic Company, he continued, but Great Britain. They should be ashamed of themselves. John Bay snored gently while Valerie took out her false teeth and put them in her handbag before attempting the precarious climb to rectitude. Dickie retreated into his bedroom with great dignity and shut the door on the scene. I think it was Joss Ackland who came to Valerie's rescue and helped her to her room.

It was the turn of the third play in the repertoire to have its opening night, Oscar Wilde's *The Importance of Being Earnest*. It was a strange evening. Every line we spoke was translated in a whisper, the whisperer sitting in the stage right box. The laughs were delayed by a beat when someone in the box led the laughter. I came off stage ready to do battle about the noise when Maia, our lovely and friendly interpreter, came towards me, finger on lip. She took my arm: 'Don't say anything, please, it could be very difficult.' There was something in her manner. I looked at her closely; she was clearly terrified.

It transpired that Nikita Khrushchev had come to see his favourite play. Madame Foortsova, his Minister of Culture, was with him, together with the whispering interpreter. Khrushchev did not come to the reception after the show but Madame Foortsova and other dignitaries did. There were a great many toasts and rapid vodka consumption. It was almost impossible to catch at a leg of chicken and certainly impossible to eat it between toasts to Russian culture, English culture, lasting and abiding friendship, and the need for international cultural exchange.

The date of Khrushchev's visit to *The Importance of Being Earnest* was 19 January; just three days before, British Intelligence had uncovered the biggest Soviet spy network since the war. Was there a political move towards appeasement or did Nikita really love Oscar Wilde?

The company moved on to Leningrad. The temperature was -25° F. I had not long finished reading *To the Finland Station* by Edmund Wilson, with its account of Lenin arriving at this same station in 1922. There had been shooting and cheering and killing and dying – the reorganisation of power only forty years earlier. As our bus passed through this extraordinarily beautiful city, I was aware of Johnny Moffatt sitting beside me singing softly, 'With a ladder and some glasses, you could see to Hackney Marshes if it wasn't for the houses in between.'

On the street the people appeared as depressed and unsmiling as the people in Moscow and here, too, there were queues at all the shops. Our hotel, almost opposite the Winter Palace, was a splendid building with wonderful panelling and glorious cut-glass mirrors; its vast public rooms spoke cryingly of the middle of the last century.

We settled into our rooms while the indefatigable Julia Wootten sorted out passports, lost luggage, emotional problems, anything we could throw her way.

There was a letter from Julia: the girls were well, and delighted with the postcards I had sent them from Moscow: one had been of a scene from *The Three Sisters*, the other of a sculpture of Pavlova's dancing feet. While we had been in Moscow, I had received a letter from Julia, saying that the bank was being 'difficult'.

By that, she meant that we didn't have enough money and they didn't want to extend our overdraft. I was, in fact, technically bankrupt; my assets did not meet my commitments. I was being paid £75 a week by the Old Vic which, by most standards in 1961, was a very good wage indeed but it was the old unpaid debts which were the grievous problem. Julia now wrote to say she had again had to borrow money from her rich brother, architect Raglan Squire.

I sat looking out at the River Neva, wondering how long this marriage could take the strain. There was no lack of love on either side but, as our family friend and accountant, Justin Daly, had said, 'You two will never be solvent while you are together.' There was no question that I was uxorious. And from years of financial insecurity I had learned to shrug the shoulders with Mama's phrase, 'Ah well, God will provide!'

The People's Palace of Culture was a bus ride from the centre of the city, a vast mausoleum of a place. Not at all like the beautiful theatre in Moscow we had played in. The staff weren't as friendly either, but the press and the public were. We opened in the same order: *Macbeth*, *Saint Joan* and *The Importance of Being Earnest*. Oscar Wilde again proved immensely popular; the Russians look on him as a wonderful social satirist and socialist at heart. The Russians believe his characters are drawn from life. Personally I think his exaggeration for comic effect is very slight.

The plays went well, were a triumph. The Old Vic was invited by the artistic community of the city to share a cultural evening with them. It was to be held in the vast rehearsal room of the Kirov Ballet. Now why the British Council could not have found out that this sort of thing might happen and given us time to prepare, God knows.

We had just three days to prepare something. Dickie Hudd was voted in charge and a wonderful job he made of it. David King, a good actor, a fine musician and scholar, had started learning Russian as soon as he knew that the tour was on. He sang a poem by Pushkin in Russian which he had set to music and accompanied himself on the piano. Mark Kingston and John Moffatt gave a bravura performance of 'Any Old Iron' to an incredulous but enthusiastic Russian audience. David accompanied most of the evening on the piano, Joss sang jazz, others recited or played short two-handed scenes from Shakespeare plays. It was quickly established that as I had no party tricks I wouldn't be appearing.

Dickie tried desperately hard to prevent Valerie Taylor from doing anything, but she was adamant that she would do 'The quality of mercy' speech. The ad hoc concert was going tolerably well, and then came Valerie, the penultimate turn. She swept on to the stage like a wild dervish, swirling her cloak and clacking her teeth. She stopped, took in her audience and began.

'The quality of mercy is not . . .' She paused, searching for the *mot juste*, circling her hand as if to catch it from the air. Dickie got the picture at once – she had dried stone dead. 'Strained' he sang out from his seat in the front row. After that, it became a free for all; even the Russians supplied some of the more obscure phrases like 'him that takes'. She did remember 'One drop of Christian blood'; oh yes, she did and said it triumphantly.

She came to the end and there was polite applause. When she took her gracious bow, I honestly believe she had no idea she had fucked up.

Barbara Jefford put our evening back on the rails with a beautiful rendering of Katherina's 'Fie, Fie! Unknit that threatening, unkind brow' speech from *The Taming of the Shrew*. We got away with it. Phew!

Came the interval, when there were canapés of red and black

caviar, tea from the samovar or vodka for those who like that sort of thing, and then it was the Russians' turn to entertain us.

The chorus of the Kirov Ballet gave us a quick burst of Tchaikovsky's *Swan Lake* with stunning ballerinas; there were jugglers, acrobats, pianists and, the *pièce de résistance*, a puppet film so many light years ahead of anything we had seen in the West that it took our breath away. It was the most momentous event. So much talent.

The Russian leg of the tour finished with a performance of Wilde's *Importance*. At the final curtain we took our bow ... and then the unexpected happened. The applause swelled, people stood up, stepped forward and threw flowers on the stage. As we came downstage to shake the hands of the enthusiastic people, the rest of our company came on stage to be part of the Old Vic Company saying goodbye to our wonderful Russian audience.

We left Russia the next morning for our last stop, Warsaw. Although we were still in a communist country, there appeared to be a spirit of freedom at large in the streets compared to Russia. The Hotel Bristol had a European faded grandeur about it. There was actually a bar where you could get a gin and tonic.

Our interpreter found out that I wrote poetry and arranged for a broadcast, which involved Barbara, Paul Rogers and myself. We were delighted to be paid a few zlotys for our work.

Once more, the Old Vic Company was a triumph – but, after twelve weeks away, we were more than ready to come home. As John Moffatt so succinctly put it, 'All I want is to sit in my own chair and drink a nice cup of Nes.'

16

I WAS COMING HOME TO A TIME OF DISTRESS, TO A TIME OF DISASTER, TO A TIME OF LOVE AND A TIME OF LYING, TO A TIME OF WORK AND, MOST OF ALL, TO A TIME OF DEBT. I could not service the interest on my loans; the Inland Revenue was after me. I could not pay the interest on the interest. We continued to spend.

We had taken on a home help, Carol Wilson, who was to stand by us through thick and thin. One good thing at least: my two younger brothers were no longer a financial liability. Patrick had finished his National Service; he had been commissioned in the Green Jackets and had served in Libya. He successfully applied for a job in Singapore and was off to eastern climes. He had always been quite wonderful with Candy and Tessa and there was no doubt that we would all miss him. Julia had been an exceptional surrogate mother to him and he a dear son to her. Yes, we would miss him.

Terence had left school when he was sixteen and had been cutting a swathe of pleasure through the West End and adjoining boroughs. Si Laurie's jazz club was one of his haunts and as I was getting into the car to go to the studios in the morning, I would sometimes meet him coming home. 'Wonderful evening, danced all night and then had a cup of coffee with this girl, back at her place.' Having a cup of coffee was, I think, an allusion to a more fundamental pastime.

After leaving school Terry had worked as a trainee at the Dorchester Hotel and hated it. He had gone from there to the Richmond Theatre as an ASM; he loved it but life in the theatre wasn't for him. After his National Service, Second Lieutenant Baker,

Royal Ulster Rifles, joined a new theatrical agency run by Richard Hatton. Here he became a theatrical agent but found that his true forte lay in representing directors and writers, of whom he gathered an imposing list. He became a partner, and the theatrical and literary agency Hatton and Baker was born.

So, now, the boys had gone and our responsibility had gone with them.

Mother was still working at the Electrical Development Association and as usual throwing all her energies into her work. She had the enviable ability to find everything she did interesting.

For me, the work came bustling in, some good, some not so good, but work to keep us afloat. I had a succession of bank managers who told me how irresponsible I was, but as I managed to keep a steady cash flow going, they looked upon me as trying to do my best.

Peter Lambda wrote two episodes for the long-running series *Probation Officer* in which I played a convict about to be released into society. It was a play of two parts and Lord Stonehouse, then the Home Office spokesman in the House of Lords, arranged for their Lordships to have a private showing. I don't know if it was instrumental in changing the probation laws but it was good to have done something of worth.

Three weeks out and then *Boule de Suif*, an adaptation of a Guy de Maupassant story with Isabel Jeans and Barbara Jefford, Peter Barkworth and Ian Hunter, directed by Lionel Harris.

During the break before rehearsals began, we went to the cottage and I exercised in the rubble room, making a couple of rockeries with the contents of the fireplace. The roses I had planted at Christmas were coming into bud. The potatoes planted to clean the soil could have fed the army. Kerr Elliot had lent me a fell pony, Beauty, which grazed with the cows in the field opposite the cottages. I enjoyed teaching Candy to ride.

Then a script arrived: *The Glad and Sorry Season* by Irving Ravetch and Harriet Frank, an American husband and wife team. They had jointly written a number of films and I think they were the main money behind the venture. They had a good cast: Juliet Mills and I were the love interest, and Madge Ryan and Robert Beatty were her parents. This may do the trick for me, I thought. I counted without the director and the Ravetches.

Philip Wiseman was a fussy, nervous director; he picked and picked until he had almost unravelled us. The Ravetches would come to rehearsal and add their pennyworth. Willie Donaldson, the producer, was a smiling cipher.

We opened in Bath to good houses and rehearsed every day for no good reason. I stayed with one of Julia's great friends from her school days, Clare Brakspear, at Pickwick Manor. It was no great distance to drive and was a haven from the management.

Once actors begin to interact with each other, the play takes on the feeling of an ensemble company. That company feeling is often what makes the magic for the audience. The play moved on to Brighton and then the Queen's Theatre in Southsea. Our friend from Walton Street days, Birdie, had married a colonel in the marines, Michael Wilberforce. Julia brought Candy and Tessa down for the week and we stayed in the comfort of the commandant's quarters in the marine barracks at Eastney. It was here that the twins were conceived.

When I broke the news to Julia's mother, she said, 'Oh, George, how uncalled for! I assure you there have been no instances of multiple birth on our side of the family.'

My Aunt Ethel was as quick to disown the misadventure on behalf of the Bakers, but was much gentler. 'I don't recall my mother ever mentioning twins in our family.' So the burden of shame, if shame it was, fell on us.

Despite our financial troubles Julia and I remained happy and in love. We realised that the birth of the twins was another nail in the coffin of solvency but, what the hell, we could make it! A mindless bravado was creeping into our lives. Our accountant, Justin Daly, said to us one day, 'I do hope you two are taking the proper precautions, that you are doing the pools.'

We opened in London at the Piccadilly Theatre on 27 June 1962 and the following weekend, Harold Hobson wrote in *The Sunday Times*:

It is the old story of the young girl on the downward path,

yanked back on the right one by a good man. The good man in this case is dying of consumption, and fusses a lot over his temperature and medicines. Yet I say seriously that George Baker's performance of this man, still, composed and already detached from life, joyfully communicates a sense of ineradicable virtue and – this is quite wonderful – of mastered fear that is neither mawkish nor self righteous, which in turn is exquisitely reflected, criticised, and responded to by Juliet Mills's captivating and touching girl. Listen to Mr Baker's telephone call to his mother, and to Miss Mills's last cry, and be moved to tears.

Although we had had an excellent run in the provinces, the play came off after only a few weeks in the West End. In 1962, if you earned more than £100 a week, you did not receive rehearsal pay or a touring allowance. You were obliged to provide seven changes of costume yourself. If you could settle into a long run you could recoup, but a five-week run is a financial disaster.

That summer, running water came to Rousham. Charles Cottrell-Dormer had taken over the estate from his father, Tom. He told us that he would bring the water as far down the village as the first cottage, which was us. The pipe was behind the wall in the field where the now pregnant fell pony, Beauty, grazed. Most of the village inhabitants clubbed together to get the water from where it had been left to the other end of the village. George King helped me with the task of joining the main pipe in the road outside to our cottage via a trench leading to the back door. He was not going to put the water in for himself. He was cowman for the Home Farm and since his was a tied cottage, he did not see why he should enhance the landlord's property. When we got to digging the trench up to my back door, his sister May was leaning on her gate, crying. She wanted running water in the house.

'Come on, George,' I said, 'we're going to dig the trench into your house, too.' I could see he was about to refuse, but then he looked at his sister's face.

There was a bit of a race to get the water into all the cottages at the same time, but we did it and there was an almighty party that evening. Dancing in the street, everyone supplying what food he or she could rustle up. Oh, it was a celebration! After all, it was quite something to get running water by 1962. Progress is slow in some villages.

May King produced a half-bottle of whisky, which had been lying in a chest of drawers since before the war. Neither of the Kings drank. It must be my imagination but I'm sure it tasted better than any whisky I have drunk since.

The cottage had water and then there was talk of putting in a bath.

I did some more work for television, guest starring in an episode of *Glide Path*, directed by Silvio Narizzano. It was good to work with him again; the last time had been on *Death of a Salesman*.

I had long talks with Geoffrey Russell of Linnet and Dunfee, the highly respected management under whose auspices the play was to be produced, Lionel Harris director of *Boule de Suif*, composer Julian Slade and lyricist Robin Miller. They wanted me to play Rawdon Crawley in the musical of *Vanity Fair*. I wanted to play the part but resolutely would not sing. God had kept the promise he made to me behind the laburnum hedge: I was only able to sing in church. Finally they agreed and it was stipulated in my contract that I would not have to sing.

Nevertheless, the musical director Michael Moores was absolutely determined that I should sing. He had this theory that there wasn't anybody who couldn't sing. I proved him wrong.

Vanity Fair was the maddest production in which I have ever been involved. The cast was spectacular: Sybil Thorndike, Naunton Wayne, Joyce Carey, Frances Cuka, John Stratton, Eira Heath, Gordon Boyd and Michael Aldridge. The chorus was hugely talented, as were the many small, and entirely beautiful dancers in the *corps de ballet*. Norman Main was the choreographer and I felt envious of the dancers. They had a schedule, a timetable and, most importantly, they knew what they were doing. We didn't.

We rehearsed in an old Gaumont cinema in Kennington which doubled as a bingo hall at night. I realised that Lionel had seriously lost the plot when he called Sybil for rehearsals at ten o'clock one morning and released her at eight o'clock that night without her working at all. Sybil would be celebrating her eighty-fifth birthday in three weeks' time. Why allow an old lady, a great actress and the most loving person, to sit doing absolutely nothing for ten hours?

If Frances Cuka had been cast as Becky Sharp in a dramatisation of *Vanity Fair*, all would have been well, but she was cast in a musical. Fanny's voice was not a trained voice. She was an actress singing. That's not good enough for a West End musical, particularly if you then cast Eira Heath as Amelia Sedley, Becky's great friend. Eira's voice was magical.

We were to open at the Hippodrome, Bristol on the Tuesday. It was to be a charity evening in the presence of Princess Margaret. It was only at the last minute that Geoffrey Russell found out that the show before us was an ice show and it would take days for the ice to melt. Too late, all the arrangements had been made with Buckingham Palace. The fire brigade was called in to get rid of the ice; I think every blow heater in Bristol was in action but the ice did not finally go until the Monday morning. Our scenery was still not up by the time we came to do a dress rehearsal on Monday evening. While we desperately tried to rehearse, pieces of scenery came in from the flies or went up into the flies. The pandemonium would have been a joy to behold had it not all been so serious and frightening.

We never did finish our dress rehearsal. We broke to go home at three o'clock in the morning. We were back in the theatre at 10 a.m. We staggered through the play again, trying to forget that we opened to a charity premiere at 7.30 p.m.

We didn't get through the play that rehearsal either so we didn't rehearse the ballet in which the bailiffs take away Rawdon's furniture. I enjoyed this part of the play hugely. Fanny ran off-stage in the black-out and was replaced by the prima ballerina dressed as Becky. I had been taught the steps and danced the routine with her. We had never rehearsed it with the real furniture so the first night was to be a bit of an eye-opener as the stagehands, dressed all in black, tried to empty the stage of its contents while we pirouetted around them.

The orchestra played the overture, full of some very good tunes. You could hear the expectant audience giggling and trilling in the auditorium. Little did they know what they were in for.

The opening number went off tolerably, Lord Steyne (played by Michael Aldridge) and I crossing from one side of the stage to the other for no apparent reason, stopping for a moment to hold an inconsequential conversation with the Prince Regent, played by John Stratton. Becky Sharp sang her first two numbers and then Amelia sang of her love for William Dobbin, played by Gordon Boyd. There was a burst of applause. Well, so far so good.

I went to collect Sybil, playing Miss Crawley, to make our entrance together. 'My dear,' she said, 'God must put his hand on our shoulder this night,' whereupon we marched on to the stage.

Sybil played her scene standing foursquare to the audience. None of this profile nonsense for her, she played everything out to the audience. I stood beside her and did the same. I had been very doubtful that there could be any connection between us if we weren't looking at each other. But I was wrong: by turning to look at each other from time to time, we established a very palpable communication, whilst allowing the audience to see us full face throughout the scene.

Came the moment for the ballet. My partner was quite brilliant at getting out of the way of stagehands lugging furniture away, and we danced our way triumphantly to the end of the scene. As we danced off-stage I noticed that the vital piece of furniture, the desk where Becky had hidden the jewels, was still on stage. This complication could quite ruin the plot, but what to do?

The next scene was the Sedley house; some of the set had come to a shaky stillness on the stage, and some of it had not yet been lowered from the flies. Just as Joyce Carey and Naunton Wayne, who were playing Mr and Mrs Sedley, were about to make their entrance through the front door, the flymen decided a particular part of the scenery was not wanted and began to haul it up.

'Oh, fuck,' said Joyce while Naunton continued as though nothing had happened.

Then I noticed an extraordinary apparition making its way across the stage on all fours. It was our director, crawling his way over to get the desk off-stage. The poor Sedleys came off second best. How can you play a scene while the walls of your house are going up and down like yo-yos and your podgy director is busy pulling a piece of furniture off the stage, very slowly, presumably believing that he could not be seen?

He got a round of applause for his valiant efforts. We heard later that when he had taken stock of what he had done, he went to the stage door and ordered a taxi and departed for London. Things didn't get much better and the play took nearly five hours to perform. Princess Margaret stayed to the bitter end and, because she did, so did the audience. The applause at the end, however, was scant and tired. I studiously avoided reading the notices. For the rest of the week, Julian Slade took rehearsals, rewrites, cuts; it never stopped.

There was a wonderful moment at the end of the Saturday matinée when Sybil was taking her bow and her husband, Lewis Casson, came on with a birthday cake.

'Lewis, what are you doing here?'

The orchestra struck up 'Happy Birthday'. The audience rose to their feet and sang lustily. We finished with 'For She's a Jolly Good Fellow'.

'What can I say? Well, at my age it doesn't matter what I say. Thank you, thank you. Oh, Lewis!' And she went over and kissed him.

I tried very hard to persuade Geoffrey Russell not to bring the show into London but he was determined and we opened at the Queen's Theatre on a bleak Tuesday at the end of November. The fog that night was as bad as any we had seen; the buses were crawling and the cars stationary. The theatre was empty and the notices dreadful. Bernard Levin gave us a real corker.

On the other hand, we had the living proof that love rules the world. Lewis, at ninety, would brave the King's Road, get himself on to a bus and come to Shaftesbury Avenue to collect Sybil from the theatre every night.

'Can't you stop him?' I asked her, because I could see how worried she was.

'I just pray, dear, I just pray.' Her prayers were answered.

The weather during the first two months of 1963 was wicked and getting home was a nightmare for everyone. No one was really surprised when we came off in the first week in February.

The twins were breech babies and Julia had to go to the Charing Cross Hospital, then still in the Strand, for their birth. And an extremely long, painful and unpleasant business it was but we were the proud parents of two more girls whom we named Eleanor Louise and Charlotte Jane.

It was an exhausting week: visiting Julia and the twins in hospital, looking after the older girls at home, and rehearsing for *It Happened Like This*, based on stories by Sapper. At least there were many pluses there. I met Peter Sallis and Paul Eddington, who both became good friends. The director, James Ormerod, was most understanding and would release me early so I could go and look after family.

My sister Evie and her husband Keith now had two children, Richard and Andrew. They had moved out to a cottage in Buckinghamshire but their life was not easy. Keith was working as a driving instructor and Eve found it almost impossible to cope with the smallest tasks.

Eve had become ill, diagnosed as schizophrenic and was committed to Stone Hospital. On my way down to Rousham, I called into the hospital to see her. She had just had electric shock treatment and was lying bemused and wounded in her bed. She was hardly able to speak, but managed to tell me she had been making wicker baskets. Dear God, my beautiful sister.

I kissed her forehead and told her I would come again.

I stood outside the grey stone building. There were bars at the windows of the top floor, and from the wards inside there came screams and shouts. Nothing seemed to have progressed since Bedlam.

I need not have feared for my dear sister, she had a mother second to none. Mother drove up to the hospital and took Eve into her own care. She took her home to her flat in Victoria and called in Nita Smith who had been her partner in the Roehampton nursing home. Nita knew all the best people, including Sir Ronald Bodley-Scott, the Queen's physician. Sir Ronald referred Evie to Mr Lynford-Rees who diagnosed her as mildly schizophrenic. He treated her for some time in his rooms in Brooke Street, then he referred her to St Bartholomew's Hospital where he continued to look after her under the National Health. It was decided that she should go to the

Bethlem Royal Hospital at Beckenham in Kent as an in-patient until he had established the best treatment.

Mother drove her down in the Mini, with the usual adventures on the way. First, they got lost around Forest Hill, and then they stopped at a garage where the pump attendant had just squirted spirit in his eye. Mother calmly got her medical bag out of the car and gave him first aid. I should add that she also always carried a tool bag with every conceivable wrench, spanner and screwdriver in it.

When they arrived at the hospital, they were told that the papers had not yet arrived although they had been appraised of their coming. 'Never mind, dear,' they said, 'you can leave your mother with us, she'll be quite safe.'

It was Eve who was safe, thank God. Our mother worked unstintingly to make sure her schizophrenic daughter had as good a life as possible. She, Mr Lynford-Rees and Evie herself succeeded so well that Evie got a job with the National Coal Board, where she worked for many years. She married again and was exceptionally happy until her husband died in 1999. Her indomitable nature helped her through her bereavement. My sister is a witty, joyful woman, with a wonderful sense of humour; we are the greatest friends and speak on the phone every day.

17

AT LAST, SALVATION! I was offered a part in *A Shot in the Dark*, an enormously successful comedy from Broadway. Rosemary Harris played the female lead in New York and Judi Dench was to play it in London. It was to be directed by Harold Clurman, founder of the Group Theatre and precursor to Lee Strasberg and his Method school of acting. Wow, here was the fulfilment of a dream. A long run in the West End and solvency was beckoning.

The cast was strong: Peter Sallis played the clerk of the court and I played the examining magistrate; Polly Adams played my wife, Kenneth Edwards the presiding judge, Judi Dench the accused and Anthony Newlands her lover.

It was a well-made comedy by Marcel Achard, adapted from the French by Harry Kurnitz. The play had been tailored to be a vehicle for Josefa, the part which was originally played by Rosemary Harris. Harold Clurman had brought over the blueprint and we were to follow every move exactly.

Peter and I sat behind desks at opposite sides of the stage, facing slightly upstage. We were more or less chained there and had very few moves. A chair had been set in the middle of the stage where Judi sat facing the audience, to answer questions from the magistrates.

There is no need to give you more than two examples of the great Method director's way of working. He said to Judi: 'OK, Rosemary would hear the question, take three steps to centre stage, stop, pause to think, just a beat, count one, turn to the audience, speak the line, get the laugh and sit.' After that rehearsal, Judi had a drink with John Neville and burst into tears.

Then it was my turn. 'See here, this is what you do. You pick up the phone with your right hand, you put your left hand over the mouthpiece, you speak your line to Morestan ... you know, um ... Peter, and then you direct your question to Rosemary ... JUDI, hell, yes!'

That's when I felt the tears running down my cheeks. My redemption was not nigh. Not in this production.

We opened on 30 April and after the show Harold came to the dressing-room and, in tones of great surprise, said, 'Congratulations, you made the part your own.'

The next morning the *Liverpool Echo* gave our hearts a lift:

In bringing together George Baker and Judi Dench as a comedy team, they have scored a resounding success. Judi Dench is the main suspect in a case of murder being investigated by a French examining magistrate, a role taken brilliantly by George Baker.

Maybe all the agony was worth it.

We came to London and opened on 16 May 1963 at the Lyric Theatre in Shaftesbury Avenue and the notices were dire. The first night of a play is its first night in London; provincial notices can be exultant but it is the London notices that count. Hopes faded.

Judi's mother and my mother met in one or other of our dressing-rooms after the first night. They had not seen each other for nearly fifty years. This is how Mother wrote to Aunt Eva in Dublin:

I met Mrs Dench who used to be Olive Gregg, who lived down the road, remember?
    Well, there she is on the first night in George's dressing-room. Also Reggie Dench, now a doctor in York. Reggie turned out to be my old pal from the Sandymount Methodist Church. Little did we think that our children would be playing together on the West End stage when we were kids in Sandymount fifty,

nearly fifty-five years ago. Really I can't have been more than nine or ten when we were in Guildford Avenue.

She told me Mabel Dench has four kids and Turner Huggard has died. So that's all the *craic* at George's first night in the dressing-room.

Well, thank God somebody found the play stimulating ... My mother tried to save the play single-handed by bringing friends to the very few performances we played. Peter Sellers came with Harry Kurnitz, the author of the play; he was, of course, later to play Inspector Clouseau in the film version of *A Shot in the Dark*.

The failure of the play put paid to any hope of financial recovery. We sold what remained of the lease of Lower Belgrave Street and decamped to our Oxfordshire cottage. Well, not to our cottage, which wasn't ready to take us while a septic tank was being dug and a bathroom put in. Josie Baird kindly lent us her cottage. I don't quite know how we all squashed in but we did.

The Pickfords van that brought some of our furniture down from London was bigger than the two cottages put together. Most of the furniture had to be put into store. What arrived at the cottage was put into the centre of one of the downstairs rooms and we worked around it.

We kept the copper in the corner of the kitchen; it was wonderful for boiling the nappies. Our invaluable mother's help, Carol, trotted between our cottages and Jo's on an hourly basis. We took the old Victorian range out of the kitchen of no. 1 and replaced it with a Rayburn. David Tuckey from the village had set up his own building firm and was plastering, decorating and generally putting us together. We hoped to be in by September.

The stress of moving, coping with the twins and, even more the blow to her self-esteem in having to retreat from Belgravia, made Ju very vulnerable. On top of all this, she was having to learn to drive in her late thirties. Michael Campbell and Bill Holden would come down at the weekend and drink. That was one of their pastimes; the other was to come in and demand that we play cards. Hearts was the game. A great deal of drinking and shouting went on late into the night.

I was still robbing Peter to pay Paul. Luckily I made a film, *Lancelot and Guinevere*, with Cornel Wilde playing Lancelot and his wife, Jean Wallace, playing Guinevere. It paid enough to bung a few holes and pay for the septic tank and building work.

I commuted to Pinewood every day. I was up in time to give the twins a bottle and a change of nappy before driving off at five to be at the studios at seven. I never got home before nine-thirty at night. It was putting a tremendous strain on the marriage. While I could keep the money coming in, and my overdraft below its limit, I was able to juggle the other creditors. A little here and a little there kept bankruptcy at bay, but it was all too close for comfort. It would be better, I told myself, when we were in our own cottage.

I was offered a play with Phyllis Calvert and Renée Asherson: *Portrait of Murder* by Robert Bloomfield. An extraordinary American, George Shdanoff, directed it. George was an acting and voice coach in Hollywood and had never directed a play before. He didn't direct very well but he was a superb acting coach and I learned a great deal from him, most particularly about focusing one's centre and harnessing one's energy.

Phyllis Calvert could be quite prickly. 'He doesn't know how to do it right, but I'll tell you what, even a bad director can tell you when you're doing it wrong.'

I got on famously with Phyllis; she was splendidly down to earth and had made her way from an impoverished childhood in the less salubrious parts of Chelsea to become a Gainsborough Lady. She had very little time for airs and graces, and possessed a raucous sense of humour.

Barbara Hicks, also in the play, was one of the funniest women I have ever met. Peter Bull told me the story of the day on location with *Tom Jones* when Tony Richardson invited those people playing villagers to ad lib when Diane Cilento emerged from the church in her bridal gown. 'You think she's a slut,' said Tony, 'so nothing can be too vituperative, but keep it in period, eighteenth century.'

Barbara picked up a piece of turf and, hurling it at Diane, shouted, 'Take that, you eighteenth-century cunt.' If you watch the film carefully you can see the turf hit Diane's shoulder and you can see Barbara's lips forming the words, but no sound cometh.

We went on tour with *Portrait of Murder* for three weeks and then into the West End's Savoy Theatre. The expected ghastly notices assured us of a short run. The Queen and Prince Philip came to the show, unannounced. The story ran in the tabloids the next day and we struggled on for a few weeks on the back of Her Majesty's visit.

The cottage was as near ready as damn it and in September 1963 we moved in. It was warm, it was clean, and the two living-rooms were a decent size as were two of the bedrooms, the other two being quite small. Cows grazed in the parkland, and Beauty's foal, Hester, ran happily beside her. Candy and Tessa were at the village school, and Candy was about to try for Oxford High, one of the leading girls' schools in the country. If only I could get on top of the finances, life at the cottage might yet work.

However, the driving up and down to London was soon killing me. I began staying with friends for the odd night, or even at the Turkish baths in Jermyn Street.

Portrait of Murder closed early in 1964 and I took the opportunity to go into hospital to have some polyps removed from my nose. Just one week later, I was rehearsing for what was to be one of the highlights of my career – Shaw's *Man and Superman* at the Theatre Royal, Windsor. It was a joy to play Jack Tanner; I had wonderful flowing speeches which would be punctuated by glorious laughter from the audience. Shaw was not only a consummate writer but also a natural director and understood actors and their way of working. The theatre at Windsor has a truly theatrical atmosphere; it breathes plays and work and pleasure.

There were friends in the cast – Charlie Carson, John Humphry, Gillian Lind, Brian Peck and Duncan Lewis. I was particularly pleased to see Duncan again; he had been such a part in my life when I was an ASM at Richmond.

Charlie Carson had been in the original production of Shaw's *The Apple Cart*. Charlie was finding a line rather difficult to say and asked Shaw about it.

'What do you want to say?'

Charlie told him.

'Oh, that'll do me fine. Go ahead, say it.'

The author was much easier to get on with than the Shaw Society, under whose fist you are not allowed to alter a comma.

After Windsor, I started work on a six-part serialisation of *Rupert of Hentzau* playing King Rudolf/Rudolf Rassendyll. In the cast was Sally Home who was playing Helga von Tarlenheim. It was not love at first sight; it was quite slow to grow. Sally had a spare room in her flat in Upper Montagu Street and asked me if I would like to use it while we were rehearsing. It seemed a sensible idea. She shared the flat with her brother, John, and his wife, Janet. The flat was divided so that each had their own bedrooms and sitting-rooms but shared the kitchen and bathroom.

On the first recording afternoon, Peter Wyngarde, who was playing Rupert of Hentzau, came on stage wearing tight breeches, the crutch of which had been stuffed with cotton wool. Sally, who had been with Peter in the cast of *Duel of Angels* both in London and on world tour, looked him up and down, focusing on his crotch.

'Go and take at least half of that out, Peter.'

'Do you think it too much, darling?'

'Yes, I do. In fact, why don't you take it all out?'

'I couldn't do that, darling. I'd feel naked.'

We went on location to Bury St Edmunds and filmed in Lavenham. There was a spooky moment in Bury: I stood outside the eighteenth-century Theatre Royal knowing quite certainly that one day I would have some connection with it. At the time, the theatre was a barrel store for Greene King, the brewers. It was about to be restored.

It was a summer full of blue skies and sunshine; we sunbathed on the lawn and swam in the Cherwell. Candy and I took Hester, the foal, for walks. She would soon come when called. One very welcome visitor was brother Frank who had come home on leave from Calcutta. He had married Anne Gilmore, a Scots girl, in Singapore in 1957. He brought his family down to visit us, staying in Josie's cottage. His son was called Frank, thus keeping up the barmy Baker tradition of naming son after father.

I was living a double life with Sally in London and Julia in the country. This toing and froing was to continue for five years, everybody behaving well and hurting badly.

While we were making *Rupert of Hentzau* Sally would come to the cottage and stay. She and Julia got on very well; they liked each other and had similar tastes in books. There was one great difference, however: Julia had begun to drink heavily and, as the wear and tear of life overtook me, I joined her.

Of course Julia suspected that Sally and I were having an affair but, for a long time, said nothing. Then, one day she broached the subject. This was cataclysmic because I could not deny that I had fallen in love with Sally; I could not say that I had fallen out of love with Julia. To be honest, I never fell out of love with Julia. We decided on a triangular arrangement and Sally agreed to be part of it while the children were growing up. Well, the twins were only two years old so we were all kidding ourselves. Julia was slipping into alcoholism and I into heavy drinking.

Somehow or other we managed to keep this arrangement between ourselves, our friends knowing and not saying anything or just not knowing. Sally got to know the girls, she liked them and they liked her. So we lived.

Greatly helped by Sally, I began to try and sort out my finances in a sensible way. Then *Any Other Business* introduced me to Jean Anderson of *The Brothers* and *Tenko* fame. She was to become a great friend and, later, ever willing to come and act in my company at Bury St Edmunds.

Like Wilkins Micawber, I was full of desperate schemes to make money. Like Wilkins Micawber's, they seldom came good.

A new venture was making records for HMV's Laureate Series with Denis Comper. I went to see Christopher Fry in the hope of getting his permission to record his play, *A Phoenix Too Frequent*; unfortunately the rights were not available but the meeting started a friendship that was to last for life.

One evening I went to the Hampstead Theatre Club to see the music-hall John Moffatt had devised. Our discussions in Moscow had borne fruit. The production, while splendid in its way, was not sufficiently well mounted to transfer to the West End. I would have to find the money to mount a new production. In other words, I would have to go into management; this seemed to be the way forward.

In the meantime there was work to be done – plays for television were keeping me very busy. But there was also the stage: *The Glass Menagerie* by Tennessee Williams was presented by H. M. Tennent and, after opening at the Yvonne Arnaud Theatre in Guildford, we toured Brighton, Golders Green and Bournemouth before coming into The Haymarket for a limited run. Ian McShane played Tom and Gwen Ffrangcon-Davies, Amanda. Anna Massey was Laura and I had the great pleasure of playing The Gentleman Caller.

We got the most superb notices and it was a joy to go into the theatre every night. Gwen was a wonderful woman and, in her youth, a great beauty, but it was the spirit that shone out of her and embraced everyone in loving kindness.

I often visited her at her home and have two notable memories of her. She was well into her eighties when she said to me, 'Don't come and see me on a Wednesday, darling. Wednesday is my day for helping with the old people in the village hall.'

Then she had her cataracts removed when she was ninety-odd. She clutched me by the arm and led me upstairs.

'Now, I want you to see the view.'

'But, Gwen, I've seen the view many, many times.'

'No, darling, no. Look, look, you see the copse? I've lived here for sixty years and last week was the first time I've seen those trees. Aren't they wonderful? You know what I'm going to do? I'm going to write to Tidy [John Tydeman, head of drama at BBC radio] and tell him that now that I can see there's no reason why I can't work in radio.'

In her hundredth year she did a master class for the Royal Shakespeare Company, and when she was a hundred, she appeared in a film. The part was written for her and to make her life easier they wrote it for a woman who was chairbound. They thought that Gwen would be able to sit in the chair all day and not get too tired. As it was, she treated the chair as a character prop and leapt out of it the moment the shot was finished.

Her memory was crystal clear to the end and Nigel Hawthorne made a programme of her reminiscences for the BBC, 'Always a Juliet'; I treasure my copy. It was Nigel who arranged her memorial service and although there were four of us who read – Nigel, Anna Massey, John Gielgud and myself – most of the readings were Gwen's own words, relayed from her broadcasts.

The Glass Menagerie finished its run on 8 January and the first of Julia Jones's plays, *The Navigators*, went out on 20 January. Life was full for the actor then: we had Armchair Theatre, The Wednesday Play, Play of the Month and many other slots for single plays. Now there are series and serials and the Channel 4 Film; little imagination and not much hope for a burgeoning Dennis Potter, Julian Bond, Donald Churchill or Julia Jones.

John Moffatt's 'Victorian Music-Hall' was taking shape nicely. Leslie Grade took some units (a unit was backing to the tune of £500) and with the help of other 'angels' or backers, including both John and myself who had taken units, we were nearly ready to produce.

It was to be an evening of humour and song, recreating the golden age of music-hall. Music-hall had its roots in the 'glee clubs' of the Georgian coffee houses in the 1830s, but soon made itself a more permanent home in the Coalhole Tavern in the Strand. When the taverns and supper clubs first drew the audiences, the manager of the house would act as 'chairman', announcing the various singers and acts, but then the job became too burdensome for one man and 'Your Chairman' was invented.

By 1852, the Canterbury was opened. This was a specially built hall behind the Canterbury Arms in Pimlico. An elaborate proscenium arch was built to house the stage. The Chairman sat at a desk between the stage and the proscenium, entertaining the audience, announcing the 'turns' and generally holding the evening together. The early music-hall was given the option by the Lord Chamberlain of becoming either a theatre with a dramatic licence but without the privilege of selling alcohol in the auditorium or a tavern concert room without the right to produce stage plays. Most music-halls took that option. But the Lord Chamberlain still held the right to censor and veto lyrics. When Marie Lloyd sang, 'I sits among the cabbages and peas', there was an outcry. Sensible women changed it to 'I sits among the cabbages and leeks'.

Looking back on it, the next five or six years were quite extraordinary. Full of work which was good. Full of a tangled marriage which was causing us all pain. Full of too many cigarettes and too much drink.

18

As we had handled little Hester since she was a foal, it was not difficult to pop a saddle on her and ride her out. She learned very quickly and was a careful and steady pony for Candy to ride. Yes, there were moments of great joy. The twins were a comedy double act. Arms entwined, they came running in from the garden one afternoon and, as they approached the kitchen door, Ellie stopped in her tracks, 'Good gracious me, I'm a human being.' Then, of course, they were curious to know if they could marry each other when they grew up.

Little girls and growing up: Gareth Davies and James MacTaggart offered me the part of Charles Dodgson (Lewis Carroll) in Dennis Potter's play *Alice*. Deborah Watling played Alice. In the exploration of the character I came to the conclusion – and I believe that Dennis, at that time, was of the same mind – that Carroll's paedophilia was mental rather than physically sexual.

It was from seeing this play that John Schlesinger cast me in Marguerite Duras' *Days in the Trees* for the Royal Shakespeare Company. Rehearsals for the play proved difficult since Peggy Ashcroft and I didn't seem to be able to find common ground in the parts of mother and son. We both rang John Schlesinger and told him we wanted out. The play was impossible.

Then we found a way through: mother has eaten son. It was a well-made play, exploring human emotions in a form which could hardly be simpler, or more immediately compelling. She ate him with love and indulgence, she ate him for his bright golden hair, and she ate him for his laziness and his good looks. She adored him for his 'days in the trees'.

Once we realised that the umbilical cord had never been severed, that mother and son were Siamese twins, we were able to play our love and hate with a binding ferocity. It was an extraordinary experience working with Peggy. One critic said that her performance 'is set fair to pass into legend'.

Also in the cast was Frances Cuka playing Marcelle, the son's painful mistress, for whom he procures seedy lovers so that he can take the money they give her and lose it all on the gaming table. Fanny Cuka gave a breathtaking performance. You could see why she had become what she was by the way she stood.

Days in the Trees played in repertoire over a period of eight months. We often had two weeks – and, on one occasion, a month – between performances so I was able to produce the music-hall with John Moffatt, apply for an Arts Council grant to form a new touring company to be called Candida Plays, rehearse for three television plays, do the seventy-fifth anniversary performance of *Charley's Aunt* at Bury St Edmunds and, when I could, go home – to Julia at Rousham and Sally in London.

Loving two people at the same time is a hard row to hoe and one not to be recommended. The fact that they both love you in return is an added complication – and I am not talking about sex, 'that purple palace of sweet sin'. On the one hand was Julia, the loving mother of my four children who was spending too much and drinking too much, but I could never forget how she had supported me by being a surrogate mother to my brothers as well as a loving wife to me. She was a person whom I loved deeply, but I knew that if I stayed with her, I would be sucked into drinking more than I did already, and the financial situation would never improve. I don't know whether I made myself feel a failure, or Julia made me feel a failure. I was not the actor she wanted me to be. I was not the star she had wanted to marry.

On the other hand, Sally was somebody who was quite happy to accept me as I was. Having your cake and eating it is a load of bollocks.

Towards the end of the run, Noël came to see *Days in the Trees* and we had supper at the Savoy Grill after the show.

'You look absolutely worn out,' he remarked.

I told him something of my life – not a very pretty tale.

'You'd better go to Les Avants and take Julia.' Les Avants was his home in Switzerland and the next morning Cole rang me to confirm the details.

'We've only two people looking after the place. They'll do everything, cook and so on. Will two be enough?'

Can you imagine? The idea that we might not be able to manage with two people looking after us was delightfully laughable.

We had a blissful week there. It was a great holiday – but not a solution. Julia began to look for a house in London. I suppose she thought that Rousham was too far away from me and my work, and that moving back to London would be better for the family.

Between the engagements with *Days in the Trees* at the Aldwych, the music-hall became a reality. We called it 'Candida Plays Presents A Victorian Music-Hall – Your "Chairman", Mr John Moffatt'.

Our casting genius was Richard Price. He and his partner, Fraser Kerr, lived in a flat next door to Sally in Upper Montagu Street and they had all been friends for years. I had met Richard at the Palace Theatre in Walthamstow when, years earlier, we had worked together in *Damaged Goods*. Richard had an encyclopaedic knowledge of actors, which is why he became such a respected casting director at LWT. Even when he had gone to work for LWT, I consulted him about casting and he always came up trumps. His casting of Mary Wimbush in *The Killing of Sister George*, for instance, was masterly.

I put together a crew. We employed Brian Curragh to design us a proscenium arch and a beautiful backcloth of Piccadilly Circus in the 1880s and Julia designed the costumes. John Moffatt was our director, devising the show and bringing to it his great knowledge of music-hall. Alice Lidderdale was our stage director. We were on our way.

A chance meeting with Elizabeth Sweeting of the Oxford Playhouse was serendipitous. She suggested that I contact Neville Blackburne, managing director at the Theatre Royal, Bury St Edmunds to discuss playing there. Three Blackburnes jointly ran a prep school at Nowton, just outside Bury: Betty, Charles and Neville. Betty had an awesome figure, which stood foursquare and could not be budged. She was the school matron, 'and I teach the little buggers how to dance'. Charles was the headmaster and Neville was the bursar. The Blackburnes were eccentric, civilised and compassionate, and they cemented in my mind the idea that people were the most important thing in life.

They had been instrumental in restoring the Theatre Royal and Charles was the chairman of the management committee. I put my proposal to them and they were thrilled, they would love to have our music-hall in their theatre. Prospect Productions, under the direction of Toby Robertson, had brought one of his productions there from the Arts Theatre in Cambridge, but the Blackburnes were finding it difficult to get shows. But Guildford came first.

'Your "Chairman", Mr John Moffatt, will introduce the following artistes: Miss Doris Hare, Mr James Cairncross, Miss Sally Home. Mr Basil Hoskins, Miss Anne Carr, Mr Tom Watson, Miss Jean Muir and Mr Peter Street.'

We played to packed audiences for two weeks in Guildford. The press was ecstatic and so was the cast. I really thought we might be able to get the production into the West End. Then came a sobering lesson in the shape of the Winter Gardens, Morecambe. This enormous barn of a playhouse, with two thousand-odd seats, was empty. I had managed to get a guarantee out of the management but it only just covered the expenses.

Two weeks at the Theatre Royal, Bury St Edmunds restored our hopes. The first-night audience turned up in Victorian costume and took the show and the company to their hearts. John Neville came to see the show and asked us to go to the Nottingham Playhouse for one of the weeks that his company were on holiday. And that, I'm afraid, was the last week of the tour. I had tried everything to get us into London but had to admit defeat.

On 30 July 1966 I drove to Nottingham to tell the cast that the show was closing. On the way, I heard England beat Germany 4-2 in the World Cup. I arrived at the theatre and told Johnny, then went round all the dressing-rooms with the bad news before putting the notice on the board. Elated by England's win, my news came as a great dampener. However, there is something magnificent about actors – they were playing the show for the last time and it was the best of all the brilliant performances I had seen. They all used their considerable talent to make sure the audience enjoyed themselves.

As the last curtain came down there was a strange commotion in the audience. A group of young people, dressed in Victorian costume and carrying baskets of roses, ran to the stage. They stood throwing their flowers at the cast, covering the stage. The audience rose to its feet and clapped and cheered and sang.

A letter sent by a lecturer in English at Nottingham University explained all. He respected the work done by John Neville at the Playhouse and had been appalled to learn that a music-hall would be one of the entertainments offered during the seasonal break. He sent his students to the show to see what theatre should *not* be. His students disabused him and even took him to see for himself. And, at the end of the week, they paid their floral tribute. He was kind enough to write to John and tell him this.

Sally had befriended our ASM, Lynn Dalby, who had given up her room in London when the tour started. With its premature end, she urgently needed to have somewhere to put her head while she looked for a place to live. Sally was able to offer Lynn a bedroom since John and Janet Home had bought their first house and departed for north London. Lynn came to stay in Upper Montagu Street for a week and stayed for five years.

I had come down from London to see the music-hall and was sitting with Charles and Neville Blackburne, having tea on the lawn on a hot summer's day in July 1966, when they asked me if I could form a company to supply theatre for Bury St Edmunds. It was a fleeting idea I had already had and the music-hall experience had made me think that I would like to try my hand at production. Here was the spur, a theatre that needed plays.

I prepared a brief working document of how a touring company could run out of a home base at Bury, and this I sent to Dick Linklater and Joe Hodgkinson of the Arts Council. As with any request for funding, they took their time in reaching a decision.

Elizabeth Sweeting had introduced me to Laurence Harbottle of Harbottle and Lewis, a firm of solicitors who represent a great many of the theatrical, film and musical interests both here and abroad. Laurence became chairman of Candida Plays and guided me through the first steps of becoming a charitable company and dealing with the Arts Council. At about this time, Peter Hall, who had just taken over the National Theatre, took me to lunch and asked me to join his company. I turned him down because I had committed myself to Bury St Edmunds; although we were still waiting to hear from the Arts Council, I had set my heart on setting up my own company. There's no point in wondering how my career would have flourished there rather than on the path I had chosen for myself.

The work came rolling in; I had to get into training for *The Paraffin Season*, a splendidly funny play for television by Donald Churchill. There was a pause in the day of the character, Helen Penfold, after her husband, Frank, had gone to work. This pause was happily filled by 'the paraffin man', who began to deliver on a very regular basis. Pauline Yates, Donald's wife, played Helen, Joss Ackland her husband and I had the great pleasure of toning up my muscles so that, as 'the paraffin man', I could use Pauline as a lifting weight. I stopped drinking, went on a diet, trained daily in a local gym, lost weight and finally was able to pick Pauline up. Their fantasy was for the paraffin man to kneel on one knee with his hands above his head, she would then lie on her back across his upturned palms and with a one, two, three he stood with her above his head. Next he dropped her lightly and caught her to his bosom. What happened next was never shown.

Rehearsals for *The Paraffin Season* sadly came to an end and it was duly recorded and shown in the Armchair Theatre's autumn season. Mike and Helen no longer enjoyed filling the afternoons with physical exercise. As I walked the streets round Marylebone after the play had been shown, lorry drivers rolled down their windows, 'How's the paraffin going, George?' or 'Don't you sell any to my missus'. And once, 'Cor, some people, that Pauline Yates!'

Between the closing of the stage version of *Days in the Trees* in November 1966 and starting rehearsals for the television version early in the new year, I recorded two other plays – the first was for ATV, *The Four Triumphant*, in which I played St Patrick; it was directed by Peter Potter. This was followed by a play for ABC Armchair Theatre, *Love Life* by Hugh Leonard. Pauline Collins was in the cast with me.

Waris Hussein directed the television version of *Days in the Trees* for the BBC and my old friend of *Vanity Fair* days, Lionel Harris, produced. On the evening the play was due to be taped in the studio, Peggy Ashcroft and I were waiting for our first entrance. Peggy began to work herself up into her stage performance. I tried to get her to calm down but she was away, the bit between the teeth. Her subsequent performance was wildly over the top. Waris was enormously brave at the end of the first half of filming: he asked the studio if they would allow us to do the first hour again. Everyone had seen the genius of her performance at the dress rehearsal and to a man they agreed that we could start again. This, of course, meant extra expense and overtime for the BBC. Peggy gave a great performance which will live in the archives for ever.

There was still no news from the Arts Council but, while we waited, I prepared a seventy-fifth anniversary production of *Charley's Aunt*. With high hopes and second-hand scenery, the play opened, under the auspices of Candida Plays, at the Theatre Royal, Bury St Edmunds on 28 February 1967. The production cost £300; there were three backers, each being responsible for one act. We had a diamond in the cast, Sarah Badel; her playing of the proposal scene between Kitty and Jack, played by Rodney Diak, light and hysterically funny. The show played to a full house for two weeks so we made a profit. Jevan Brandon Thomas, the author's son, said that of all the Fancourt Babberleys he had seen – and he had seen dozens as the play was translated into many languages and at one point was playing in forty-eight countries – John Moffatt's Babberley was the best.

After the first night, I was handed a small brown envelope which looked so unimportant that I left it until later to open. It was a cheque for £100 with grateful thanks from the Brandon Thomas children; Amy, Kitty and Jevan had all signed it. I wrote to Jevan thanking him, saying that I could not afford not to cash it. I asked him, however, if he would be kind enough to return the cheque to me after it had been through his bank. It hangs on the wall of my office. It's all the more precious because the play was out of copyright.

Finally, a grant came through from the Arts Council. Candida Plays was awarded £14,000 to mount four productions.

I had managed to persuade Noël to come to London and record Sheridan's *The Critic* for Ember Records. He was to play Mr Puff and Mel Ferrer played Mr Sneer.

We had dinner the night before we recorded and I asked Noël what he thought of the script. 'About as funny as a baby's open grave, dear.'

I didn't pursue the conversation. The record was not a great success.

In his diary, Noël wrote: 'I did my recording of Mr Puff in *The Critic*. I think it will be all right but the other acting, except for George Baker and John Moffatt, was not of the highest order. I went to *Hay Fever*. The cast was as good as ever ... Celia [Johnson] was quite enchanting and very, very funny.'

I actually went to that performance of *Hay Fever* with him. We were just about to sit in our seats when he saw someone he knew sitting behind him. He turned and kissed her on the cheek. Then introduced the woman to me. 'Darling, do you know George Baker?'

It was Jackie Kennedy.

After the show, we went back stage and as I realised that a great deal of finger wagging was about to go on in Maggie Smith's dressing-room, I took the opportunity to have a scotch with Robert Stephens.

Working with Noël put an idea into my head. I was planning the first season for Candida Plays at Bury. I went into it with great enthusiasm, planning three plays in repertoire: *Private Lives* by Noël Coward, *Ghosts* by Ibsen, and then a double bill of *Augustus Does His Bit* by George Bernard Shaw and *The Resounding Tinkle* by N. F. Simpson.

I planned to open the season with *Private Lives*. Jane Hilary played Amanda to my Elyot. Tandy Cronin played Sybil and Geoffrey Colville was Victor Prynne. Julia had designed the sets and costumes and I was the director. Rehearsals of this difficult play had gone well and we were all ready to open on Monday 12 June 1967 with the gala night the next day.

I wondered if I could get Noël to come to the opening; after all, his refusal would be every bit as memorable as John Gielgud's, 'Do ask me again, I've done sillier things in my time.'

I rang him at Les Avants. 'When is this grand opening to be?' he asked.

I told him. There was a pause while he consulted his diary. 'I do have to be in London then. All right, Dainty, we'll come and support you.'

'We' turned out to be Noël, Graham Payn, Cole Leslie, Joyce Carey and Gladys Calthrop. I told Noël that there would be a party at the Angel Hotel afterwards and asked him if I should book rooms for them all at the hotel but he preferred to return to London immediately after the show. It was now quite simple to get publicity both in the local and the national press. Anglia TV couldn't wait to interview Noël and me before the show.

Years later, I read what he had written in his diary: 'On Tuesday next I have to traipse to Bury St Edmunds to see George Baker's production of *Private Lives*. I have promised to do this but I wish to God I hadn't. I hope my virtue will be rewarded but doubt it. No good deed goes unpunished.'

The curtain was to rise at 7.30 p.m. on Tuesday evening; it became customary to always open a new play on the Tuesday. I had warned the cast that I might not be about until the last minute since I would be talking to journalists and waiting for Noël to arrive. Anglia was to film the arrival and then I would whisk Noël into a room where the interview camera had been set up.

The car drew up by the steps of the Angel Hotel at 6.50. Noël stepped out of the car, aglow with presence. It may just have been the small cathedral town of Bury St Edmunds but you would have thought he was arriving at the New York premiere of his latest play. We kissed on both cheeks, then Gladys, then Joyce, then Graham and last Coley, a lot of kissing for a country town in the sixties. The friendly Anglia producer suggested that Suffolk wasn't quite ready for such theatrical greetings.

Noël and I rushed through to the interview room. He always walked with purpose, the getting from A to B was irrelevant; it was being here or there that mattered. His elegant fingers held a cigarette, his shoulders hunched slightly forward, his eyes were alert while he waited for me to introduce him to the director and the crew. They were greeted with a dazzling smile.

'Do I sit here?' He made for the chair set in front of the camera. I could see the director visibly relaxing; he knew he was dealing with a consummate professional. His life was about to be made easy.

'Shouldn't you be at the theatre?' he asked me.

'Yes.'

'Well, go. You don't have to mollycoddle me, you know. I'm grown up.'

He gave the most wonderful interview, which went out live at 7.05.

I sprinted up to the theatre and sat for a moment in my dressing-room to calm down. Rather than calming down, however, all I could think of was what I had done. What can I have been thinking of, inviting Noël Coward to come hundreds of miles to see me play Elyot in possibly his most famous play? I knew that I must stop that line of questioning at once or I would be jelly before I spoke the first word.

There was a buzz of excitement from the front of house. The public was reluctant to take their seats as they wanted to see Noël arrive. Alice Lidderdale, my stage director, came backstage to tell me that we would have to hold the curtain for a few minutes. Noël and his party were to sit in the centre box of the balcony, flanked by the Blackburnes on one side and civic dignitaries on the other. The officers from the American air base at Lakenheath had taken the first three rows of the stalls and arrived in full Mess dress – black trousers, black bow ties and white monkey jackets, and all wearing medals.

The curtain went up at 7.40 p.m. There was a wonderful air of expectancy in the auditorium; they had come to enjoy themselves. We sped through on light wings, there was no 'cough of boredom', only an exhilarated audience with us barely a step ahead.

The Blackburnes entertained Noël in the interval and it was reported to me that when Noël said to Betty Blackburne that he felt sure he had met her before she had replied, 'Not in your wildest dreams, dear.' Apparently, Noël was fascinated by the eccentric Blackburne siblings who had lived and worked together all their lives. He was enjoying himself hugely.

The final curtain came down to an ovation, then the audience called for the author. The play had been written thirty-six years before and here was the audience clamouring their appreciation. Noël stood up in his box and took a bow, but it was not enough to satisfy. Alice Lidderdale brought him on to the stage and he stood between Jane and me and took another bow. I know he was very moved; weren't we all?

He didn't go home immediately after the performance as planned; he and his friends stayed and partied until two o'clock in the morning. 'When Amanda slapped your face,' he said to me, 'the ruffled dignity was a delight. I've never seen it played like that before. You looked very nicely on your high horse.'

That and many compliments for the cast and the production made the night memorable and set the season off with a swing.

The entry in Noël's diary records: 'I made the noble gesture of driving all the way to Bury St Edmunds, to see George Baker do *Private Lives*. Ninety miles there and ninety miles back, but my virtue was rewarded because he was very good indeed; in fact, the whole production was excellent.'

Thanks, Master.

The next day I received a phone call from my old friend Richard Leech. 'How did Noël enjoy it?'

'How did you know Noël was here?'

'Bully [Peter Bull] told me. Noël was in my dressing-room on Monday and I mentioned I'd heard he was going to see you. "Yes," he replied, "I go to Bury not to praise him."'

It has always been a further source of pleasure to me that he quotes that in his diary.

Our second offering at the Theatre Royal, Bury St Edmunds, was *Ghosts*. If I had triumphed in bringing Coward to see *Private Lives*, I also triumphed in casting Jane Baxter to play Mrs Alving. She was my first choice for the part. I had seen Mrs Alving played by strong, dramatic actresses and could never believe that Alving would have got away with any of his misdemeanours or indiscretions. Mrs Alving had to look vulnerable and have a powerful and hidden strength. Jane was a superb Mrs Alving.

The Stage of 6 July 1967 wrote:

Audiences for *Ghosts* at the Theatre Royal, Bury St Edmunds, are finding that any ideas that they may have had about Ibsen being dull or outdated are being dramatically dispelled by a production that turns the stage into a battlefield – a conflict between human beings as well as social ideals ... Jane Baxter makes Mrs Alving a woman of great joy and courage, fighting furiously to prevent the Victorian shibboleths, which had destroyed her own life, from destroying that of her son ... George Baker has directed the play as though this were a world premiere, with a freshness and vigour that wins the utmost approval.

After *Ghosts* came the double bill of *Augustus Does His Bit* and *Resounding Tinkle*. I was playing Augustus in the Shaw and Bro Paradoc in the Simpson. I had had a pain in my chest all through rehearsals, then I began to break into cold sweats as well but I decided that if I could get to the end of the week and could spend Sunday in bed, all would be well.

After the Saturday night performance of the double bill, I broke into another cold sweat and passed out on my dressing-room floor. Hard work had at last caught up with me. I can't remember playing the last few minutes of the play or taking the curtain call. I came to in my dressing-room and took myself home – a little town house the Blackburnes had found for me to rent during the season. Sally was staying with me.

I determined to spend Sunday in bed but, as it was a glorious day, I put up a camp bed in the garden. The effort made me sweat so much I collapsed again. Sally rang the Blackburnes, they rang Dr McKenzie who gave me an ECG which showed I had obviously had a mild heart attack towards the end of the performance. The doctor rang for an ambulance which took me to hospital.

As we were playing in repertoire, Michael Cottrell learned my parts in the double bill in a couple of days and took over while I was in hospital; in fact, he finished the run. Dr McKenzie released me from hospital with strict instructions to rest for six weeks. I went back to Rousham. I had a difficult task to face. I had to tell Julia that Sally was pregnant with my child.

19

JULIA FOUND A HOUSE IN TUNLEY ROAD IN BALHAM, WHICH
I BOUGHT, AGAINST MY BETTER JUDGEMENT. We were going to
try again with Julia and the family now living in London. The plan
was that I should spend four nights a week in Tunley Road and
three with Sally. The whole thing was doomed to failure.

Candy was deeply hurt when told of Sally's pregnancy. She was
twelve and the whole thing was very personal: in her opinion, her
father had rejected her, her mother and her sisters. There is nothing
to say that can mend this alienation. What could I say in justification?
Nothing. Tessa, on the other hand was thrilled at the thought of
having a brother or another sister. The twins were still too young
to take it in.

The birth was to take place in a small maternity home in Olney
in Buckinghamshire. When Sally went into labour, our next door
neighbours in Montagu Street drove her there, Richard counting the
contractions while Fraser drove.

I was at Rousham and as soon as they got to Olney, Fraser rang
me. Julia answered the phone.

'You'd better go quickly,' Julia said to me, 'Sally's in labour.'

My fifth daughter, Sarah, was born at 3 o'clock on 29 October
1967.

My mother had always been very censorious of my affair with
Sally. There was no reaction from her to the birth of Sarah. She
had disappeared some weeks earlier and could not be found. She
surfaced a week after the birth of Sarah, having been to Ross-shire

in Scotland where she had bought two derelict cottages in Fortrose for £500. My brother Patrick was responsible for finding the money for their renovation.

There was plenty of work both before and after Sarah's birth. After resting as instructed following the heart blip, I had been keen to get back to work and a timely phone call from Guy Verney lifted my spirits. He suggested a guest appearance in *Mrs Capper's Birthday* by Noël Coward, starring Beryl Reid. In fact, the cast was full of friends – Arthur Lowe, Pauline Yates, John Humphry and many others. I think it would be an excellent idea if we could have a channel especially devoted to showing old programmes from the good old days of television. This would be a wonderful candidate and another *The Sex Game* with Sian Phillips, Eileen Atkins, Anne Jameson and Marie Kean.

In fact, I was kept incredibly busy. Candida Plays produced thirty-five plays in five years and toured the length and breadth of the country. At one time, we had six companies out on tour; and 158 actors and stage management working for Candida Plays. David Coe ably assisted me in the early days, but he moved on to the Young Vic, his place being taken by John Baylis. Nick Kent, now of the Tricycle Theatre, was my assistant director. Of all the people I have met in my career, Nick Kent's enthusiasm, loyalty to his friends and his political and philosophical principles make him a man to be loved and admired. What he has done in the Kilburn High Road is a truly Herculean achievement.

Another invaluable assistant in the enterprise was an actor, Peter Dennis. He had been in the regular army as a sergeant clerk when he saw an advertisement for a personal assistant to the chairman of a major industrial company. He answered, was given an interview and got the job. It was while he was working for this company that he went to the theatre for the first time in his life. He fell under the spell of the grease paint and at the ripe old age of thirty-three he got himself to RADA.

I met Peter through Sue Pulford who did the research for *Room for Company*. This was a compilation to be presented by the RSC at the Aldwych Theatre during the Festival of London while the

RSC moved to the Barbican. I was part of the company with Paul Rogers, Gaye Brown and John Kane. It was a joyous piece of work, so full of laughter. A mongrel called Dinah was acquired from the Anti-Vivisection Society; she played 'Crab' to my Launce in an excerpt from *Two Gentleman of Verona*. Candy was adamant that Dinah would not be sent back to the Anti-Vivisection Society to be put down after the run of the play, and so it was that she came to live with us.

There was no change in London: Julia had the new house in Balham on which to spend a small fortune, and there was nothing I could do to stop her. It was a beautiful house, but not one we could afford. We kept the Rousham cottage, and Julia went up there at the weekends with the children and dogs, Minnie and Dinah.

Although Peter Dennis did appear in several plays for me, I needed him initially not so much as an actor but for his typing and clerical skills. Minutes were typed and circulated, schedules written and posted, reports landed on various desks, often bringing a financial contribution in return. We plotted and we planned; we were always low on finance as the town council, the district council and the urban district council could not find it in their hearts to let us have more than £4,000 between them.

We ran a programme for schools, the children coming to us. We would take one of their syllabus plays and, choosing a scene from it, would rehearse it. The actors had precious little time to read the play so the rehearsals were very much a matter of discussion about the meaning of the scene in context to the whole. We always played to full houses on these school matinées. When the time came for me to leave Bury St Edmunds, John Hill, the Education Officer, wrote saying how well it had worked.

One of the plays we put on in Bury was *The Sleeping Prince* with Susan Hampshire, Jean Anderson, David Hutcheson, myself and a strong supporting cast. We opened on Tuesday 26 March 1968. As Susan had just finished appearing in *The Forsyte Saga*, I thought we had a good chance of getting it into London. We opened well, and Susan's performance was a joy. Julia had designed the show with great taste. It certainly looked like West End material. We toured for several weeks, playing to good houses and, mostly, good notices.

We did not have Terence Rattigan's permission to allow the play to come to London until he had seen it, which he came to Newcastle to do. In the dressing-room after the show he said, 'Thank you for making me like my play.' He also said that he had some reservations and would I go up to London to talk about them. The next day was a Wednesday and a matinée day, so after the show that night I took the sleeper to London, and saw him at Claridge's for coffee at eleven.

The reservation he had was a scene between the Grand Duchess, the Arch Duchess, the Countess, the Baroness and Louisa. He wanted me to cut it. By cutting the scene, we completely lost the part of the Arch Duchess played by Viola Lyle. Viola was a very good but elderly actress who no longer worked very often and I dreaded telling her the news. I rehearsed my speech to her on the train back to Newcastle.

When I got to the theatre I talked to Jean Anderson. 'He is quite right to cut the scene,' retorted Jean. 'It doesn't work. It's regrettable that it is Viola's only scene, but she's used to the theatre. She'll understand.'

I wish it had been as easy as that. Viola took a lot of persuading that it had nothing to do with her acting.

With Rattigan's approval in the bag, we opened at the St Martin's Theatre on 9 May 1968. The notices were mixed and we were not to last long. Noël Coward had it sussed, writing in his diary: 'In the evening we went to see George Baker in *The Sleeping Prince*. He was very charming and looked very handsome, but the play is no good and never will be, as I know to my cost. When I think of all the lovely music and lyrics I wasted on *The Girl Who Came to Supper* [the film version] I grind my plates with frustrated rage.'

In 1969 I devised an anti-war recital, *The Hungry Tigers*, for Candida Plays, taking the title from Winston Churchill's *While England Slept*: 'Dictators ride to and fro upon tigers which they dare not dismount. And the tigers are getting hungry.' Peter Dennis, Sue Pulford and I drew on the broadest material – from Cicero and Caesar to Dean Swift and David Garrick, from Napoleon to Hitler, Truman and Eisenhower.

I had just made a picture for Columbia, *The Executioner*, directed by Sam Wanamaker so for once I had a little money and when Nick Kent said he had managed to get the Arts Theatre in London to give us a showing, I could not resist the risk and put up the money to take *The Hungry Tigers* there. It had gone very well in the provinces. David Hersey's lighting was imaginative and innovative, now showing the destruction of Warsaw, now making Tony McKeown ten feet tall in Lilliput. The cast were versatile, able to speak, sing, dance and play musical instruments. I really thought we had a chance of making it a success.

Sally and I went off to Crete for a much-needed holiday and Nick saw the production into the Arts Theatre and it opened there on 20 July 1969. But no one was interested – the whole world was watching the landing of the first man on the moon.

Luckily I was coming back to work, and it was the nearest I got to playing James Bond. I was cast by Peter Hunt to play Sir Hilary Bray in the film *On Her Majesty's Secret Service*. Sir Hilary was Master of the Royal College of Heralds, and Bond was to impersonate him while trying to explain to a character played by Telly Savalas what sort of a coat of arms he might be entitled to.

I had a scene at Pinewood Studios, supposedly Sir Hilary's office, with George Lazenby. George was really living the part. He had been given the suite that Cornel Wilde and Jean Wallace had made over for themselves when filming *Lancelot and Guinevere*. He had a bedroom, a kitchen, a sitting-room and a dining-room. He had a butler and a chef.

He wanted me to have lunch with him so he could go over the lines with his dialogue coach, Job Stewart. Job was an old friend; we had been at the Old Vic together and had traipsed all over Russia together. Now here was Job doing his best with George Lazenby's accent.

We went to his suite for lunch. The butler served drinks, the chef cooked up a storm. Job avoided catching my eye and I avoided catching his. We ran the lines over lunch, at which time it seemed to us that George didn't mind how he said them. Neither in what order, nor which accent. We played our scene and I went on my way.

Some months later I got a call from my agent who said that Peter Hunt wanted me to dub George Lazenby's voice for the section where he is supposed to impersonate Sir Hilary. But while we were in the dubbing theatre, Peter found other scenes he would like dubbed.

Most of the newspapers pretended they hadn't heard anything about this but the *Guardian* was not that kind.

> The general level of everything is quite as good as it ever was, except for Mr Lazenby who looks like a Willerby Brothers' clothes peg and acts as if he has just come out of Burton's short of credit. The only time he passes muster is dressed as a Scottish genealogist and dubbed with the voice of George Baker (who also acts a scene with him supplying both voices).

Lawrence Durrell's *Justine* took me to Tunisia and then to Hollywood. I was booked into a hotel in Tunis; it was a dreadful place and I determined to move myself out as soon as possible. A large man, with his left leg in plaster, was standing at the bar looking as unhappy as I felt. I introduced myself to the person who turned out to be the French actor, Philippe Noiret. He agreed with me that anything would be better than where we were.

There were a few days to go before filming started so the next day I hired a car and set off in search of a decent hotel. First stop was Sidi bu Said, a fortified town dating from the eighth century, but the hotels were not what we wanted. A friendly receptionist told me to try the Abwnawas just outside Tunis.

This hotel had chalets on the beach and there was a good fish restaurant a mile down the beach. Yes, it would do and they had plenty of room. I booked a chalet for Philippe and one for myself. I met up later with Dirk Bogarde who had arrived for the film and he and Tony Forward moved in as well. The last to join us was the director, the extraordinary Joe Strick, a most amiable companion when not working, but much more difficult as soon as he got behind the camera.

I arrived back in England to have a hilarious meeting about Candida Plays' Christmas production of John Moffatt's version of *Aladdin*. We discussed the laundry, the donkey, the Imperial Baths, outside the magic cave and inside the magic cave and how Michael Cottrell would play Widow Twankey.

David Hersey, later of *Cats* fame, had joined us as lighting designer but sat there, contributing nothing. We discussed the Flying Palace and the fact that the robbers would live in a marmalade jar. It was this that galvanised David.

'OK, you've had your fun! What kind of a joke is this?'

We suddenly realised that we were in the presence of a man who knew nothing of pantomime. Being a North American, the great panto tradition had completely passed him by. What a thrill! We had to teach him and, first, he had to learn that the old jokes were the best jokes. He entered into the spirit of the thing and the Flying Palace was a triumph. It flew and the children gasped.

After Christmas, it was off to Hollywood to finish *Justine*. Changes had been made. Joe Strick had been replaced by George Cukor. The producer, Pandro S. Berman, saw a rough cut of the footage shot by Joe in Tunisia and decided that it was not good enough.

On Cukor's first day on the set, he meant to let everyone know how he worked.

'When I say cut, everyone stands still. There is no movement, no tweaking of lights, no fiddling with clothes. When I speak to my actors, nobody else speaks. When we have discussed all we need to discuss, you can have your turn.'

And that is how it was.

Anna Karina, playing a prostitute, was wearing a white skirt and a tight, fitted top. Edith Head, the dress designer, was sitting on the set with Cukor when Anna came on to model the costume for him, looking most uncomfortable. Without a word, Cukor got up and, taking a pair of scissors (God knows from where), he started slashing at her dress. Soon it was in rags. Dirtying his hands on the studio floor, he rubbed the dirt into the material. Anna was delighted and lay down on the floor to ensure the whole dress was filthy.

A triumphant Cukor turned to Edith Head, 'That's much more the sort of thing I was looking for.' Edith, the three-time Oscar winner, got up and left the set.

Nothing could save *Justine*. John Simon wrote of it in *Halliwell's Film Guide*: 'Despite leaden forays into homosexuality, transvestism, incest and child prostitution, it remains as naïvely old fashioned in its emotional and intellectual vocabulary as in its actual verbiage and cinematic technique.'

One of us is going to die – and it isn't me!

Tiberius with author Robert Graves

Above The Bakers at
home in their kitchen –
a photo opportunity

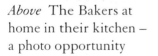

Right Reg and Dora, aka
George and Louie

Candida Plays presented seven plays and a Christmas production between September 1969 and January 1970. I commuted from Hollywood.

Gigi, directed by Nancy Poultney, was a difficult play to mount since there was no flying space in the eighteenth-century theatre and all the scenery had to trundle on and off stage into the wings. I was standing in the wings one day, watching the dress rehearsal with great pleasure, when I saw our leading lady, Petra Markham, trip and fall into the orchestra pit. She narrowly missed the percussion which could easily have impaled her but she broke her fall by landing on the drummer. No harm was done to anybody, thank God. David Coe, the director, and I had a moment of fear as we both stared at a possible court case.

I then directed *Springtime for Henry*, a Benn Levy comedy with Patrick Newell. The next play was *The Promise* in which Susan Tebbs, Roger Davenport and Peter Dennis gave moving and well-thought performances. Unfortunately, the good people of Bury thought they could give the play a miss.

After much persuading, I got Geoffrey Palmer to come down to play Torvald Helmer in *A Doll's House* at Bury. He was quite marvellous in it.

To make some money so Candida Plays could afford to mount *The School for Scandal* as a hundred and fiftieth birthday celebration of Bury's Theatre Royal, Sarah Badel and I embarked on Jan de Hartog's *The Fourposter*. It was a two-hander and the settings were extremely simple. I had a magnificent fourposter made which dominated the stage. The walls were black drapes, and almost invisible picture wires suspended three pictures. Mick Hughes lit the set with great imagination. *The Fourposter* was an enormous success wherever we went and did exactly what we had intended – it made money for the ambitious production of *The School for Scandal*. Sarah Badel, John Woodvine, Maria Aitken and I led a strong cast. We played to ninety-eight per cent of the house for the run of the play.

My marriage to Julia was finally over and we set about getting a divorce. Not that a marriage like ours could ever finish, divorce or no divorce. There were children, there was friendship, and there was more work to do together – Julia designed many sets and costumes for me and for Candida Plays. We continued to see a great deal of each other for the rest of our lives, and I carried the guilt of the marriage's failure about with me for at least twenty years.

It was as amicable as any divorce could be. I had unfettered access to the girls. I was to pay the debts and to pay maintenance to Julia, the mortgage on Tunley Road and the girls' school fees. Candy and Tessa were at a comprehensive called Mayfield College, and the twins were at school in Streatham. Julia was to keep the cottage and I was to pay for that. So really nothing had changed except that I was now living permanently and, up to a point, legally with Sally. We had decided not to actually get married.

Laurence Harbottle, the chairman of Candida Plays, and his friend Helge Magnusson were selling the lease of their Hasker Street house. In a generous act of friendship, they sold Hasker Holdings to Sally and me for a nominal price. For the first year of her life, Sarah's cot was in a tiny room under the stairs which we had used as a broom cupboard. Being short of space we moved out the brooms and moved Sarah in. The cot was a snug fit but since there was a small window giving on to the area, we reckoned it would do. However, with the purchase of 34 Hasker Street, we were able to give the child a room of her own. Lynn Dalby came too.

One morning I was setting off for work when a company of the Household Cavalry came down the street on early exercise. Lynn, who was always pining for a knight in shining armour to scoop her up and take her off to his castle, said to Sally as they stood in the doorway watching the procession, 'I only asked for one knight in shining armour. I don't think I can manage a whole regiment.'

I was dazzled by the workload of the seventies. I seemed to be running three jobs at once: managing a company, acting and directing.

In March 1970, I had the great joy of working with an actor who was something of a hero of mine, Raymond Massey. I still have a clear mental picture of him in Michael Powell's wondrous film *A Matter of Life and Death* made in 1946 with David Niven. Although I admired David Niven and Roger Livesey and fantasised over Kim Hunter, Raymond Massey's counsel for the prosecution made a lasting impression on me. The quirky, ugly face, so full of life and expression, riveted me.

We worked together in Robert Anderson's *I Never Sang for My Father*, which was an American family drama in the manner of Greek tragedy. I had an immensely long part, and was off-stage for only two and a half minutes in the entire evening. Both Raymond Massey and Catherine Lacey, who played my mother, were very elderly. Catherine looked extremely frail but gave a fine performance. Raymond was electrifying when he was on form. They weren't always quite sure of the words or where to move next.

Vivian Matalon, who was directing, suggested that as I was on all the time I might as well learn all the parts. Therefore I learned every line in the play and if things looked as though they were about to grind to a halt, I was able to heave them back on track by either asking a pertinent question or simply making a statement.

Alec McCowen came to the first night in Brighton. 'Have you ever thought of taking up nursing?' he asked.

After Brighton, we all went home and waited for a theatre in London. Finally, the Duke of York came free and we were to open there. We had a week of previews and, after the first preview, Vivian Matalon went on holiday in Jamaica – to my mind, quite extraordinary that a director would leave his play to go on holiday the week before the London opening. Raymond Massey had not appeared in London since 1938 and was delighted to be coming back. We did not enjoy a long run but I think Raymond, at seventy-three with chronic arthritis setting in, was glad to finish. He had been welcomed home. He had acted in the London theatre again, which was what he'd wanted.

The Memorial Theatre at Stratford-on-Avon closed for the winter season. The manager, Robert Vaughan, asked me if I could mount a Christmas play for him and I chose the dependable *Charley's Aunt* again. Most of the cast had worked with me before: Michael Cottrell, Tony McKeown, Julian Holloway, Jean Anderson as Donna Lucia d'Alvadorez and David Hutcheson as Sir Francis Chesney.

One of the great pluses of Stratford was the Dirty Duck pub run by Ben Shepherd and his wife Margot. They loved the theatre and actors, and were most generous to us all. They became very good friends and remained so for life. Their son, Robin, took the Howard Arms in Ilmington and my daughter Tessa once worked for him as his chef. Robin, a superb chef himself, taught her a great deal. His second son, Simon, is a national heart-throb in *Peak Practice* on ITV.

In February 1971, we opened in Stratford in *The Constant Wife* by W. Somerset Maugham. The cast included Gwen Watford, Phyllida Law, Gillian Raine, Basil Hoskins and myself. Nancy Poultney, who had directed so many plays for the company, was directing; Julia designed the costumes and David Hersey did the lighting.

I had warned Nancy that I had to have a couple of days off to film a TV commercial for Castella in Paris. This was great fun as I liked both the producer, John Nicolls, and the director, Don Leaver. But most of all it was a golden opportunity to see Philippe Noiret.

I was determined to get to London with *The Constant Wife*, and we very nearly did. We opened to splendid notices in Stratford-on-Avon and began a long tour through the country. Every day I worked on the phone, trying to get us a London theatre. Tony Peake of the Theatre Royal, Haymarket showed great interest. I tried to persuade him to come to one of our early touring performances but, as he knew we were coming to Wimbledon, he decided he would see it then, bringing Mrs Watson, who owned the Haymarket with him.

When we were playing in Wilmslow outside Manchester, I motored to London after the show three times in the week to have meetings with Tony Peake. We would meet in the morning and I would drive back at lunchtime to be there for the evening performance. On my return, I was always greeted with enthusiasm by Gwen and Phyllida; I think it was mainly relief that they had a leading man for the evening performance.

The upshot of all this hard work was that Mrs Watson, the Haymarket's co-owner, was in the habit of having tea with Binkie Beaumont, the great London producer at H. M. Tennent once a month, and Binkie told her that *The Constant Wife* was not one of Maugham's better plays and that Gwen Watford and George Baker would mean nothing to the public.

Tony Peake rang me the next day and said the deal was off. Three months later, Binkie mounted a vastly inferior production with the husband and wife team, John McCallum and Googie Withers; it died a richly deserved death.

And I am not in the least vindictive.

After we finished with *The Constant Wife*, John Roberts, sometime manager of the Royal Shakespeare Theatre and now a London producer, came in on a joint venture with Candida Plays. We were going to try and revive four of Christopher Fry's plays to tour for the Arts Council. Laurence Harbottle had introduced John Roberts to me as someone he thought I could work with. He was right; John and I hit it off together from the very first moment.

Before we embarked on the project, BBC Television offered me a part in Shaw's *Candida* with Geraldine McEwan in the title role. I had known Geraldine slightly for many years and admired her greatly. One of the performances that has stayed in my mind was her playing of Olivia in *Twelfth Night* at Stratford opposite Dorothy Tutin as Viola; I don't think I shall ever see again the magical joy those two actors brought to the characters.

John Roberts and I had the pleasant task of driving to East Dean in Sussex to see Kit Fry. Kit was going to direct our first play, which was to be *The Lady's Not for Burning*. We arranged to have auditions to find a Jennet Jourdemayne and an Alison Eliot. Kit came up to London and we held these at the Globe Theatre. We found a splendid Jennet in Jennifer Hilary and a demure and beautiful Alison in Jenny Quayle. Tony Quayle had two daughters, both ravishingly beautiful and exceptionally nice women. The rest of the cast was recruited from the Candida Plays' stalwarts – Jean Anderson, Brian Oulton, Brian Smith, Jeremy Longhurst, Michael Howarth, Dudley Jones and Dermot Kelly.

It was a great joy working with Kit; he was a gentle and lucid director. He was patient in rehearsal and let the player come to the part at his own pace. But then he became, quite rightly, merciless about the text; not a word could slip. I don't think I have ever enjoyed a production more. Jennifer Hilary was a joy to work with and quite brilliant in the part. I loved playing Thomas Mendip and was so comfortable in the part that I really began to think I could act.

We opened in Guildford where we played for two weeks to full houses. Kit and I would communicate by telegrams in rhyme while on tour. This one came from Leeds:

> There was a young person called Candida,
> Whose performance got grander and grandida.
> All roads roam to Leeds
> At various speeds
> And that was the place where they landed her.

Sadly, we failed to get the play into London and Kit was as disappointed as we were.

The Arts Council now had a special touring arm called DALTA. It was run by Jack Phipps whose dictum seemed to be: 'Let's get the big boys out on tour and forget about the little fellows.' It didn't take him very long at all and the next three Fry plays were cancelled.

Jack now held the purse strings and was much happier funding the RSC's and the National Theatre's touring arms than the small touring companies like Candida and Frank Hauser's Meadow Players. Without money, I had no option but to wind up Candida Plays. It was the end of an era in my life.

20

IT WAS NOW TIME TO BECOME SOLVENT. I was still in the position of not really being able to service the interest on my debts, never mind about paying them off but something had to be done. My friend Bob Redwood, the landlord of the Plumbers Arms, had retired and was looking for something to do to while away the hours. He came to work for me at a risible salary and his job was to try to make sense of the debts. In all, I was £32,000 the wrong side of solvency.

Sally and I set some serious rules. Stop smoking, stop drinking – in fact, stop almost everything, really. We had started on the road that would take nearly ten years to cover.

At about this time, Angela Halliday, a bookkeeper, joined the rescue team. I made sure that my VAT monies were paid by separate cheque into a separate account. I found a new accountant. I wrote to my inspector of taxes, suggesting he took a percentage of the earnings from every payment I received. This would mean I was not faced with an unpayable bill each year.

Yes, I was on the road. Luckily the work came tumbling in: *Fraud Squad*, *Girls About Town*, *Z Cars*, *Doomwatch* and *Paul Temple*. Richard Price, our neighbour, was now head of casting at LWT and he asked me to play Mr Bowler in *The Fenn Street Gang* which I was glad to do. Brian Izzard, the director, encouraged me to go far, perhaps too far, with the characterisation of Mr B. I thoroughly enjoyed the part. Humphrey Barclay, head of light entertainment, thought the character might translate into a situation comedy of its own and not long after John Esmonde and Bob Larbey set about writing *Bowler*. It was to run to a series of twelve episodes and I had the great pleasure of playing Mr Bowler.

Throughout the time I was running Candida Plays and getting through the breakdown of my marriage to Julia and my making a commitment to Sally, I had many staunch friends, but none so steadfast as Laurence Harbottle and Helge Magnusson. Laurence not only gave me support as a personal friend, but also was unfailing in his support of my endeavours in the theatre. It was the laughs we had; I do believe the whole world revolves on laughs.

Michael Miles asked me to do the first episode of *Some Mothers Do 'Ave 'Em*. I had heard it said that Michael Crawford was difficult to work with but, on the contrary, I found him stimulating. He worked enormously hard himself and, not unreasonably, he expected others to do the same. I played Mr Lewis, the manager of an ironmongers' store, and Frank Spencer came to me for a job. By the time he had finished with the unfortunate Mr Lewis, the man was a gibbering wreck, with his office in shambles and his mind in tatters. Michael is a comedy genius, has a delightful singing voice, a keen sense of humour and an absolute determination to become the best in the world in his field. Good luck to him, he's done it.

In 1973 I did a tour of Ray Cooney's *Not Now Darling* with Ian Lavender, a wonderfully true yet underrated actor. We opened at Stratford. The RSC was getting ready for its season and some of the directors and designers were there. One afternoon, Buzz Goodbody, a director for the RSC, came running down the stairs as I was going to my dressing-room. After she had passed me, she turned to her companion and said, 'We've got to get the theatre back. We can't have commercial drivel like this going on here.'

I did another episode of *Z Cars* and a programme called *Who Done It?* Then followed an ad for Pedigree Chum with Willie Rushton, directed by Richard Lester. It was a couple of very funny days in the studio. Willie was a very witty man. I always think that we're lucky to work in a business where laughter is the norm, where jokes are welcomed in discussion and where a good-humoured day is a successful one.

A Warm December, a film with Sidney Poitier, was next; he also directed. In the cast were Esther Anderson, Johnny Sekka, Earl Cameron and T. P. McKenna. Working with Sidney was an exhilarating experience. He acted with energy and power, and directed in the same way.

We became friends. I was patron of the Dark and Light Theatre Company, whose directors were Frank Cousins and Norman Beaton. I asked Sidney if he would come down to Brixton and see a performance, which he did. The sixties and seventies were a dreadful time for most black actors, and any publicity we could get for this theatre was a good thing and money in our pockets for future productions. Sidney's presence there brought out the entire local and some of the national press.

Three for All was a film directed by Martin Campbell. It was not a good film, but Martin was a good director and we were to work again. It was fun because I met young Richard Beckinsale who was making his film début; he was a charismatic actor even then.

My old friend Di Dors was playing a small part, but it was so sad to see her – she was a shadow of her former self and died a couple of months later of cancer. When she left the set on her last day, I blew her a kiss and we both knew we would not be meeting again.

Sometimes it was hard to believe how fast time was going. Candy had left school, gone to secretarial college and was now working for John Birt on *Weekend World*. Tessa had left school and was working as a waitress at Spot Three, a restaurant which was run by our great friend, Andrea Leeman. Tessa had decided she wanted to be a chef and through Andy's good offices she went to learn her trade in Switzerland. She seemed to me to be awfully young to be going off on her own.

I had sworn to myself that I would not allow to happen to my children what I had gone through, but due to my own weaknesses and indulgences, it was being repeated. Certainly their education was a little better than mine, and I suppose their home life was a little more stable. But I had not been able to create the world I would have liked them to inhabit.

After long discussions with my accountant and my bank manager I had to agree that there was nothing for it but to sell the house in Tunley Road, Balham, and be rid of the mortgage. Julia was very understanding. The deal we came to was that, after the mortgage had been paid off, Julia would keep the rest of the money as her part of the divorce settlement; she then moved back to the cottage in Rousham. She took the dogs, Minnie and Dinah, with her. Because we didn't want to disrupt the twins' education, they came to live with Sally and me during the term and were with Julia for the holidays. When Julia had settled in, they too moved to the cottage and went to school in Bicester.

My eldest daughter, Candy, decided that she would like to do something in the theatre. I had seen her playing Elizabeth in *The Witches of Salem*. She was good but she was not an actress. Fortunately, Candy was sensible enough herself to realise that acting was not for her and she went to work with Frank Hauser as an ASM at the Oxford Playhouse.

In 1994, my youngest daughter, Sarah, was walking upstairs, having just come in from school; she was about six years old. 'I wonder if you two would mind getting married,' she said. 'And, by the way, we never have any puddings in this house.'

Sally and I had made a conscious decision not to marry and Sarah's request threw us. 'Why, darling?' we asked.

'It would make things easier at school.'

That decided us. We would get married, which was a first for Sally. My mother had by this time long accepted the situation between me and Sally, becoming great friends with her, and was as fond of Sarah as the other girls.

But first things first. No puddings, eh! I went into the kitchen and concocted a very good pud out of what I could find in the fridge and store cupboard: cream, bananas, ratafia biscuits, sugar, lemon and a little drop of brandy. Whip it all up and it's amazingly good. Andrea Leeman stole the recipe for her restaurant and called it Mr Scroggins' Pudding. God knows why. I invented one or two other recipes for puds, and these were also pinched. I decided to treat it as a compliment.

For some time, Julia had been a little tricky about signing the necessary forms for the decree nisi but when I rang her and told her Sarah's comments and that we wanted to get married, she said immediately: 'Oh, my dear, I'll sign them straight away.'

Well, not quite.

When she said the papers would be signed immediately, we made plans to get married on 12 October 1974. I was in Birmingham making *Spy Trap* and, at the same time, was writing a script for Pilkington Glass for an audio/visual presentation to be made in Paris. The producers were Gill Best and Bernard Braden. The wedding day was approaching and still no papers had arrived.

I rang Ju. It had slipped her mind. She signed them straightaway and sent them to Harbottle and Lewis. There, with the help and advice of Laurence Harbottle, we finally got the signed papers properly attested. Bob Redwood took them to the court and we got the decree nisi on 11 October. This was the recording day for *Spy Trap* and I got a cryptic message from the director in the control room. 'I'm to tell you that the papers have been delivered to the Chelsea Registry Office. What's it all about, Alfie?'

Paul Daneman, also in the cast, shouted out, 'He's going to marry my friend Sally!'

When I arrived at Euston that evening, Sally was there to meet me with the news that she had invited a few people in for a celebration after the ceremony.

'How many exactly?' I asked, dog-tired.

She counted the names off on her fingers. It appeared that there would be forty-two.

'I'm sorry, darling. That's quite a lot of catering, isn't it?'

Having bought up half the local Europa foodstore, I cooked all night.

Our marriage was witnessed by Laurence Harbottle and Andy Leeman. Sarah squatted on a chair with both hands held up to her chin, in the manner of a squirrel. All my hard work the previous night was worth it – we had a wonderful party.

Sally had been offered a telly part in Manchester so the honeymoon consisted of a night in Kendal, a night with Jean Anderson's daughter Aude and her husband Airlie Holden-Hindley, and then off to Manchester for a week where Sally rehearsed and recorded and I went to the art gallery, saw friends at the Royal Exchange Theatre for coffee or drinks, and lounged about reading my script for *Dial 'M' for Murder* which I was to start when I got back to London.

We spent a gloriously romantic weekend at Blanchland, a wonderfully preserved eighteenth-century village in the heart of the Pennines. We often returned there; the drive from Brough to Blanchland is simply one of the most spectacular I have ever driven.

Back in London, I got a call from my agent that Buzz Goodbody from the RSC would like to come and see me about *Hamlet*. I was broadcasting some of my poetry at the BBC for Reggie Smith, so I suggested that she might come and have some lunch with me at the BBC Club. I remembered that it was the little person who had come flying down the stairs at Stratford, commenting that commercial theatre was rubbish but, beyond her words, I couldn't remember her face or figure. I could not have been less prepared for the little person that arrived to see me.

She was quite short and squat of figure, a round face, a good Jewish nose, brown eyes and black eyebrows, black curly hair. She was wearing winkle-picker shoes, a long black skirt, black blouse, a waistcoat of dark purples, blues and greens and a long black coat down to her ankles. The curly head had a black hat with a red feather on it.

I felt very old.

We got our food from the buffet and sat down. 'I see Claudius as one of the most powerful businessmen in the world,' she said. 'Certainly more ruthless than Tiny Rowland or Robert Maxwell. It's one of the greatest whodunnits ever written. The murder is committed, the ghost tells his son who did it and leaves him to prove it. Exciting! Ben Kingsley is going to play Hamlet and I would love it if you could join the company and play Claudius.'

We talked a little about her way of working, her hopes for The Other Place and for herself at the RSC. I was also to play Worcester in *Henry IV* in the main house, and Clarence in *Richard III* at The Other Place. I wasn't entirely sure but I felt it might break the pattern of my career if I were to work with this dynamic young woman; she was just twenty-six years old and full of ideas. Once the plays were on and in repertoire, I would have time off to write and to do some telly.

On 3 February 1975, the company of the RSC met at the rehearsal rooms in Floral Street and, for the next two days, we all sat on little hard chairs, sort of pub chairs, facing the great and the glorious of the RSC. Trevor Nunn took nearly four hours to tell us that he wouldn't be around a lot as somebody called Terry Hands was going to be in charge of the season. Terry Hands took five hours to tell us how he was going to run the season. Then the accountant took two hours to tell us how little we would be paid for working all the hours that God gave plus some extra ones invented by the RSC.

Then we had an extraordinary talk, for a further two hours, by a funny little New Zealander, Des Wilson, who told us how he was going to try and collect sponsorship for the RSC and how, in the spare time we were not going to have, we could help.

I knew then that I had made the greatest mistake of my life. But there was no way out and I had to make as good a job of it as I could.

Rehearsals with Buzz were certainly a new departure for me. I had been used to going to the rehearsal room, reading the play, blocking the moves and rehearsing the scenes. Discussions on motivation came out of the rehearsal process; sometimes many hours were wasted by actors who had not done their homework but were getting it done for them by the director in other people's time. Or, of course, there is the actress (I realise that this is politically incorrect and I should be saying 'actor' covering both sexes, but that would not be conveying what I mean) who fancies the director, and hangs upon his every word. And vice versa, of course. Immensely time wasting.

However, Buzz talked at length while we listened. She made a great deal of sense to me and the hours of the great and glorious began to fall away, and interest in the work in hand to reassert itself. We did a fair amount of moving round in circles and touching hands to communicate. Sending out positive vibes and negative vibes. I opened myself to it and began to feel all sorts of preconceived prejudices falling away. I was gaining a freedom of emotion I had not bothered to touch before.

Sally had gone down to Ilmington to make ready the cottage that we were renting from the RSC. I was to arrive the next day. The cottage belonged to Dennis Flower, chairman of the Shakespeare Trust and on the board of the RSC as well as chairman of Flowers Brewery. We walked over to the Manor to introduce ourselves to

Dennis Flower; he was the gentlest and most courteous of men. He had been captured by the Germans in 1940 and spent the war in a prison camp, not being released until 1945. The first his family knew of his return was when he rang from Moreton-in-Marsh. 'Mum, I'm at the station in Moreton. I wonder if there's anyone free to come and fetch me?' I think that says it all.

We were soon very warm and very happy in the cottage. What I didn't know was that we would be staying in Ilmington for the next eight years.

Just before we opened, Buzz organised a macabre rehearsal; in order for us all to realise the magnitude of suicide and burial in an unconsecrated grave, she got permission from Holy Trinity, Stratford's parish church, to allow us to dig a grave in unhallowed ground. Yvonne Nicholson, who was playing Ophelia, was wrapped in a shroud and put on a two-wheeled trundle. The gravediggers pushed her to the grave and the scene between the priest and Laertes was played.

Not only were the basics of my Christian belief offended, but I sensed a deeper atmosphere of distress in the whole game that was being played out. I turned away from the scene and heard myself say, 'Don't go looking for death, Buzz, it will find you soon enough.'

'Well said,' said Griffith Jones.

I don't know if it was well said or not; it just came out of me.

We played our first performance on 8 April – not in fact our official press night. We played again the next night and then two nights later. We had the evening off on the Saturday and Sunday. I had a long talk to Buzz before the show on Friday 11 April, and she told me of her plans for a *Macbeth* to be staged at The Other Place in the next season.

She said goodbye.

On Sunday 13 April, Ben Kingsley rang me at the cottage to tell me that Buzz Goodbody had taken her own life.

The band played on. We opened with *Henry IV Part One* on 22 April, and the other Henry plays followed in their due season. The great and the glorious did not come to see *Hamlet* at The Other Place until after the press night when we had received ecstatic notices.

The big plus of the season was that, in the main house, I shared a dressing-room with Trevor Peacock. Not only was he an immensely original actor but also a writer and musician. He had a house in Chipping Campden for the season and was always surprised when I called on him on horseback while out exercising Ginger, my friend Richard Organ's large hunter.

Emrys James, who was playing King Henry IV, was an old friend and we had worked together on a number of television productions. We were able to renew our friendship. Also in the cast was Charlie Dance who became a very dear friend and we still meet as often as we can.

Away from Stratford, we had a marvellous time, especially revisiting the friends I had made in Aston Subedge, and making new ones in Ilmington. The Red Lion, with the church, was to become the focal point of our stay. There was Dennis Flower and his mother, Bob and Barbara Webb at the Red Lion, Ruth and Jimmy Last at the Howard Arms, also in Ilmington; Bertie Wyton, Kim and Winifred Holman of Foxcote House, my everlasting friends; Michael and Shirley Dingley, witty and generous; Dilwyn and Kate Davies, the vicar and his wife, and Father Murphy.

Dilwyn and Father Murphy were the greatest of friends. When Father Murphy died, the Roman Catholic parish asked Dilwyn to make the address. The whole village, irrespective of denomination, went to the funeral service.

A visiting American Episcopalian minister, seeing Kate, Dilwyn and Father Murphy standing together at a cocktail party, asked, 'Which one of you is the Anglican?'

'The one that gets to sleep with Katie,' answered Father Murphy.

Barry Rutter, actor and later director, put together an old time music-hall, which he chaired with great panache. He devised it to tour the surrounding villages and brought it to the village hall at Ilmington for a hilarious evening of bucolic fun. It inspired Bob Webb, landlord of the Red Lion, and he and I put together our own music-hall, based largely on Johnny Moffatt's script. Our problem was to find a pianist. We found an ex-schoolmistress who could play the piano for our rehearsals but she certainly couldn't play for the performance. I managed to persuade Michael Tubbs, pianist and musician for the RSC, to play for our show. Charlie Dance, Trevor

Peacock and Barry Rutter all came and augmented the village talent of the Halls, Brudenhalls, Peachys, Boyd and Helen Sabin.

Of course, our music-hall was amateur, rash and ill-advised; after all, it was in the main performed by the young of the village, but it was an evening to remember. Charlie Dance sang 'Champagne Charlie' and Dilwyn Davies 'The Miners Dream of Home'. It made the village teem with life and a Nativity play was planned for Christmas, but not before the music-hall had returned by popular request.

The most extraordinary happening that year was the announcement that I was entitled to ten days' paid holiday. I had seldom had a holiday and certainly not a paid one. My twin daughters (who had brought Dinah, the rescue dog from *The Two Gentlemen of Verona*, with them), Sarah, Jesse the springer, Sally and I squeezed into a Ford Cortina and at 11.30 p.m., after the show one Saturday night, we set off for Fortrose in Scotland.

I had promised the twins that they would see red squirrels and they did. When we arrived at the Queen's View above Pitlochry at five-thirty in the morning, the view was covered in fog but I proposed we had breakfast there, whatever the weather. In due course, the mist began to lift and the twins wandered over to the edge to look at the view. As the mist moved away from a fir tree, it exposed two red squirrels sitting on a branch.

We motored to Fortrose in slow stages, pitching our tents where the fancy took us. Although we had seen pictures of my mother's cottages, this was the first time we had seen them. They had been splendidly converted, and it was no wonder she was so happy there. The magic of that holiday has never left us and we have never been foolish enough to try and repeat it.

Candy, who had been working as an ASM at the Oxford Playhouse with Frank Hauser and then with Prospect Productions, was out of work. She came over to Ilmington so that we could discuss any possibilities and write application letters. I left her writing the letters in the cottage and went into the theatre.

David Brierley stopped me in the corridor and asked me if I happened to know of an ASM who would be free to go on a tour of *Pleasure and Repentance* and *The Hollow Crown*, going to the Middle East, the Far East, Australia and New Zealand. 'As a matter of fact, I have one sitting at home, writing letters for jobs at this very moment.'

Candy had a meeting with Billy Jay of the Paul Elliot Organisation and was offered the job that would shape the rest of her life. Our dear friends Annie Firbank and Charles Kay, who was to be with me in *I, Claudius*, were in the company as was Edward Petherbridge. They gave her a spectacular twenty-first birthday party while on tour. She arrived home eight months later saying that the only place she wanted to live was Australia. She is now a highly successful journalist and novelist, living in Sydney with her two children and her husband, Robert Drewe, arguably one of Australia's best writers.

During my time in Stratford, I augmented my meagre salary by making a film for Martin Campbell and Tudor Gates, and a most enjoyable episode of *Z Cars* for the BBC, directed by Derrek Goodwin. It was enjoyable because of the content: a sleazy itinerant preacher gets away with the collection and as many female parishioners as he can. When the time comes for him to make his escape, he drives off in his camper-van humming 'There is a green hill far away.' Playing villains is always so much better than playing good guys; the villains always have a much better sense of humour.

The downside to the filming was the heat; 1975 was one of the hottest summers on record and filming in the enclosed space of a camper-van was sweaty work.

Martin Lisemore and Herbie Wise asked me to play Tiberius in a television adaptation of *I, Claudius* for them. I had already worked with Herbie on *Voyage in the Dark* by Jean Rhys and was very excited at the prospect of working with him again. Martin's office sent me seven episodes of the script to read. Jack Pulman had adapted the book with great flair and not a word was changed in rehearsal. Martin Lisemore was the most meticulous of producers: everything was checked and double-checked.

There had been a conscious decision not to go on location. We rehearsed for ten days and then had two days in the studio to record each episode. Studio days were long but so efficiently run by the stage management team that we seemed to glide through them.

My first problem was to get myself looking twenty-two – that's how old Tiberius is when we first see him. I was forty-five.

I could still hear my daughter Tessa's birthday greeting to me on my forty-second birthday. 'Hi, Dad! How does it feel to be middle aged?'

'What do you mean, *middle aged*?!'

'Well, you don't expect to live until you're eighty-four, do you?'

No answer to that.

Up at six for a six-mile run round the perimeter of Hyde Park and Kensington Gardens with Jess the dog (if I had to be fit, so did he!); home for breakfast and no dairy products; on to the bike to go down to swim at the North Kensington baths before pedalling up to the BBC rehearsal rooms in Acton. And certainly no alcohol. I lost the weight and put on muscle and by the time we came to rehearse, I had lost enough to make a very passable thirty-year-old. Make-up would have to do the rest and I was assigned to Lisa Westcote, one of the best make-up artists at the BBC.

Having conquered the young man, we then had to set about the old man. This was to be achieved with latex rubber. Both Lisa and I realised that it would be very inhibiting to the performance if I couldn't move my face, so as she was applying the latex I would move the muscles on my face and grimace and smile until all the lines on my face and around my eyes were coated in rubber. I was then able to move my face quite naturally within the latex mask.

Brian Blessed, playing Augustus Caesar, was the first to don the latex and he had been given explicit instruction by Pam Meagre, the make-up supervisor, not to move his face at all. He was sitting behind the Imperial desk dashing off the Imperial edict when I happened to stroll by.

I picked up a piece of charcoal. 'Brian, if you stick this bit of charcoal between the cheeks of your arse, you'll be able to harvest a diamond in two thousand years' time.'

'Oh, for fuck's sake, fuck off. I can't laugh, you sod.' His latex crinkled round the edges of his mouth and Pam Meagre was not best pleased.

The latex was very hard on our faces. Sian Phillips went home in her latex mask one evening to show her mother and when she took it off she put it on the windowsill. Next morning when she came to pick it up to throw it away, it had taken the paint off the sill.

Sian and I would forget the cantankerous relationship between mother and son and go to the bar for a couple of sausages on recording days. Although as Tiberius I had little to do with Derek Jacobi, Claudius, on screen, we became great friends off-stage. I was to direct him in *The Lady's Not for Burning* at the Old Vic for Prospect Productions.

Most of my scenes were with mother, Sian Phillips, or nephew, John Hurt. John is a consummate actor with the great gift of simply becoming the character he is asked to play. Alec Guinness disguised himself into many roles but always remained Alec Guinness. John Hurt disappears and re-embodies himself.

Days in the make-up chair got longer and longer as Tiberius got older and older and more and more disgusting to look at. By this time, I not only had the latex, but I had a bladder over my head to hide my hair and make me bald. Then I had two bladders, one over the hair on which I stuck thin string and another one over that to keep the string in place. Lisa touched in the string with light blue to achieve, very realistically, the effect of veins. Then came the moment when the poor syphilitic old bugger had to have scabs all over his head.

My make-up was now taking up to nine hours to accomplish so we had to start incredibly early each morning. Lisa and I had become a little peckish and, at about 5.30 one morning, were eating bowls of Cornflakes. The texture and the crinkle of the flakes fascinated me. I picked one up and put it on my bald head.

'What do you think?'

'Yes!' She got the glue and stuck it down and, with the help of a little make-up, it looked like the most disgusting scab. We were so pleased with ourselves.

Until I got to the *Inspector Wexford*s, I had never experienced such a happy job with so many talented, intelligent and pleasant people.

21

In March 1977 I took off for New Zealand to play Inspector Alleyn in four of Ngaio Marsh's books – *Vintage Murder, Colour Scheme, Died in the Wool* and *Death at the Dolphin* – for television. John MacCrea was the head of South Pacific Television; he had worked in the BBC for many years and was trying to introduce indigenous production into New Zealand television.

The joke current at that time amongst middle Britain was that New Zealand was closed. I must have been lucky for, within two days of arriving on North Island, I had been to the trotting races and to a concert in the theatre of Auckland University. I had a week to acclimatise before starting rehearsals. There was some magic in the air that was to keep me buoyant through the five months I was to spend in New Zealand.

I still had a few days before rehearsals began so, taking my rented car and my camera, I set off for the North Cape; the idea of a ninety-mile beach fascinated me. I was on my way by 5.30 a.m. Out of the mist at Warkworth, the head of a white horse leaned over the post and rails and noded his 'gu' day' to me. I took his picture. I was very surprised at the light reading; I felt sure my meter had gone wrong, but then I realised the sky was blue and the air was pure.

Miles of pasture and rolling hill followed, the Dalmatian vineyards, towns with broad streets, picnic places with tables and benches, hot spring baths and children overweight and eating take-aways. I walked on black sand and swam in the clear sea. I marvelled at the size and breadth of the trees, the wild boar, and the feeling when I was travelling north that I was travelling south.

I had just unpacked the car on my return to Auckland when John and Ainsley Sullivan drew up in their car; I had met John at the races. They told me they had a Lockwood – a prefabricated bungalow – on their property and I was welcome to use it. Since the four films were to be made in different locations all over the country, it would certainly be easier for me to have a base from which I could work. I could pack what was necessary and leave the rest of my belongings in the Lockwood. I accepted their generous offer but insisted that I pay them the hotel allowance given to me by the company. They finally agreed to let me pay for phone and electricity.

The first film was to be *Died in the Wool*. There were costumes to be bought and I was delighted that a bright and knowledgeable costume designer was to do all four films. Barbara Darragh was then just starting out on her career; she now shuttles between Hollywood, Sydney and Auckland.

I had brought one or two things which I thought might be suitable and she had some very forties suits made by a local tailor who had been apprenticed in Savile Row. The costumes were interchangeable and so would do for all four films. I was delighted with my dresser, who was to be with me all the way through the filming. Revell Troy was gay, willowy and unashamedly camp. He possessed a sparky sense of humour and caused much surprise and disbelief in country locations. But he was the best dresser I have ever had.

Alan Feonander, friend and casting director at J. Walter Thompson, had given me the name and address of a friend, Adrian White, who had been the only equestrian representative of the New Zealand Olympic team in 1947. Adrian White was now running his own sheep station. I rang him from Auckland and learned that his farm was near Hastings, which apparently was only a few miles from Napier. He told me to ring him as soon as I got to Napier.

Our first location was to be a sheep station owned by John Gordon. The Gordons were an old New Zealand family of Scottish descent; John had been educated at Winchester. They were interested in the filming and tolerated our strange hours and inexplicable working practices with great good humour. Like everyone else in New

Zealand, they were generous and hospitable. They came to see my production of *The Lady's Not for Burning* when they came to London. The sheep station was down the road to Houmana, past the Hawkes Bay Vinery. The wooden clapboard house on two storeys overlooked the sea and was backed by the Kaimanawa Mountains; the property extended all the way out to Cape Kidnappers.

I would drive out early to location, take a stock pony up the hill and ride through the property, marvelling at my luck. What a privilege to see this beautiful and unexpected country with its hills, ravines and plateaux and go where only ponies can get. Some parts of the station were not accessible to the noisy motorbike, the modern farmer's workhorse. After a swim, I was ready by 8 o'clock; even the crew never turned up until 8.30. That had to be changed – and it was.

Our director, Brian McDuffy, had only ever directed six minutes of film before. When he had completed his BBC directors' course, he had been allowed to film six minutes of a *Z Cars* episode. Our other director, Peter Sharp, had never directed film at all, and nurtured some novel and undistinguished ideas.

New Zealand boasted some very good actors, but there was not much work for them and most of them had 'day jobs'. There were theatres in Auckland, Wellington and Christchurch, which had resident companies, and a touring theatre in Dunedin and that was it. There were some home-made television series and serials but most of them had an English or Australian actor in the lead. Elona Rodgers, an English actor married to a New Zealander, was a genuine star of small screen and stage, and still is.

While we were filming *Died in the Wool*, I made a particular friend. Robin Bowering, an Englishman who had played in *Charlie Girl* at the Aldwych for years, had decided to settle in Australia and found himself working a great deal in New Zealand; now here he was in Napier. We laughed a good deal and he suggested that I should go and stay with him in Sydney when I had finished filming.

The film was going well if slowly but the great joy was to get away at the weekends. I had followed up Adrian White's invitation to make contact with him and he, Muff, their children and friends were all hugely hospitable and took me to their hearts. I would spend hours riding in the beautiful countryside surrounding their sheep station. Adrian introduced me to the master of the Hawke's Bay Hunt, John Pattison, and I was invited for a day out with the hounds. So at the end of the shoot, I stayed on in Napier.

John Pattison was a remarkable man, remarkable in that he was shot down into the Channel three times whilst flying Spitfires in the Battle of Britain. The third time in, he spoke to the Lord: 'If I get safely out of this, I promise you that I will enjoy every single moment of my life.' He was eighteen at the time. He was seventy-two when I last saw him and there is no doubt he kept his promise to the Lord.

They hunted hares as there were no foxes and they were sensible enough not to import them. Hares run in circles so it is easy to know where you will end – where you started. The horse boxes made a circle and by the time we got back, a spread was on the table and the whisky in the glass. As we moved off I rode behind the field master with everyone else. As we approached the first barbed wire fence, however, the other riders drew back, the better to watch a Pom come to grief. The Pom did not give them the satisfaction: I had been jumping wire for a month and sailed over. It was a wonderful day in the sun.

Returning to Auckland, we started rehearsals for *Colour Scheme*. Filming was to take us to the hot springs of Rotorua and Taupo, with its vast lake and golf course. Golfers have been known to lose their feet as small geysers erupt and boil them down to the ankle. I decided to give the place a wide berth. We moved on to Dargaville where the main street is straight out of an American Western. This is where the Dalmatian immigrants settled to fish and grow their wine.

I thought I had seen nearly every form of horse race, under hunt rules, on the flat, in Hong Kong, which is crooked, point to points in England and a similar sort of thing only livelier in Ireland, but Dargaville was something else! I went to a race meeting which might have taken place in Ireland fifty years earlier. A grassy, hillocky course; a hand-held rope at both start and finish, and a commentary yelled out of a small wooden tower. But some things never change. Cars lined the track, the boots were open and the liquor was flowing. People wandered from car to car, helping themselves to their neighbour's good things to eat and drink. The bookies did a brisk trade as most people reckoned they knew something that no one else did – but then they hadn't taken the course into consideration.

In the first race alone, three jockeys were unseated because their mounts tripped over hillocks. The penultimate race was held up while the starter implored the crowd to provide jockeys for spare horses. A jockey who had already ridden was sporting enough to take his chance a second time, and a young man wearing shorts was apparently prepared to have his calves cut to ribbons by the stirrup leathers in order not to disappoint the punters. Finally, that race was run but the last race was cancelled because there were no entries. I have never been so happy in my life.

In the evening, I went to the theatre in Whangarei. Michael Redgrave was there with a recital, 'Shakespeare's People'. He was not too good with his lines but his power as an actor shone through and saved the night. We met for dinner after the show, joined by David Dodimead and Ros Shanks, and made plans to meet again in Auckland the following week.

When I returned to Auckland, I was told John MacCrea wanted to see me. When I found him in his office, he was looking very pleased with himself.

'I just wanted to wish you a happy birthday.'

'My birthday was five weeks ago.'

'I know, but I just couldn't arrange your present in time.'

The telephone rang. 'It's for you,' said John, handing me the receiver.

'Hello?'

'Hello, darling,' said a very familiar voice. 'They're flying Sarah and me out to be with you for the rest of the time you're there.'

That was a birthday present indeed!

As we'd arranged, I saw Michael Redgrave for supper a few days later and it was then I realised that he had Parkinson's. He was witty, urbane and gentle. I always found him the most courteous of men, and have a wonderful memory of his reading a fairy story to my daughters before they went to bed while we were filming *Goodbye Mr Chips*.

We talked of Micheal Mac Liammoir and *The Importance of Being Oscar* which Micheal and his partner Fred Sadoff had produced in

London and then toured all over the world. It seemed strange to be in a small restaurant in Auckland talking about the Haymarket, the Globe and his *Hamlet* at Stratford. Sadly, that was the last time I saw him.

Vintage Murder was next to be filmed. Plot: the leading lady is killed in the middle of a performance by a magnum of champagne dropping on her head. Alleyn investigates. We were using the theatre in Christchurch; it had just been refurbished and looked a million dollars.

John MacCrea brought Ngaio Marsh down to meet us all, and she and I hit it off at once, and we spent a good deal of time in her cottage in Valley Road. Sally and Sarah arrived via Hollywood, Sidney Poitier and Disneyland. Some shots were needed of the audience and Ngaio and Sarah sat happily in the fourth row of the stalls during the filming.

There was one more film to go, *Death at the Dolphin*, and we returned to Wanganui for the shooting. It was supposed to be London! Ah, well. I have a photograph of the six survivors of all the films: myself, Lilias Munroe, Barbara Darragh, Vic Yarker, Pete Stems and Revell Troy.

One of the other actors, a young man called Peter White, asked me if I thought he would make it in London. Because he was really very good, I replied that I thought he would. Some months later, Sal took a call from a rather hungry, cold Peter White. He was finding the streets of London were not paved with gold. He also had bronchitis and Sal was only too pleased to ask him to stay with us. He was finding it difficult to get an Equity card, and as there was already a Peter White on the Equity books, he was going to have to change his name. I suggested that he took his mother's name, so he became Peter Land.

He was ambitious, personable, charming and hard working. He also had a very good singing voice. It was not long before he was offered a job and got his Equity ticket. He played Freddie in *My Fair Lady* and married our old friend, Gillian Lynne, director and choreographer of the show. Subsequently, he worked at Stratford and appeared in many West End musicals. We are still the very best of friends, and some years later he was to play an important part in my life.

* * *

After filming finished in New Zealand, we had some time off in Napier where, once more, we were wonderfully looked after. Sally and Sarah flew back home and not long after, on 13 September, I flew to Sydney to see Candy. She was then working as the results secretary on the London–Sydney rally which was due back in about ten days' time. I was collected from the airport by Robin Bowering whom I had met in New Zealand and he gave me a quick tour of Bondi Beach. Like so many people, I fell in love with the place and whenever I return there to see the family, I stay in a self-catering apartment in Bondi.

Robin had a small house in Camperdown, which he shared with two girl lodgers; he kindly let me have his bedroom while he slept under the stairs. Was I getting that old? I had not been two days in Australia when I was offered a commercial – back in Auckland. The producers were quite happy to pay the fare and my hotel for a two-day shoot. The money was good and meant that I would be able to leave Candy a lump sum so that she could find her feet more comfortably in her chosen country.

However, when I got back to Sydney, I found a message from her saying that she had had a recurrence of glandular fever and would be arriving home earlier than expected. This did not faze Robin in any way. 'You sleep on the veranda, Candy has the bed.'

And so it was. I fed her on home-made soda bread, stuffed peppers and live yoghurt. Camperdown is a predominantly Bulgarian and Greek quarter and the yoghurt was wonderful. While I left her to rest, I walked all over Sydney. It was my first visit to Australia, and I was loving it.

Robin introduced me to his agent, Liz Mullinare, but she didn't think there would be much future for me in Australia, even though my friend Michael Craig was already well established there. However, her partner Hilary Linstead and I got on very well and Hil thought she might get some work for me on Channel 9. In the event, there was nothing doing but we did eat some splendid lunches.

I was on the steps of the Opera House when the London–Sydney rally arrived, and I am glad to say the results secretary was well enough to be part of the cavalcade. I was hugely proud of her.

Twenty-two years earlier, I had watched her forehead grow and the bridge of her nose appear and here she was starting a new life in a new world. She introduced me to her new boyfriend, Doug Stewart, who was one of the rally drivers. At a guess, I thought he must have been at least two years older than me. When I got to know him better, I found out I was right. He is a dear family friend to this day.

Now it was my turn to do some introducing. I took Candy to lunch with Hilary Linstead in the hope that she could find her a job. Candy went to work at the agency itself; the job didn't last long, but their friendship has. Hilary is my grandson's godmother.

The six months of magic were over and it was time to go home. The direct flight flew overnight and I woke as the dawn was breaking. We flew over Turkey and across the Black Sea. It was cloudless and clear and as we approached Varna I could see the harbour and I could see the house where I was born.

Of course, being home was everything in the world I wanted – except for a looming VAT inspection. However, the system that Angela Halliday had set up, whereby a proportion of all my earnings was paid straight into a special account out of which the VAT bills could be paid, was working well and the inspection went without a hitch. I now tried to persuade the bank to work on a similar system but to no avail. I could only pay my debts via the well-known method of robbing Peter to pay Paul, with poor Peter suffering in consequence.

I had no work so it was time to sign on at the Labour Exchange and look for work. After Kenneth Carton retired, I had moved to Denis Sellinger, who was now my agent and was digging away to little effect. If you go away for six months, everyone you knew seems to have moved, given up the business or died.

However, I was not long without work. Peter Fozzard at BBC Schools commissioned me to write some plays for him, and Richard Imison, Deputy Head of Drama on Radio Four, commissioned a 'Saturday Night Theatre'.

I spent a great deal of the writing time in Ilmington. We had rented a cottage in the village from Tim and Jill Royle. Tim was a director of Hogg Robinson, a vast City firm incorporating travel and insurance agents. At dinner together one night, Sally commented that, as she had been almost forgotten by the acting profession, she had tried to get a job as an ambulance driver, partly for the money and partly for something to do. She had passed all the tests but because she would have to be on call for twenty-four hours when on duty, she would have to pay for someone to look after Sarah and that would negate the purpose of the exercise.

Tim said his company was looking for a driver, and offered her the job. Sally agreed so long as she could have time off if a play were to come up. She slung a light blue Granada Ghia hatchback in and out of the City, to and from the airports, all round the countryside; she enjoyed the people she drove, and when she got to know some of them better, put her left-wing views in their right-wing ears. She was a very good driver and it was good to see her confidence returning.

Of course, the moment she looked confident and assured, she began getting work as an actress. John Glenister, always a great fan of hers, employed her in the television serial *Madame Curie* with Nigel Hawthorne and Jane Lapotaire. It was a good part and she was good in it. The best of it all was that we made friends with Jane and Nigel. As soon as she had finished filming she went back to drive for Hogg Robinson.

Meeting Derek Jacobi one day, I suggested that he would be wonderful in the part of Thomas Mendip in *The Lady's Not for Burning*. He wasn't too sure but was open to persuasion. He suggested the idea to Toby Robertson of Prospect Productions at the Old Vic. Toby thought it a good idea and asked Eileen Atkins to play Jennet Jourdemayne. I was to direct. Kit Fry was delighted that the play would again be seen in London after a thirty-eight-year gap.

Prospect were on tour with *Saint Joan* and we had to rehearse wherever they went – Malvern, Nottingham, Cardiff. Michael Denison and Robert Eddison were in the cast and Robert gave a definitive performance as the chaplain.

Toby had also contracted me to direct *The Rivals* with Tony Quayle for Prospect. He and I saw eye to eye about the best way to do the play, and worked well together. The production of *The Lady's Not for Burning*, however, was not a happy one for me; there were too many undercurrents. Toby had already sacked Frank Hauser from an earlier production. He tried to warn me Toby was not the easiest man to work with.

I had employed Sally Gardner, a young designer, to design the set and costumes. Her father, George Gardner QC, was sometime member for Billericay. Both her mother, Nina Lowry, and her stepfather, Dick Lowry, were judges. The Lowrys were my Sally's oldest and best friends, and kindly countenanced me through the difficult years. We grew in friendship as the years rolled by. Sally Gardner did a superb job on the set and costumes. She later went on to be successful in opera but now writes and illustrates the most ingenious children's books.

After the dress rehearsal I went confidently into the first night. Ah, foolish boy! Toby, incited and applauded by his friends, was relighting my production. I ran up to the control room to find a distraught lighting designer looking haplessly on while Toby relit the set in the middle of the play.

Kit was delighted with the production and that's all that mattered to me. I just pulled a veil over the rest.

The writing was tumbling in but so was work in the theatre. I did *Cousin Vladimir* by David Mercer for the RSC. Jane Howell directed with great intelligence and flair. I'm not sure how good the play was. For television, there was *The Mouse, the Merchant, and the Elephant* by Valerie Georgeson. It was directed by a wonderfully funny Irishman, Jeremy Swan. We were visited by Mrs Thatcher — neither she nor the elephant knew what to make of one another.

My writing work was dominated by scripts for children's radio, 'Listening and Writing', but an idea I had put to Anne Head, a BBC Television producer, was commissioned and it was something which gave me immense pleasure.

I had been commissioned to write the play at the end of 1978 but the excitement came on 15 May. Anne Head rang me to say that *The Fatal Spring* had gone through all the bureaucratic hoops and been given the go-ahead for production. To crown a memorable day I was opening in *Measure for Measure* directed by Peter Gill at the Riverside Studios.

The Fatal Spring was a play about three poets who fought in the First World War: Siegfried Sassoon, Wilfred Owen and Robert Graves. Graves and Sassoon were both in the Royal Welch Fusiliers. Sassoon was exceptionally brave and should have been awarded the VC; he had already won his MC. The fighting sickened him. He turned against the war, the generals and the establishment waging it. He published his views, spurred on by Bertrand Russell, and was about to be court-martialled when Graves used influence to have him sent to Craiglockhart, the sanatorium in Scotland for officers suffering from shell shock, run by Dr Rivers and Dr Brock. Alan Seymore was a kindly and erudite script editor; the play was directed by Michael Darlow, who was shortly to have a great influence on my life. I suggested my friend Charles Dance for the part of Sassoon. It led him directly to *The Jewel in the Crown* and the rest is history. The play won the United Nations Media Peace Price, Award of Merit which, I have to say, chuffed me enormously.

Michael Darlow was forming a company to make programmes for the newly formed Channel Four and asked me to join as a writer. I thought it a great compliment. There were too many of us, about twenty-six in all, resulting in an awful lot of talk and little action. However, John Pett made a beautiful film about his childhood in Somerset.

Partners in Production commissioned me to write and produce an in-house corporate video for English China Clays, which John Pett directed. The research took me to the USA. First was Baltimore: the harbour and waterfront of that city must be as beautiful as anything in the world. Then we travelled to Atlanta and some miles out of the city is a small village in the middle of clay quarries. I was in the South and I have to tell you that if you think that the great American democracy has achieved racial harmony, you are wrong.

Savannah, I could have stayed for ever in Savannah. The whites are Irish, there's a Fitz this, a Fitz that, and a Fitz the other. There is Guinness on tap in all the bars but, most remarkably, it is one of the biggest Madeira-drinking cities in the world. I stayed in a wonderful hotel, where I was able to do the rewrites on a play I was writing for Capitol Radio, *Just a Hunch*, in which the part of Elena was played immaculately by that great actress, Miriam Karlin.

Savannah also boasted one of the best restaurants I have ever eaten in – the Pink House.

English China Clays took me to Australia where I had a wonderful time with my two daughters, Candy and Charlie. From there to Finland to see the trees speeding down the rivers to the sawmills, and then to the paper mills. And finally, we went to Denmark and Sweden. The round trip covering half the world took ten days.

While researching *The Fatal Spring*, I had discovered that the troops that General Gage sent out to find a cache of arms in Concord after the Boston tea party were mostly Welch Fusiliers. I also found that, because of a series of mishaps, misunderstandings and sheer stupidity on the part of the English, the first shot fired in the war of American Independence was fired on that march in Lexington. Richard Imison commissioned me to write a play about it. At first it was called *The Way to Concord* but it was transmitted as *The Marches of Wales*.

I was commissioned to write seven plays for schools and three for radio. I would hide myself in Ilmington to write, where I gathered inspiration from the Cotswold escarpment – and my friends. The Organs, whom I had now known for over thirty years, held open house, and their son Richard always had a horse for me to ride.

I landed a part in *Triangle*, a desperate television series set on the Harwich-Esbjerg ferry but, what with that, the writing and an episode of *The Gentle Touch*, the finances were slowly getting better.

At the birth of each child, I had taken out a small insurance policy in their name to mature at eighteen. Charlie wanted to take it early so that she could go out to Australia to see Candy. Having seen her there looking so happy, I had a sinking feeling that she too would settle in Sydney. I was right: she came back from her holiday just before Christmas 1979, saying she wanted to live there permanently. She went to Australia the following February and, like Candy, became an Australian citizen. Of the other daughters: Tessa was doing her cookery course in Switzerland and Ellie had come to live with us and do her 'A' levels at a college in Bloomsbury. So, three girls abroad and that is virtually how it has remained to this day – two in Australia and Tessa in France.

Sally and I were in London and a very lonely Julia was in Rousham. Her brother, Rag, ever generous, paid for her to visit the girls in Australia. I fetched her from Rousham to stay with us in London before she flew. A funny family with many misunderstandings that only time could heal but with a great deal of love about.

22

NEIL ZEIGER WAS PRODUCING *IMAGINARY FRIENDS*, A PLAY FOR THE BBC STARRING PETER USTINOV AND LILLI PALMER. Peter didn't like the script and demanded rewrites. Michael Darlow was to direct and suggested that I did the writing. As always it was a rushed job, hardly time to read the play let alone rewrite. I had some ideas and jotted them down; Neil and Michael were happy, now the task was to sell them to Peter.

Michael and I flew over to Paris and over dinner I explained to Peter what I wanted to do. He was delighted with the concepts for the changes but, naturally, he wanted to see the finished script first. Ilmington beckoned and off I went for the inside of a week and did the work. The news from Paris was good and the production got under way.

Peter Ustinov must have decided I was a competent writer since he later commissioned me to adapt his book *Krummnagle* for television.

In the meantime, we went into a third series of *Triangle*. The North Sea is not a pleasant place and can sometimes be very rough. On two occasions, the ferry had to stand out at sea until the weather had blown itself out. There was a considerable bonus, however: Joan Greenwood was in the series. We had first met when Julia designed the costumes for *Father Brown* and had been firm friends ever since. I was lucky to have my old chums Michael Craig and Larry Lamb in the series. We managed to keep each other sane as we lurched backwards and forwards across the North Sea.

I did the film *Hopscotch* with Walter Matthau; Ronnie Neame directed and Arthur Ibbetson did the lighting – the same Arthur who had run the hundred yards with Robert Shaw. Sam Waterson was one of the protagonists, a man of gentle manners and great talent. Walter Matthau had always been one of my favourite actors and, luckily, all my scenes were with him. We sat in the Salisbury pub and instead of putting in our stand-ins we sat and talked while Arthur lit the scene. Walter's humour could not be found anywhere but in America. I was laughing till the tears were running down my cheeks – and that at the story of his heart bypass!

In November 1982, Sally's mother was knocked down crossing the road; she died in the ambulance. The plan had been to rent a bungalow in West Wittering, both so we could be near her over Christmas and so I could adapt *Krummnagle* for Peter Ustinov. In fact, we did spend Christmas there – doing the round of the coroner's court, the funeral parlour and the crematorium. Sally's brother John and his wife Janet came down to help with all the necessary arrangements. Sally's mother left her some money and for the first time we really did see the light at the end of the tunnel.

I had a new bank manager to whom I would have to try and explain the matter of my complicated finances in all their boring detail. Bob Farrant sat across the desk with a large grey folder of my sins and omissions open in front of him. I tried him with my oft-repeated idea of repaying my loans via the bank taking a regular percentage of my income.

'I know what you owe this bank,' he said, 'but what exactly do you owe altogether?'

I told him.

'If I give you a loan account that would clear those debts and consolidate everything in this bank, you could repay us by our taking a percentage of your earnings.'

Glory be! It was the beginning of a sensible world.

Things were moving very quickly. The Grosvenor Estate renewed our lease on the house in Hasker Street, with permission to reassign. It had always been too small for us so we sold it and were able to get a mortgage on a bigger house in Baron's Court. Poor Sally had to do the move to Margravine Gardens as I had been offered a part in *Hart to Hart* in Athens and Rhodes and it seemed churlish to say no.

Uncle George, my mother's brother, died in Fortrose and my mother asked me to go to the funeral. Mother had long given up Fortrose herself, and was now living with my brother Pat and his son, Christopher, in London. Pat had married in Singapore but, unfortunately, it hadn't lasted and Pat and his son had returned to England. I was appalled at what I found. George's wife, my Aunt Avie, who had inherited so much from the Irish property dealer, Uncle Fraser, had bought and sold houses at a time when everyone was making money in the property market; Avie managed to lose the lot. She had gone from The Deanery, a splendid house in Fortrose, to a fisherman's cottage on the sea front. Avie was beside herself with grief over George's death and had tried to commit suicide by walking into the sea.

Avie needed to move back to Ireland. A little house was found and I went over to supervise Avie moving in with her dog. Everything had to go like clockwork since I had to get home by Sunday because on the Monday I had to be in Birmingham to film *Dead Head*, directed by Rob Walker and with a young Simon Callow in the cast. That was accomplished – well, give or take a long and hairy journey.

We had left Waterford bright and early in gale-force winds; the driving was difficult and slow. We were nearly at Duncormick when a white Garda van approached us, driving very slowly in the middle of the road. I pulled over and stopped. When the policeman drew level he opened his window about two inches, 'There's cats on the road. Close your windows.' With that he drove off. Our windows were shut; the wind was too strong to have them open. We drove on and first we saw the circus transport lying in the ditch and then we saw the cats. A pride of lions was stomping about in a front garden, watched by a frightened face peering out of the window of the bungalow. One of the lions jumped over the garden wall and walked up the road towards us. I drove slowly on and passed it within inches. 'I had no idea they were so large,' said Sally.

We got to Rosslare and boarded the ferry. It was obviously going to be a very rough crossing. It was not long before we got the announcement that the boat couldn't get out of the harbour because of the conditions and there we stayed for nearly ten hours. They couldn't open the bar because they are only licensed when sailing. The food was almost inedible and soon ran out. I just managed to catch the nine o'clock train to Birmingham. I had been given a first-class ticket so I settled myself in the carriage, prepared to sleep all the way. No such luck!

The irrepressible Miriam Margolyes popped her head round the carriage door and decided to join me. Her lively conversation kept me entertained all the way from London to Birmingham. Our fellow passengers seemed to show no interest and stayed hidden behind their newspapers. But as we left the train at New Street one man turned to us and said: 'Thank you for a most enjoyable and informative journey.' Nothing on *Dead Head* could equal the joy of that journey.

Work was plentiful. I did a few happy episodes of *Robin of Sherwood* which sent me to Bristol for a time; Michael Craig was in them too so we had a great time. A play I had written, *Sister, Dear Sister*, was produced by Jane Morgan for 'Saturday Night Theatre'. I had the enormous pleasure of working with Lenny Henry on *Coast to Coast* which was directed by Sandy Johnson.

This led to Lenny asking me to do a sketch with him in support of Actors Against Apartheid at the Donmar. I was to play a theatrical agent trying to persuade his client that there was no reason for him not to take a job in South Africa. Lenny had written a very funny but hard-hitting script. We were on after Harry Belafonte who had made a powerful and moving speech. There was dead silence and we could sense considerable antagonism as we started the sketch. Luckily, somebody saw the joke and began to laugh, and we were all right after that.

After the show Harry Belafonte said, 'I don't know if you two were very brave or just foolhardy. Brave, I guess.'

It wasn't until afterwards that I realised we could have been torn to pieces.

Roger Davis of Interlink asked me to write and direct a corporate film for a national safety organisation. It made me think seriously that perhaps that was the direction my life should take. I was thoroughly enjoying the work I did for Roger and that, with my writing – and a fair wind – might mean I wouldn't have to act again. The older girls were on their own feet – in 1983 Ellie had met and married Craig Sherwood, road manager for Depeche Mode and Siouxsie and the Banshees – and Sarah was the only one still at school.

Life doesn't work out like that. HTV Bristol offered me a part in *The Canterville Ghost*, starring John Gielgud. Work on this film conjures up a fond memory of John. The scene is a lunch party for thirty people, a charger is set on the table and when the lid is lifted, the ghost's head is lying there, nestling in a bed of lettuce, tomato and cucumber. John was sitting under the table with his head stuck through a hole, talking of things theatrical as though he was sitting by his own fireside.

'I don't want to go scrambling in and out of here while they reset. Stay and talk to me,' he said. And so we talked of cabbages and kings, of *Forty Years On* and Alan Bennett, and of the need for actors to constantly reinvent themselves. 'Of course, some, like Ralph [Richardson], are so brilliantly invented in the first place they don't have to bother. Makes you sick.'

I was working on yet another corporate script which I was writing for Roger Davis when I got a call from my agent telling me that Mary McMurray wanted to see me about playing a part in a Miss Marple. I was contracted to direct the corporate video so I wasn't at all sure I would be able to do *At Bertram's Hotel*. However, I went along to see Mary who entirely won my heart by saying she thought I would have to have my hair greyed at the sides as I looked far too young. We discussed dates and, praise be, they fitted so she let me have the script to see what I thought of the part. The wonderful thing about Mary McMurray is that she likes and respects actors; so many directors are either frightened of them or have no time for them.

It was a splendid part and I wanted to work with Joan Hickson again. Joan and I had worked together in both films and television on and off since 1956. I accepted the part and found myself working in the happiest of companies. Joan and I sailed into our friendship where we had left it which I believe was on a laugh, because it was on a laugh that we picked it up.

Mary wanted me to play the part with some sort of country accent. I decided on a West Country burr and presented it to her for her approval. We had enormous pleasure making the episode. Mary is not only a talented film director but also a civilised one and the four weeks of filming sped past.

I was working away on another script for Roger when Denis Sellinger telephoned to say that Southern TV was sending round a script of Ruth Rendell's *Wolf to the Slaughter*. I read it with great pleasure; the novel had been adapted by Clive Exton and was being produced and directed by John Davies. I told Sally that I really thought I must do it, as it was a smashing part. I confess I had never heard of nor read any of Ruth Rendell's work at this time. It was an offer: John didn't want to meet me except to renew our acquaintance.

It came as a slight shock to hear they were thinking it might run into a series. I booked into Greyshots Health Farm for five days and took ten novels by Ruth Rendell with me. At the end of my time there, I had read all the books and knew that it was going to be a very successful series if it were made. I had a final talk with Sally – and together we agreed I should accept. The comforting difference was that I had, by this time, whittled down my debts to manageable proportions which is why Sally and I were able to consider whether I should take the part or not. It was a decision I was never to regret.

Some time later, I asked John Davies why he had cast me so confidently. Apparently he had been walking through the cutting rooms at the BBC in Ealing and had heard my voice in the Miss Marple which Mary was editing. John had asked her which actor was playing the part of the inspector. She told him and, without further hesitation, he cast me as Chief Inspector Wexford.

On such slight threads hang our opportunities.

I was contracted for the one title, *Wolf to the Slaughter*, with the producer's right to exercise an option on another three. There was a long pause between the showing of the first episode and the go-ahead for the other three. *Wolf to the Slaughter* was made in the summer of 1987 and the series proper didn't really start until the spring of 1988. Louie Ramsay was chosen to play Wexford's wife, Dora, and Christopher Ravenscroft got the job as Reg Wexford's sidekick, D/I Burden; his wife was to be played by Ann Penfold.

Filming was to take place in Hampshire, in and around Romsey. In March 1987, we rented Tiled Cottage from the Barker Mill Estate, just north of Southampton which Sally had heard about through Chris Gwyn Evans with whom she had grown up and whose husband, also called Chris, was estate manager. When he drove Sally through the Nursling Industrial Estate, she wondered what on earth he was taking her to.

Through the industrial estate, under the railway bridge, turn left and suddenly one is in a simply enchanting piece of England. A lane with a farm, farm cottages, Nursling Manor, the twelfth-century church of St Boniface and, right at the end of the lane, Tiled Cottage. It had a small kitchen and study, and a long living/dining-room with a view looking out over the River Test. There were three bedrooms and a bathroom upstairs. We thought we would only be there while *Wolf to the Slaughter* was being made.

The church was fifty yards away from the cottage and we worshipped there every Sunday. The congregation had to come miles as the village and the church had been separated by the M27. However, attracted by the good Reverend Gardiner, come they did, mostly aged between forty and ninety, although sometimes children came too.

Wolf to the Slaughter was not the best of the Wexfords and it was filmed on tape. Two cameras, both shooting the scene from different angles. It was a quick way to work but not a way that produced the best results. However, it was certainly well received and we knew a couple of months later that we would be making a series based on the Wexford books.

Sally and I decided that we wanted to have our main home in the country, preferably in Ilmington where we had been so happy. While waiting for the decision about the Wexford series, therefore, we sold the house in Baron's Court and bought a small house in Ealing, just as a *pied-à-terre*. It was at the time of fast-rising house prices and the profit from the sale wiped out all our debts. Alleluia!

The Ealing house needed a great deal of work done to it but we found a good builder – there are some – and he started on the job. We put the Baron's Court furniture into store and moved into Tiled

Cottage. We negotiated a renewable six-month let for the cottage beside the River Test, reckoning to live there while work was done in Ealing and I was filming the Wexford.

When Wexford turned into Wexfords, we continued to live at Tiled Cottage. We never did get to live in Ilmington again.

At about this time, I was offered a film, *For Queen and Country*, with Denzel Washington which slotted in nicely while we waited to hear about the Wexford series. Denzel was as talented and charming as our locations were ghastly. On one occasion we were playing a scene sitting in a car outside a high-rise complex in Camberwell. A ball-bearing dropped from the top storey on to the roof of the car, smashed through the roof, on to the gear stick and out through the floor. The producers wisely decided to switch a fire scene to the car park at Wembley Stadium. I think we would all have been burned alive if we had tried to film it in Camberwell.

I was commissioned by Boxtree to write a cookery book. The title was to be *A Cook for All Seasons*. What with that and writing and directing a corporate for Roger Davis I had enough to do.

At the beginning of 1988, I was told by Graham Benson that there would be a series. Luckily, we were going to be able to get the same cast of regulars together. We had worked so well together on *Wolf to the Slaughter* that it would have been a shame if anyone had dropped out. Graham Benson had become head of drama at TVS and was therefore the executive producer on the Wexfords. I don't know what happened but John Davies was not going to be directing or producing any more of the series. This left a bit of a gap in our administrative structure.

I was having lunch with Neil Zeiger in Beotys and he was telling me that the company he had set up was not going that well and that one of his partners had pulled out. I told him about John Davies going and asked him if he would be prepared to consider working on the Wexfords. He didn't have to give it a second's thought. I pointed out that it was not in my gift and that all I could do was to telephone Graham.

I did this from the restaurant. It was a fortuitous call because the producer he had been trying to persuade had just called him to say that he had taken another job. By the time Neil got back to his office, there was a message for him from Graham. It was the start of a partnership that was to last for eleven years.

Before filming started for the next Wexford, I had a few happy but mud-encrusted days in Wales where the BBC had built trenches and dug-outs for their production of *Journey's End*. It might have been cold and wet but it was made uplifting by the splendid director, Michael Simpson, and a number of memorable performances from Jeremy Northam, Clive Swift, Edward Petherbridge and Timothy Spall. We won an award from a film festival for *Journey's End*. The jury decided that they would give the Best Actor Award to the whole cast since they didn't want to single anyone out of such cohesive ensemble playing.

Our life seemed to be settled for a moment. There was money in the bank. The work on the Ealing house was going ahead and the Wexfords were set fair to being a success. The only fly in the ointment was that Sally was getting considerable trouble with her lower back, sometimes finding it almost too painful to walk. A good friend, Michael Power, was also our osteopath. Sally would quite often displace her sacroiliac joint at the base of her spine, and speed to Michael to have it put back. She took Michael's advice and went to our new doctor in Ealing, who swiftly put her mind to rest. 'Take some Nurofen. A woman of your age must expect some backache.'

Mary McMurray directed *A Guilty Thing Surprised*, the second Wexford, which we started work on at the end of January 1988. She brought with her a wonderful sense of humour which, in part, led to the childish concept of my asking the prop department to make me a red herring. This weird piece of wood would appear on all sorts of sombre occasions to lighten the atmosphere. It has had several airings on Denis Norden's *It'll Be All Right on the Night*.

We were always lucky with our casts and crews. Going to work was like going out for a party. Christopher Ravenscroft and I did not have one cross word in all the years we worked together. Although she only came down for a couple of days on each shoot, it was always a pleasure to see Louie Ramsay, aka Dora Wexford. She did admit to being quite startled when approached by a complete stranger in

Brent Cross and told that she was the young woman's mother. 'George Baker's my father, so that makes you my television mother!' said my daughter Ellie who had approached her.

Brent Cross has not always been the luckiest of places for Louie. A woman at a check-out turned and looked at her for some time before saying, 'I know you. You play "doormat Dora" in that telly series.'

John Burgess, who played Dr Crocker, and I had worked together on a number of shows and were delighted to be doing so again. Ken Kitson, Sasha Mitchell and Colin Campbell, playing the on-going characters of Sergeants Martin, Malahyde and Willoughby, made up a very happy family. Our crews, which moved from story to story, were part of the family, too, and the camaraderie was palpable.

We were also very lucky with our guest actors – Tom Wilkinson, Jane Horrocks, Dorothy Tutin, Barbara Leigh-Hunt, Annette Crosbie, Peter Egan, Jane Lapotaire, Sean Pertwee, Peter Capaldi and many, many more fine actors.

Of all the work I have ever done in my life, I believe playing Reg Wexford has been the most satisfying and, of course, that is entirely due to his creator, Ruth Rendell. I was asked to present her with the prestigious Gold Dagger Award by the Crime Writers Association for her book *King Solomon's Carpet*. I had prepared my speech carefully and was greatly thrown when the host said, 'We're running very late. Could you make it very short?'

'How short?'

'Thirty seconds.'

So I said: 'It is wonderful and reassuring to know that when you ring up your creator, she will answer. It is my great pleasure to present Ruth Rendell with the Gold Dagger Award.'

Ruth and Don Rendell became great friends. I believe I did everything I could to ensure that her stories reached the screen as she had written them. They came down to Romsey on every shoot, and Neil Zeiger always arranged a dinner for them with the director and some of the cast. The following night they would come and eat with us at Tiled Cottage. Ruth is a vegetarian and it was a great pleasure for me to invent and cook vegetable meals for her that weren't nut cutlets. Ruth would take off her shoes, make herself at home and laugh. There is nothing grander than her deep, infectious laugh; it echoes through the room and breathes vivacity.

From my point of view as an actor what was particularly interesting was the subtle way Ruth confronted Wexford with the necessity of re-evaluating his moral and philosophic certainties in every book.

Did he convict the wrong man and send him to prison?

Is he a racist?

Is he getting too old for the job?

Yes, he is made to question himself which makes the part attractive to the actor and compulsive viewing for the audience.

The town of Romsey opened its heart to the series, the actors, the crew and, in particular, to Sally and me. We became part of the town and I have never felt so welcome. I presented the Romsey Ladies Darts League with their trophies for ten years and was very flattered to be asked back year after year. I became a life member of the Romsey Show; it is held on the first Saturday in September and I urge anyone interested in the countryside to go. I became involved with many of the local charities and was able to feel something that is virtually impossible for an itinerant actor to feel – I was contributing to the community.

In between the two Wexfords, *Shake Hands for Ever* and *No Crying He Makes*, I did the first series of *No Job for a Lady*. I had known John Howard Davies, the producer, since he was a teenager but we had never worked together, and here was the opportunity. Penelope Keith and I had worked together years ago in *Kate*, Mark Kingston was an old friend from the Old Vic days, and I made two new friends, Garfield Morgan and Paul Young.

I can't pretend that I enjoy playing to an invited audience. The rehearsals were a joy and the night of the show an agony of nerves and tension.

The cookery book was out and I was rushing about signing copies in Romsey, Winchester and all points north to Liverpool and Glasgow. I didn't like being away from home for long, however, because Sally's back was becoming more and more painful. Visiting Michael, our osteopath, one day for the nth time, he said to her, 'There's nothing out of place in your back, Sal. You must get another opinion.'

23

THE WEXFORD SERIES WAS BECOMING A GREAT SUCCESS. I was suddenly in demand for newspaper articles. My opinion, which had never been valued before, was being sought on many subjects, most of them quite out of my field. I was approached by John Rogers, a professional fund-raiser, who asked if I would join the committee which was raising money for an MRI scanner for Southampton General Hospital. It became a crusade. Of all the giving, two specific efforts live in my memory.

The first was the Romsey Community School whose headmaster, Dr Richard Skinner, was the inspiration behind the pupils and teachers who raised an astonishing £7,000 in a year towards the scanner appeal. The other was an excellent community effort called 'Beating the Bounds'. A large number of teams of eight was made up and these walked, ran, rode, cycled to and from points marking the boundaries of the town and finally pulled a float to the square outside the abbey. There was a cup for the best float and a cup for the most money raised by a team. But mainly it inspired a community spirit and was a hugely enjoyable day.

We raised the necessary £2.5 million in eighteen months. I can't explain the satisfaction I personally had from knowing I had played a small part in such a worthwhile project.

But life never seems to be content to allow good fortune to run smoothly.

The death of my Uncle George and her move from Scotland had greatly affected Aunt Avie. She needed me to communicate with her constantly; I had to phone her every evening. If ever I had a long weekend (from Friday to Tuesday morning) I would leap into the car and drive to Waterford. I would get up at the crack of dawn and start the five-hour drive to Fishguard, to catch the ferry which arrived in Rosslare in the afternoon. Then on to Waterford to sort out her latest escapade. Sometimes Sally would come with me but more often than not I was on my own.

I would take my aunt for drives; go into town to shop. I would spend hours listening to music with her, and reliving old memories. Sometimes she would sing; her voice was still true and strong. I would cook meals in the hope that she would eat and prepare food that could be frozen. She stopped taking it out of the freezer. Aunt Avie was old and becoming ill; like many old people she had virtually stopped eating.

Then came the time when Avie was ill enough to have to go to hospital but refused point blank to do so. The doctor rang me up and asked me to go over and see if I could talk her into it. Avie cried a good deal at the prospect of leaving home, but when the ambulance arrived, she dried her tears, wiped her eyes and greeted the ambulance men like long-lost friends. I saw her into her ward and promised I would return the next day before driving back to Romsey. When I went in the next morning as promised, I took with me the sampler she had made years before of a W. B. Yeats poem; wherever she had lived, it had hung above her bed:

Had I the heavens' embroidered cloths,
Enwrought with golden and silver light,
The blue and the dim and the dark cloths
Of night and light and the half-light,
I would spread the cloths under your feet:
But I, being poor, have only my dreams;
I have spread my dreams under your feet;
Tread softly because you tread on my dreams.

One evening when I rang the ward, the sister said, 'Wait while I take her the phone. Now, can you hear her?' Avie was singing 'Down by the Salley Gardens'. I learned she had been entertaining the ward and been singing requests for them since she had been admitted.

Avie died of malnutrition three weeks later. It was a merciful death and, thank God, not too prolonged. She faced up to the last weeks with great courage but it was not an easy passing.

She lay in the chapel of rest and we said our farewells to her there before we all went to the cathedral for the funeral service. There was no way my mother could make the journey over. Her comment at the death of her old sparring partner was, 'Ah well, George, at least it was merciful.' The wake at Dooly's was good fun, everything Avie would have wanted, especially the fact that Brian McGrath was there. He was an Irish actor who had been in *At Bertram's Hotel*. His parents lived in Wexford and whenever he visited them he went to see Avie. He was a kind man and grew fond of her; he was right to do so, she was a good woman.

I had to return to England to finish *No More Dying* but we then went back to Ireland to clear the house and put it up for sale. I was over there when my daughter Ellie rang to tell me that her mother, my first wife, Julia, had tripped and fallen down the stairs and had broken her neck, dying instantly. A friend of Charlie's from Sydney had been staying at the cottage and found her. Julia's drinking had escalated over the years and this was a kinder end than liver failure. She was sixty-three.

Julia's funeral was on 19 August 1989 in Rousham village church. Candy and the other girls wanted me to read one of Julia's favourite poems by Shelley. I suggested that it was a little unorthodox to have an ex-husband reading at the funeral, or even attending, but it's what they wanted. I was even more surprised when, before the service, Candy took Sally down to the end of the garden and read her the eulogy she had written for her mother.

'Now, Sal, you'd better sit up at the front with me because if I break down I'm going to hand it to you and you can finish the reading.'

A great many people thought the whole business of us being there very odd but I was glad we were. Julia and I had remained friends and you can't have four daughters without loving their mother very much.

And I'm glad that my first four daughters loved Sal so much.

While at Oxford, Sarah had gone out to Rousham to see Julia on a regular basis. She would cook meals for Ju and they would talk about their love of Jane Austen into the small hours. I got an ecstatic phone call from Julia one day to tell me that she thought Sarah was the best of all our daughters. A little farfetched but I realised that the love of Jane Austen has a compelling effect on the emotions. Julia left all her Folio Society Jane Austens to Sarah in her will, and Candy mentioned their friendship in her eulogy, which was big-hearted of her.

Tess and I got quite drunk afterwards, and took all the flowers that had decorated the house up to the grave and stood there, sobbing into our whisky.

I had a couple of days off before starting the next Wexford, *The Veiled One*, so I took the opportunity of going to see my mother in London. She had not been well enough to come to Julia's funeral. The nice thing is that Julia and my mother had always remained close. Brother Pat, with whom she was still living, was away so I took her in some fish and cooked it for her lunch. She looked very frail and tired, but she was of the rallying kind and we had a few good laughs. It was a desperately hot August day and I sat beside her with an old fan Frank or Pat had brought back from Singapore and acted as her punkah-wallah.

'Did I do well?' she asked me.

'You did better than that, you did wonderfully.'

'But, did I do well?'

'Yes, darling, you did well.'

Candy had always been very close to her grandmother and I am so sorry that she went back to Sydney on 27 August because her grandmother died the following day. If I could, I would wish my mother's death on all human beings.

It was still and hot and she was sitting by the open window when Pat came in from work.

'Are you all right, Mummy?'

'Yes, thanks, just a little tired.'

'Would you like to change your blouse for something cooler, or would you like a drink perhaps?'

'I'll have a drink, thank you. A little white wine.'

Pat brought it to her and she took and raised it to her lips. It never got there. She stopped with it halfway to her mouth.

'Are you all right, Mummy?'

'Just a little tired, darling,' she said and died.

Mummy was buried in Ealing on 2 September. The date had an attendant difficulty, as Sarah was being bridesmaid to her great friend. We did the funeral in the morning and got ourselves over to Clapham Common for the wedding in the afternoon. Mother would have liked that.

The show had to go on. *A Sleeping Life*, with Bill Hays directing, took us to Honfleur so that Reg Wexford could talk to a French colleague about the case he was solving. I seem to remember the scene entailed eating a great many oysters and drinking quantities of Chablis.

Sally came with us although her back was very bad and hurting a great deal. She had had X-rays and scans but nothing had shown up. She was now looking for alternative medicine to provide her with a clue. Blood clinics, allergists and faith healers were all visited to no avail.

Sally had always been fascinated by Velázquez's paintings of buffoons and dwarfs and, in particular, she liked the kindly face of 'Aesop'. A major Velázquez exhibition was showing at the Prado and we had received an invitation from Cuz Hardee to visit them in Mijas. As the closing months of 1989 had been hectic and the opening months of 1990 saw me writing and directing a corporate video with all the attendant annoyances of 'the client', and as Sally's back was giving her more and more pain, we decided to fly to Madrid on 8 February, hire a car and, after seeing the exhibition, head on side roads over the mountains to Mijas.

When we arrived at Madrid airport, Sal was in such pain that I suggested we flew straight back to England. She was adamant, however, that it was the flight and sitting in one position that had exacerbated the pain. We made our way to the apartment which was old-fashioned and comfortably run down but well-equipped and very clean. I poured her a scotch and sat her on the bed, making her comfortable with pillows and cushions banked up behind her.

We went out to dinner, eating earlier than is the Spanish custom so were alone in the restaurant and very happy for that. By the time we got back to the apartment, Sal was close to exhaustion. I propped her up on the pillows again and she went to sleep.

The Friday morning was bright and cold and inviting. Having been out for an early walk and seen the queues for the Velázquez exhibition already forming, I told Sal that I thought we should get back to the Prado as quickly as possible. She found it difficult to walk and would often rest on one of the benches that line the Madrid streets. I went on ahead and joined the queue. She found herself a seat opposite the front entrance and watched my progress in the queue, joining me just before I bought the tickets.

We shuffled past 'The Surrender of Breda', 'The Spinners', and 'The Maids of Honour' and found 'Aesop'. Sal was tired and couldn't stand any longer but urged me to go and see the rest of the exhibition while she sat near 'Aesop' and waited for me. I wanted to see the Goyas – the Maja nude and Maja clothed, and some of the war pictures – but I got back to Sal as quickly as possible. On our way through the ground floor to the exit we passed the Elder Breughel's 'Triumph of Death'.

We sat in the gardens until she felt comfortable enough to walk back to the apartment. There, we discussed our trip to Mijas, which would take us over the mountains on very minor roads and which we had planned to do before leaving Nursling. I suggested we change our plan and drive down the motorway but Sally wouldn't hear of it.

The next day we set off on the twisting journey to Mijas. It took everything out of Sal and she had to retire to bed where she remained for most of our stay with the Hardees. We returned from Spain on 19 February.

We started to film the next Wexford, *The Best Man to Die*, on 1 March. It was good to be back at work. Chris Ravenscroft was very solicitous and Herbie Wise a pillar of support.

About three weeks later, on Sunday 18 March, we were going across to church. It had been raining and there was a puddle outside the house. Sal found she couldn't make her legs step over it. We didn't go to church, we went back into the cottage and sat down to wonder what was happening to us. The next day she was due to drive up to London with Sarah to see Dr Sherwood in Harley Street so we held on to the hope that he would tell us what was wrong. Throughout that day, her condition got worse and worse. She was only able to walk very slowly and in great pain.

Sarah had been going up to London on her way to visit Amy, her great friend in Spain, but felt she should cancel her trip. Sally, however, was determined that everything should continue as arranged.

The next morning I kissed the girls goodbye and went to the *Best Man* set. The set was in the ward of the disused maternity wing, which was now housed in another part of the Southampton General Hospital and we were due to be filming there for four days. There were some good strong scenes to be played but I can't pretend I wasn't hugely worried about Sally. Barbara Leigh-Hunt, with whom I had worked at the Old Vic, was in the cast and it was a great relief to have an old friend in whom I could confide.

Not that there was much to tell her. In all the weeks of visiting doctors, they had found nothing. There was nothing much she could say to me but she was wonderfully sympathetic. What are old friends for but sounding boards?

We worked late but weren't able to get the scene in the can that night. When I got home at about eight, I found a message to ring Sal at the Ealing house. She told me that Dr Sherwood had taken one look at her and had rung up Mr Lange, a neurologist, who had been able to see Sal straight away. He too had acted with great speed. He had made an appointment for her at a private MRI scanner in Marylebone High Street the next morning at 8 o'clock.

When I rang a little later, Sal sounded very strong, very positive – but then Sarah was in the room with her. When I rang her to say goodnight, she was in bed and feeling very vulnerable. If only we could have been together. I longed to put my arms around her and give what comfort I could.

She had the scan next morning and we had a terrible twenty-four-hour wait before she could see Dr Lange again. Again, Sarah wanted to cancel her trip to Spain, but Sal persuaded her that all would be well and that she was to go.

The next morning, Wednesday 21 March, Sal went to see Dr Lange. He was kindly and direct with her. She had a tumour on her spine; he was quite certain it was benign but he wanted to take her straight into Charing Cross Hospital and operate. Sal told him she would rather be in a hospital near me. At first, he was terrified that I would be somewhere in the wilds and was much relieved when she told him I was working in Southampton especially since one of his close colleagues, John Garfield, was the neurosurgeon in Southampton General Hospital. Within minutes, an appointment was made to see John Garfield at 11.30 the next morning.

When I got home to Tiled Cottage that evening, she was sitting quietly in the living-room.

'How did you get home?' I asked.

'I drove, of course.'

'But you can't use your legs.'

'My feet are all right. I can drive.'

I was horrified; it had been a very dangerous thing to do. Anyway, there she was safe, but not sound. We had a great deal to think about. We had a couple of large scotches and toasted each other – God knows why; we had little to celebrate. I went into the kitchen to start cooking the supper. There was a hatchway through to the kitchen from the living-room, and Sally leaned on the dresser in the living-room and we talked while I worked at the worktop in the kitchen. I was making bisque because we had invited Bar Leigh-Hunt to dinner the next night. We were going to have a taste of it for supper. I had already made the meat loaf so it was just a question of vegetables. Every now and again Sally came into the kitchen or I would go through to her and we would have a silent hug. All I could do was to put my hands on her head in token of a hug. Putting my arms around her hurt her back.

We spoke to Sarah and reassured her that her mother was quite comfortable.

We rang Sally's brother, John, and told him what was happening. We also rang one or two other very close friends. There was nothing to panic about, we said, and we would, of course, let them know the outcome of the consultation but we were sure there was nothing to worry about. That was the gist of the message, and that's what we held on to in our hearts.

I had to help her up to bed that night as her paralysis was getting worse. I had to help her undress and wash. It was the beginning of my job as a carer. I would prop up the pillows behind her because she could not sleep in any other position. She leaned on my shoulder and wept, and through her sobs she said, 'We must never, ever ask, Why us?' It was so frustrating not to be able to hold her in my arms, but it was too painful for her.

I got up early the next morning and went for my usual walk along the river, taking the pages of script that we were working on that day. I always learned my part well ahead of time and my early morning walk was a wonderful way of revising. The first shots of the day were to complete the unfinished scene with Bar Leigh-Hunt; this was to be followed by some small scenes in the hospital corridor with Julia Ormerod. I had met her for the first time a few days before and we had played a scene together; there was no doubt she was every inch Hollywood material. There were also to be two scenes with Louie; Dora Wexford was in hospital for a hysterectomy. All pretty straightforward.

I walked along the bank of the Test, looking at the great gathering of swans in a field the other side of the river. They came every year at the end of January and stayed until April or May. Three of them were taking off from the water, running on the surface, with their wings working against the wind. They circled and were off about their business. This walk was always a wonderful start to the day and very precious to me.

When I got back, I had to dress Sally and then get her downstairs because I was frightened of her negotiating the steep stairs on her own. I left her overnight bag by the front door; a taxi had been ordered to take her to her appointment with John Garfield. I kissed her goodbye and left for work; as I drove past the house, she was standing by the French window waving to me.

The unit on location was like a home from home, all so familiar. It needed to be since I was operating by instinct only. The electricians, cabling up, shouted 'good morning' to me. Many of the unit were still arriving. The caravanserai of location vehicles was lined up in the car park of the old maternity hospital. I went to my Winnebago, which I usually shared with Chris Ravenscroft, but he was not called for the hospital scenes. I changed into my Wexford suit. I went to the catering van for a sausage – my breakfast always consisted of one sausage – and to find Neil Zeiger. I told him that Sally was due into hospital later in the morning but assured him that, as the tumour was benign, there was nothing to fear. Neil suggested that we try and swap the hospital scenes for others so that I could be with Sally. It was very considerate of him but logistically impractical; it would take for ever to get on to another location and get actors down to Southampton from London. It was a kind thought and I was very grateful.

I went to the wardrobe van and found Rita Angel, the costume designer and a great friend. I told her what was happening as I would have hated her to find out from anyone else. I had already told Chris and Louie that Sal had seen a specialist in London and that we were waiting for news.

On to the set and a wonderfully sympathetic hearing from the director, Herbie Wise. Mike Smith was lighting the set and rather than sit uncomfortably somewhere off set, Bar had elected to sit in bed. There she was in her pink bed jacket looking very pale, as her supposed condition required, but in reality buzzing with health. I sat beside the bed and we talked about the new developments in Sal's illness. She asked if I wanted to cancel dinner that evening, but I said she was to come. I knew I would need her.

After those scenes were safely done, it was time for the scenes with Dora. Imagine this – this is what I had to act while my lovely Sally was about to go under the knife in a real hospital.

Dora in her hospital bed looks well and happy and is playfully stern with Reg, telling him that there is no need to visit every day and that she is not made of glass. Why is he looking so gloomy? Reg doesn't want to tell Dora that, during the hysterectomy operation, the surgeon had found a cancer and a biopsy had been done. Reg feels it is best not to tell her until the result of the biopsy is known. He has to find an excuse for his taciturn behaviour. Reg explains that in all his years in the police this was the first time he had ever found a dead body. The body was to have been the best man at a wedding that afternoon.

Louie asked for news of Sal and, when I told her that Sal was in the hospital at that very moment and about to see the surgeon, she was very concerned and a little tearful.

I couldn't help looking at my watch. Sal would have arrived at the hospital by now. There was no point in my rushing off to see her as she would have probably been with John Garfield. At lunchtime, however, I went to the main hospital and up to Sal's ward. It was a small ward of eight beds, it was light and airy and the flowers I had sent had arrived. She hadn't yet been to see John Garfield. She was being her usual gregarious self, intent on cheering up the young woman in the next bed.

After the break, we filmed the scene with Dr Crocker in which he tells Reg that he feels strongly that Dora should be told about the tumour and the biopsy. Then follows a scene with Dora in which Reg does tell her but reassures her that Len Crocker is quite certain the tumour is non-malignant. Dora is shocked and very tearful and has to be comforted by Reg.

At 3.15, John Garfield sent a message through the production office that he wanted to see me and Herbie sent me straight off. I waited some time outside the neurosurgeon's office, helping the time pass by trying to picture what sort of man he would be; as photofits of neuro-surgeons go, I was very wide of the mark. At last, I was asked to go in.

'I must tell you that although the biopsy indicates that the tumour is benign, it is a long and dangerous operation because of where the tumour is situated. At best I shall be able to remove it cleanly and we shall hear no more of it. At worst, I might cut into it and it would then spread. In that case, it would just be a matter of time. You should also know that were a nerve to be cut during the operation, your wife might be severely crippled, unable to use her limbs and perhaps unable to speak for the rest of her life.

'I have already spoken to Sally,' he continued, 'but I have to make you aware of all the options and have your permission as next of kin before I can proceed with the operation. I would be grateful if you would go and discuss it with your wife and then come back and tell me how you feel.'

I suppose, in my heart of hearts, I had been expecting something of what John Garfield told me. At best she would live, at worst she would die, but I was not prepared for 'Your wife might be severely crippled, unable to use her limbs and perhaps unable to speak for the rest of her life.' No, I had not been prepared for that.

John Garfield had told me that he had already given Sally the news. Now I had to summon up all my courage before going in to see her. I took a deep breath before going into the ward because I knew that my courage had to match hers.

A moment later, I was sitting on the edge of Sal's bed and we hugged each other – at least, she hugged me. I couldn't touch her back.

'Radiotherapy can't do anything,' she said.

'No.'

'We'd just better go ahead, hadn't we?' she said.

'Yes, darling. We just have to trust everything will be all right.'

'So, we'll go ahead. He wants to do it tomorrow morning at eight o'clock.'

'Will I be able to see you first?'

'I shouldn't think so. I'll be doped.'

'You're sure you want to go ahead, Sal?'

'I'm quite sure, darling, aren't you?'

'I'm quite sure if you are. I have to go now and tell him that we agree to the operation. I'll come and see you when we finish.'

'You haven't cancelled supper with Barbara, have you?' she asked.

'No, not yet.'

'Don't! It will be good for you to have somebody with you this evening.'

I saw John Garfield and signed the necessary forms and then went back to work. It was so strange holding Louie in my arms and reassuring her, as Dora, that the tumour was non-malignant and she had nothing to worry about when, a few corridors away, my beloved wife was facing such an awesome ordeal.

Louie wept a good deal for Sal and me but tears were also appropriate for the scene we were playing together.

At the end of the day I went up to see Sally and Bar came with me. After a few minutes Bar said she'd wait outside, leaving Sal and me to talk of practical things, of ringing Sarah, of letting Sal's brother have the address of the hospital, of a thousand and one mundane things. John Garfield came and saw her and was full of confidence.

Before I left, she gave me a letter, saying I was to read it before I went to bed.

Sal had been quite right; it was wonderful to have Bar with me for the evening. We talked about our days at the Old Vic, about Richard Pasco, her husband and my dear friend. We even laughed, we laughed a great deal about Michael Benthall – 'Mick the blink' – who ran the Vic for many years and sustained its reputation abroad as the best of British theatre.

After she'd left, I sat on the sofa and took out Sally's letter.

Darling, darling. This is just to say what needs no saying, that I love you. I love you so much. And I love our little Saz, and am so proud of her and the way she is growing and growing. We have grown too, haven't we, and I'm happy and proud in that as well. I have loved our journey together, and goodness, I've been so happy with you. My faith is theologically rocky, to the point of absurdity, and sometimes I think a little guiltily of Matthew Arnold's 'vague half-believers of our casual creeds'. My faith, though, in the importance of the spirit is strong, and so is yours, and I'm quite certain that our journey will continue together, whatever happens. Of course I dread the prospect of being badly handicapped, but we shall go on, I know, whatever happens. I felt so sad for you, and for us – for us all, but not really for myself, despite the weedy weeping!

I have just read Sarah's essays on Political Drama and hugely enjoyed them. All I can say is that if, on the day, she had such a question and couldn't reproduce such knowledge and detail etc, etc, I would still feel delighted that she has done such work, read so much, considered so well, and has a background I positively envy. I'm very proud of her.

Well, my pet, I could write all night, there's so much to say. But there's no need, is there? We have been so blessed in our love. Such support from you always and such wonderful laughs. I hope our little Sazi will one day find someone to laugh and love with so fully. It must be extraordinarily rare, but I think she may. Love to her hugely, and to the girls, and to you, my own darling. Your Lally. P.T.O.

There's a token prezzie for your birthday (poor you, not much of a birthday, is it?) in the HMV bag in the locker. I heard F.L. singing part of it in this recording on the radio, and thought it rather beautiful.

I thought it would be cheering at the end of this most awful day to find what Sal had bought for me and play it but I couldn't find an HMV bag in the house, nor in the hospital locker when I looked the next time I went in. Sally didn't mention the present, so I decided not to mention it, either. There was more to worry about. To this day I don't know who F.L. is or what he or she was singing.

Instead that evening, I put on my tape of Brendan O'Dowda singing 'The Rose of Tralee' and other Irish songs and wept out of sentiment, fear and self-pity. I went to bed at midnight determined to be up early in order to get to the hospital in time to see Sal before she went to the operating theatre.

Not unnaturally, I hardly slept at all and got up at six. I had a shortened version of my walk and then drove to the hospital, getting there at 7.15 – but Sally had already gone down to the operating theatre.

I knew it was a long operation and that there was little point in expecting to have any news until after lunch. I felt quite certain in myself that I was behaving as though nothing was happening, while around me there were very helpful people also pretending that nothing was happening either. Lunchtime came and went and there was no news from the ward. I don't know how I resisted ringing to find out how she was but I did. It wasn't until five o'clock that news came that Sally was out of the operating theatre and in the recovery room. I was told that there was no point in my going to see her as she was still very dopey from the anaesthetic.

As we had to finish filming in the hospital that evening, there was nothing to be done but get on with the work. We finished just after seven and, without doubt, those were the longest two hours I had ever spent in my life.

I changed out of my Wexford clothes as quickly as I could and ran over to the hospital. The sister in charge of the recovery room said that Sally was just coming round. She took me into the ward. Sally was lying with all the usual tubes stuck into the back of her hand, and there was a drip over the bed. She was quite motionless. I was terrified that, although she was alive, she was paralysed. The sister whispered to Sally, 'Sally, can you move your right leg?' It seemed an age before her right leg moved, but it moved! 'What about your left hand?' Dutifully, Sally moved it.

I went over to her, 'Hello, darling.' She opened her eyes. 'It's all right, darling, I'm here.' She took my hand and squeezed it. She was neither a vegetable nor paralysed.

She would be herself again. I felt the tears mounting but at that moment the nurse told me that John Garfield wanted to see me in the corridor.

He told me that the tumour had come out cleanly and that all that was to be done now was for Sally to get as much rest as possible. I can't remember what inadequate thanks I mumbled in my relief but I do remember that the physical sensations of relief were almost sickening. I felt as if my heart would break and my stomach erupt. John Garfield turned on his heel and went.

I went back in to Sally. 'I've just seen John Garfield and he says the tumour came out cleanly and all's well.'

Sally squeezed my hand. 'You'll let Saz know?' she whispered.

'She'll be the first call. I'm going to leave you now so you can rest, but I'll see you first thing in the morning.'

'You haven't cancelled Sandy and Shelagh, have you?'

Not only was all well, but there was nothing wrong with her memory.

As I was making my way to my car, Rita came out of the wardrobe truck. We met in the middle of the car park.

'She's all right, Rita,' I said.

She put her arms out to me and I wept on her shoulder.

After all, what are dear friends for?

And that was the end of the beginning. If that was a bad time, there were more to come.

I went to the hospital to see Sal one evening, and she had been told she could come home for my birthday. Then she pointed to a young doctor in the ward who was busily avoiding her eye.

'I asked him this morning when it would be all right to make love.'

'What did he say?'

'He went bright red and said anytime but in moderation. I then asked him what he meant by moderation.'

'Do you think that was fair on the poor man?'

'He said not to swing off the chandelier.'

'Very wise.'

We had a wonderful birthday lunch with Neil Zeiger, Fiona and Herbie Wise, Christopher Ravenscroft and Shelagh and Sandy Johnson. Sally and I had a great deal to be grateful for and a great deal to celebrate.

24

SALLY WAS MENDING, WALKING WELL BUT SLOWLY. It was simply a question of the anaesthetic leaving her body, and giving it time to heal. We had been warned that this might take three or four months and that during that time she wouldn't have much energy. However, she could sit and look peacefully out at the River Test and recuperate. Not that she was much of a one for sitting about and very soon was in her car and away doing things.

I too was immensely happy. I had bought myself a new jacket and when I put it on to go shopping in Romsey on a fine spring morning, the collar of the jacket stood up and the lapels had a rakish turn to them in consequence. All the young men were wearing their jackets like this. The sun was shining as I walked jauntily down the 'Hundred' to Waitrose. I was pleased with the world. A dapper little man fell in beside me and after a compliment or two on the series, he stretched up and straightened my collar.

'We can't have Inspector Wexford wandering through Romsey improperly dressed, can we?'

'Thank you,' I muttered and noticed that the sun had gone behind a little cloud. I'm still startled that people confuse the private and public persona.

Although we always planned to keep a toehold in London (and this was the Ealing house), we were still determined to have something permanent in the country. A good friend, Jennifer Wachstein, suggested that Sally should go with her to have a look in Wiltshire. West Lavington was on their itinerary and a house had come on the market that day. It looked rather small from the outside and Sal didn't think it would be big enough. They very nearly didn't bother looking at the inside but, fortunately, over some beer and a sandwich in the local pub, they read the details again. Five bedrooms, two bathrooms, enormous sitting-room and an equally large kitchen. Surely we could fit into that. They went and looked at the inside.

Sal came back to Nursling. I had finished filming early so when she told me she had seen the perfect house, I suggested we go and look at it then and there. I bought it the next morning. The completion day was set for 26 September 1990.

Sarah had come down from university with a good degree, a 2:1 in English. She was visiting her sisters in Australia so Sal went up to Oxford to have a look at the list. She couldn't find her daughter's name listed.

'I can't find my daughter's name anywhere,' she complained to the porter.

'Have you looked in the Honours, madam?'

'No,' she confessed and that's where her daughter's name was.

While we were filming *Some Lie and Some Die*, which Sandy Johnson directed, I was asked to adapt *From Doon with Death* which gave me great pleasure. Ruth had very much accepted me as her idea of Inspector Wexford and I felt, rightly or wrongly, that I not only understood the character but that I had an affinity with and an understanding of Ruth's writing. I believe it was a good script and honest to the book. It also meant I would be working with Mary McMurray again, both as actor and writer.

On the work front, things were moving rapidly. After finishing *Some Lie and Some Die* at the end of June, we began the shoot of *An Unkindness of Ravens* on 9 July. On 31 August we started shooting *Put on by Cunning*, with Sandy Johnson directing, and Sally played a small part of a busybody nextdoor neighbour which she thoroughly enjoyed.

When we weren't filming, many of the Wexford film crew were indefatigable fundraisers for the scanner appeal. They were full of the barmiest ideas; for instance, they held competitions during the lunch break to see who could hit a golf ball the furthest. Our greatest talker decided he wouldn't speak for two days.

Ladies cooked and football matches were played and the money rolled in.

The builders began work on our new home, Holly Cottage in West Lavington, and Sally was kept very busy ordering wood-burning stoves, carpets, curtains. Our old friend and interior designer, Hermione Young, helped enormously. We moved in properly on 7 November 1990 but, since we had a punishing schedule for 1991, we kept Tiled Cottage on as well.

Then Sally became ill again. This time, the pain was between her shoulder blades, just where the surgeon had removed the old tumour. I tried to pretend it was because she had been shifting furniture, but I wasn't fooling anyone, certainly not Sally.

She was growing a visible lump on her back. We had to go to the MRI scanner in Poole since the one being installed in Southampton General Hospital had not been completed by that time. Whilst a large scanner works quite slowly, a small one – as there was at Poole – goes at a snail's pace. It took Sal forty-five minutes to be scanned and she kept herself from going mad by working through the alphabet, trying to find a name for a neighbour's new whippet.

I have never seen anyone hit by a bullet in the chest. I am told they leap into the air. Certainly Sally was lifted off her feet when John Garfield told her there was nothing more he could do for her. It was now up to the physicians.

When we came out of John Garfield's office, Sally asked, 'Is there somewhere we can have a drink?'

'Yes, darling,' I replied. 'The Woodman's at the top of the road.'

'I just think I need something,' she said.

The physicians conferred. Sally went into the South Hants Hospital, the radiology wing of the Southampton General, as an out-patient. We lived at Tiled Cottage when Sally had her radiotherapy appointments but went back to West Lavington as often as we could. Here Sal busied herself turning Holly Cottage into a home. Her spirit was indomitable. She insisted on my sticking to my routine and our wonderful neighbours, Jim and Janet Hodges, were the best anyone could ever wish for and as the crisis deepened their support became stronger and stronger. Sally was also adamant that I should keep my charity appointments. She even came to the Mayor of Romsey's Ball. Nothing was going to stop her. And, as before, we promised each other never to ask, 'Why me?'

During January and February 1991, I did a new series of *No Job for a Lady*. I would leave Sal and Splodge the cat in the early morning to face the snowbound roads between West Lavington and Teddington Studios. There was also the script for *From Doon with Death* to finish writing, always our supper to cook and Sal's lunch to prepare for the next day. Time was not hanging heavy. When we started shooting *A New Lease of Death* in February, we moved back to Tiled Cottage and the cat came too. This Wexford was to be followed by *From Doon with Death*.

During the weekend of 9 and 10 March, Sally had severe pains in her chest, accompanied by awful nausea and dizziness. She was admitted to the South Hants Hospital for further tests. I was filming *A New Lease of Death* when I got a call from Sally in the hospital, asking me to go and see her at lunchtime. I told Herbie where I was going and that I might be a little late back.

Sal was sitting up in bed when I got there. I sat beside her and she took my hand.

'Well darling, it's crunch time. I've had a long talk with Dr Williams. They can't do anything to stop the cancer. They wanted to give me chemo which is what brought all this to a head. I asked him if chemo would do any good and he said no. I would rather the cancer should run its course and I die with some dignity and quality of life. But I wanted to ask you first. I don't want my hair to fall out,' she continued. 'It isn't vanity, really. The cancer is spreading everywhere. Dr Williams says the radiotherapy will ease the pain. I don't mind the pain but I think I would like to go gently in my own, or the cancer's, good time.'

I've never heard anything so brave. I told her that, of course, she must go to her death in her own way and that I would support her with everything in my power.

We asked Dr Williams to join us and Sally told him of her decision. Poor man, he had tears in his eyes.

I returned to the set and told Herbie my news. He asked if I wanted to go home but I knew there would no point. I just had to get on with it. So I stayed and continued filming.

I told Jenny Quayle, who was in the episode and who had acted with me in *The Lady's Not for Burning*; she was wonderfully supportive.

This time it was A. E. Housman racing through my mind:

> He stood, and heard the steeple
> Sprinkle the quarters on the morning town.
> One, two, three, four, to market-place and people
> It tossed them down.

> Strapped, noosed, nighing his hour,
> He stood and counted them and cursed his luck;
> And then the clock collected in the tower
> Its strength, and struck.

Later, as I was driving back to Tiled Cottage, I thought about the future and knew that the next months would be full of moments of great sadness for Sally, for me and for Sarah and, of course, gathering pain for Sally.

Sally said she very much wanted to go to Cornwall to stay with our friends Jamie and Felicity Robertson who ran the Nansidwell Hotel on the Helford River near Mawnan Smith. At the time, I was driving a Ford Sierra, but the seat was too hard for the lump on her back. There was a Peugeot dealer in the village and I borrowed a 605 to test-drive. I drove it up to the house and took Sally for a drive in it. Yes, she would be able to get to Cornwall without too much discomfort. I bought it.

We went for four days but couldn't leave until the Tuesday because on the Monday I had a prize-giving evening with the Romsey Ladies Darts League. The first time I had given the prizes, I had made the mistake of kissing the winning team on the cheek. It hadn't dawned on me that there would be over eighty kisses to get through.

Sally didn't go with me to the dinner this year; she wanted to rest before the long drive down. We took it slowly, stopping often to stroll or look at the view. We got to Nansidwell in good time for tea and a rest. Later that evening I collected the messages from my answer-machine at home. There was one from my sister-in-law, Valerie, asking me to ring her. Her husband, my brother Terence, had died of a massive heart attack outside his home in Camberwell. He was fifty-three when he died. Sally was not up to another six-hour drive so soon so we had our few days in Cornwall and returned home for the funeral.

When, at the end of the funeral service some days later, we walked down the aisle, I looked at the congregation and my heart filled with joy. My brother's two worlds – of the entertainment business and horse racing – were represented. Writers, directors and producers, many of them having flown the Atlantic, were there, as were his racing pals, some still sporting the badges of the last meeting in their lapels.

We were about to start on the next Wexford, *Murder Being Once Done*, when Sally was offered a part in an episode of *Lovejoy*. I tried to talk her out of it, but she was determined. One evening I drove behind her to Basingstoke where they were filming the episode and stayed with her that night at the hotel. I got up at the crack of dawn and drove myself back to Romsey to my film, leaving Sally in the good hands of Ian McShane, Dudley Sutton and the director, Baz Taylor. I was relieved when she called me that evening to say she was not too tired. She had one more day's filming to do.

Work on the Wexfords continued, and work on the dying took its inexorable course. A procession of friends came to stay and to say goodbye.

Louie Ramsay came over to Wiltshire on 20 June for a couple of nights. I went back to location the next day and left her and Sal together. Louie told me later that Sal had said to her, 'You know, Louie, dying is so incredibly boring.'

Jean Simmons came to stay from California. She came with us to a day of wheelchair dancing in Winchester Town Hall. The fearsome display of courage from those bound to their chairs for the rest of their lives elicited the remark from Sal, 'You see, there are people worse off than I.' She came to the 'swimathon' arranged by John Donoghue, our chief spark. It raised a magnificent £4,000 for the scanner appeal. She returned to the hospital but not as a patient.

They had asked me if I would open the new neuro ward and we did it together, Sal supporting herself on her stick.

That year, 1991, was the heaviest on the Wexford filming schedule. We filmed five titles ending with *Achilles Heel*, which took us to Corsica. The company very kindly included Sally in the party. Unfortunately, it was not the rest it was supposed to be; for a start, the much-promised sun was nowhere to be seen. It rained. We had to lie on a wet beach pretending to sunbathe. Poor Christopher Ravenscroft had to plunge joyously into an icy sea. The Mistral blew; we drove endlessly between the locations. We nearly lost a stunt driver over the edge of the cliff. We nearly lost our director, director of photography, camera operator and first assistant when the helicopter they were using for reconnaissance was caught in a wind current and dropped 120 feet.

It is usual on a location shoot to have journalists with you. There were a few old friends in Corsica but we also had a couple of new faces, who didn't seem to want to interview or talk to anyone. I couldn't quite work out what they were doing. Then a possible explanation hit me: what a good story it would make if Sally were to die on the location. Well, she wasn't going to give them a good story. She came home.

In November, there was a gala performance at the Mayflower Theatre in Southampton to raise money for the scanner. It would be too invidious to single any one person out, but I cannot think of any other profession that would give so generously of its time and talent. We raised £16,000.

At the end of the year, John and Janet Home came for Christmas which gave us all great pleasure.

Sally told me she would like to have her hair done properly in London. I booked an appointment for a day early in January. Through Margaret Courtney's daughter-in-law who worked there, I also booked a room at the Savoy. They gave us a riverside suite for the price of a room. We had lunch there and a rest, and in the evening we had dinner in the Garrick. There were a great many old friends in the club and Sally said a cheerful goodbye to them all before we hobbled back to the Savoy. The next morning Sarah came and had breakfast with us before she went off to location; she had now become an assistant director in television.

Later, heading home in the car and going round Hyde Park Corner, Sally said, 'Thank you, darling. I've said goodbye to London now.'

The time arrived when Sally needed more care than I was able to give her. The local team of carers, the Macmillan Nurses, the district nurses and all the other helpers were exceptional in their attentiveness and care. Our neighbour, Reg Hale, who had papered our bedroom and had done a hundred and one things to make the house as comfortable as it could be for a very sick lady, had built a small ramp from the level of the hall to the level of the kitchen to take the wheelchair she now needed. She used to convey herself out of the Stannah lift, into the chair and away down the hall, down the ramp and into the kitchen at top speed. She enjoyed the speed and was reliving her dexterity in sport and physical prowess.

Reg was also responsible for introducing me to his daughter-in-law, another Sally, who came to work as my secretary soon after we moved into the house. So not only were the carers looking after Sally but the day-to-day running of the household, the fan letters, the charity letters were all meticulously looked after. Secretary Sally is still with me.

By January of 1992, Sally was very ill in West Lavington. I was filming *Unwanted Woman* at the time which was being shot around Portsmouth. I knew that I had to live at home at West Lavington and commute every day to the locations. It was three hours' driving every day. And worth every moment. I wouldn't have missed for anything watching my enormously courageous wife, slinging her wheelchair about, taking her pills with her evening whisky and enjoying every minute of it.

Each day she became more and more ill. Her hearing became so acute that it was painful; she couldn't stand any noise.

On 24 February 1992, my grandson Sam was born to Candy and Rob in Sydney; Sally was delighted and the news brought some joy to her last days.

Now we came to film *The Speaker of Mandarin* which would have locations in Hong Kong. I didn't know what I would do when I had to fly out there. Sally was so near death, but the question was how long would it be? However, I did have the most wonderful carers and felt all would be well until I got back. Sarah was working on the film as a runner.

Neil rang to tell me that we were to read through *The Speaker of Mandarin* on 5 March 1992. When he heard how ill Sal was, he offered to postpone it but Sally would not hear of it. Sarah and I got into our Sunday best to go to London. In mock solemnity, we went into Sal's room – she was now sleeping downstairs in the sitting-room – and, as good children should, we showed her our scrubbed hands. I don't think either of us expected to see her alive again.

I left my mobile's number with Tuppie Craven, friend and carer, and Sarah and I travelled to London. I left my phone on during the read-through but no call came. It was while I was walking along Exhibition Road to the Bulgarian Embassy to see Johnny Stancioff that the call came.

Sally had died that afternoon, 5 March, at three o'clock.

The funeral at West Lavington church was joyous. Four of my daughters were with me. I had decided that Sally's clothes and jewellery should be divided as soon as possible. It was glorious to see the four girls walking down the lane in front of me to the church, wearing coats and skirts and hats which had belonged to Sal.

The church was full. The nurses from the South Hants Hospital and the Southampton General Hospital had hired a mini bus to be there; the Wexford crews were there and, of course, the casts. Dear Christopher Ravenscroft, Louie, Ken Kitson, Diane Keen and Neil Zeiger, Graham Benson, our executive producer, and his wife, Christine. And all our dear, dear friends and family. Yes, it was a wonderful and happy send-off. And if you have seen someone suffer in pain for over three years, I can assure you that there is happiness in saying goodbye.

The funeral was on 12 March. I left for Hong Kong two days later. It is what Sally would have wanted me to do.

Due to the inevitable press that Sally's death attracted, I received hundreds of letters from well-wishers. I knew they would be sorted and be ready for me on my return. In the end, I received over two thousand letters of condolence and I believe I answered every single one.

I thought that by working I could escape the toll one has to pay to grief. There was *Mouse in the Corner* which I had adapted and was directed by Rob Walker; then the last of the Wexfords for TVS, *Kissing the Gunner's Daughter* which was directed by Mary McMurray. You could say that by casting me in *At Bertram's Hotel*, Mary was responsible for the happiest and saddest years of my life. Of course, the sadnesses had nothing to do with her.

Kissing the Gunner's Daughter was finished and in the can, and I was sitting in Tiled Cottage, packing boxes prior to closing it down, returning it to its owners, and going home to West Lavington, when there was a knock on the door. It was the gentle rector of St Boniface, Ian Gardiner.

'Is this a good time to talk?'

There wasn't much talking about it. I just managed to ask him in and make him a cup of tea, before bursting into tears and crying my heart out. For Sal, for my mother, my brother, Julia, my aunts. They all came tumbling out on a flood of grief.

Soon after this, I decided I wanted to see Candy and Charlie; Tessa said she would look after the house while I was away. Secretary Sally discovered that it was just as cheap to take a round-the-world ticket as a standard return fare to Australia. I went to Sydney, to Auckland to see my friends, John and Ainsley Sullivan; to the Bay of Islands to stay in a most enchanting house owned by my friends Peter and Gillie Land. On to New York, then Toronto to see brother Frank, Los Angeles to see Jean Simmons, and home to pick up the threads of life.

Apart from adapting Ruth Rendell's *The Strawberry Tree* for Blue Heaven – the company set up by Graham Benson to make films of some of Ruth's work which did not feature Wexford – and making some corporate videos, I gave myself over to working for the cancer charities.

I shall never forget the poignant opening of the MRI scanner at the Southampton General Hospital. All the nurses who had had anything to do with Sally had signed their names on a sheet of paper; this was put into a specimen bottle, sealed up and buried in the wall of the scanner room. Before the outer casing was put round the machine they had written on the cement: Sally Home, died March 5th 1992.

I am not far away: they hung a photograph of me in the scanner waiting room. Before introducing me and asking me to say a few words, the head of neuro explained this to everyone at the ceremony. I got through my speech all right but afterwards, when I was outside, I said to myself, but speaking to Sally, 'The Woodman's just up the road, Sal. I think I'll just have a drink.'

25

My daughter Sarah usually accompanied me when I had to speak at or attend charity dinners, almost always for a cancer charity, but one evening in 1993 she wasn't free and I thought to ring up my Wexford screen wife, Louie Ramsay, and ask her to join me. Even though we had known each other on and off for over forty years, we didn't really know each other at all, and here was a chance to get to know each other better. It was a delightful evening and, although we had always had many laughs on set, this was different. There was a specific attraction that had not been there before.

To say that we fell in love in an elderly and sedate way would be to misrepresent the truth. We fell in love crying with laughter and ringing each other up at least three times a day.

There was much to learn about Louie, first in the simple 'where were you born?' and 'where did you grow up?' kind of conversation.

'Dad was a doctor, a consultant physician at the Royal Free,' she told me, 'but I was born in South Africa. We came back home when I was three. My parents were both Scots.'

She went to the North London Collegiate and, for some extraordinary reason, got herself entangled with biology and physics. When tackled about her choice of subject, she hesitated to say 'because my friends are doing them' but she admitted that she would much prefer to be doing English. Nor did she quite have the courage to say she wanted to be an actress, so she plumped instead for going to RADA to train to be a stage manager. She hadn't been there many minutes before she decided she definitely did want to be an actress.

She had never sung in public but has a belter of a voice. She attended auditions for *South Pacific* for a bet, and so thoroughly surprised Gerry White, the director, that he gave her a part in the chorus and to understudy Mary Martin. She joined one of the most famous chorus lines which included June Whitfield, Millicent Martin, Larry Hagman and Sean Connery. Louie's name in the chorus was Ensign Lisa Minnelli.

After work, she would come into the Buckstone Club with her future husband, the actor, Ronan O'Casey – and that is where we first met, *en passant*.

Louie's musical comedy career flourished; she topped the bill with Max Bygraves at the Hippodrome, she was on her way. But life has a way of playing tricks. Louie became ill and was four months in plaster from calf to neck. There could be no more dancing. Life also has a way of compensating. Louie became a member of the National Theatre when it was run by Laurence Olivier who cast her as 'Lillian' in *Eden End*. She played opposite Joan Plowright. Her proudest moment was standing between J.B. Priestley and Sir Laurence Olivier at the curtain call on the first night at the Old Vic.

All this came tumbling out that first evening, and all my story too. So there is not much difference between the courtship of two twenty-year-olds and two people in their sixties.

After some months her son, Matt O'Casey, and my daughter, Tessa, sat us down in the kitchen.

'Are you two being serious about each other or just playing?' asked Matt.

'Because you're getting on a bit. You haven't much time left,' said Tessa.

We had discussed marriage with each other and decided that we should wait as there was so much of the past to be reconciled with the present and the future, but we reckoned without the *Sun*.

That July, we had been to Leeds to see Gillian Lynne's new ballet for the Northern Ballet Company and had strolled back to the Queen's Hotel, holding hands. Somebody spotted us and called the *Sun*. They didn't get much joy in the hotel as we were staying in separate rooms under our own names, but they were not to be deterred. They parked outside Louie's house in London, and mine in Wiltshire.

The following day I was in Bournemouth as a guest speaker at the West of England Writers' Association. I rang Lou just before I went down to dinner and thank goodness she warned me of the newspaper interest because, a few minutes later, I walked down the stairs and into the arms of the reporters. I made a bargain with them that if they would leave it until after I had made my speech I would give them an interview.

I went back upstairs and called Louie. 'Are you prepared to marry me so that we can get it over with and I can get back to doing some work. By the way, if you don't want to live in Wiltshire, it's all off.'

It may not sound the most romantic of proposals but the peal of laughter at Louie's end made me realise we were off on a very special journey. When you are young, you grow together in discovery. When you are in your sixties, you grow together by the accommodation of each other's long-established habits.

There were two marriage ceremonies on 25 September 1993: the first one was the civil marriage, at Devizes Registry Office. Peter Land came over from Chichester, where he was in *Pickwick*, to be my best man. Later that day, we had a blessing in our local church. Matt gave his mother away at both ceremonies and Sarah was my best man at the blessing. Our vicar, Hugh Hoskins, had arranged a beautiful service for us at which my grandchildren were bridesmaids. Maureen Lipman was supposed to be Louie's matron of honour, but Louie had inadvertently chosen Yom Kippur as the date of the wedding and Maureen and Jack Rosenthal are practising Jews. In fact, Maureen was working in Scotland at the time and it would have been difficult for her to make the journey anyway. I got to read her speech, which was a laugh a line.

Keith Ramsay, Louie's brother, read a Shakespeare sonnet, and Charlie Dance chose Dickens – the passage from *David Copperfield* describing Peggotty's proposal and containing the immortal line, 'Barkis is willin'.' The church was full of old friends and new, the singing was triumphant. There were some particularly memorable people there, considering the water that had flowed under the bridge of my life: Julia's brother, Rag; John and Janet Home; Dick and Nina Lowry, friends of Sally's and mine who had embraced Louie and given their blessing; my brothers, sister, nephews and nieces; most of the crew from the Rendells; and the nurses from the Southampton General Hospital who had cared for her.

The day had started drizzly but by the time the blessing was over the sun was shining. We had taken the amazingly ancient West Lavington Manor, which is now owned by an advertising company, but let out for functions.

And was this a function! Our location caterers from the Wexfords did the catering. The head wine steward at the Garrick Club, Peter Ellick, asked if he might bring down his assistant, Muriel, and his wife Shirley so that, together, they could buttle the champagne and wine. We had bought a great deal of champagne on sale or return, but at the end of the day, there were a lot of happy people and nothing to go back.

Matt O'Casey and his band had won 'the international street musicians of the year' award a couple of years before. Louie had put them up on the floor of her flat and made sure they had enough to eat before they went out to busk. Matt, now a respected producer/director for BBC Manchester, gathered them together again so that they could play at her wedding.

'If you're happy and you know it, clap your hands.' And two hundred and fifty people did.

We went away for one night only as we had invited the family and dear friends who had come from America and Canada to have lunch with us the next day. I had been cooking up a storm for a week getting ready for the Sunday lunch that was going to feed the forty-five guests. While we were having our honeymoon night, the girls got the house ready for the party.

Louie and I were well and truly launched.

But work called. In the spring of 1994, I had the joy of doing what I think is the best work I have ever done, *Little Lord Fauntleroy* for the BBC. The script was written by Julian Fellowes, now of *Gosford Park* fame, and beautifully directed by Andrew Morgan. I played the irascible Lord Dorincourt and my co-star was a magical young American actor, Michael Benz. Everything combined to make this production memorable. I knew it had potential and wasn't in the least surprised that it won an International Emmy in New York.

Something strange surrounds this production, however. Although it got extremely high ratings for a children's production and a clutch of good notices, including a rave from my old friend Jeffrey Bernard, it has never been repeated by the BBC. As I was paid a repeat fee built into my original contract, I have no financial axe to grind. It just seems a pity that so good a piece of work should go to waste.

We were preparing to work on *Simisola*, a 'Ruth Rendell Mystery', when I got a call from Neil Zeiger saying that he would like me to come down to the Blue Heaven offices in Portsmouth to meet and talk with Jim Goddard and Chris Ravenscroft and have some photos taken. I had already spoken to Jim Goddard about the script and there must have been more photographs of Christopher and me than any other two actors in television. However, a date was made for me to go and see them.

At the time of the photo shoot, Louie was working in London, at a fringe theatre at World's End. It was an American play, a Pulitzer Prize winner. She had eight hundred lines to learn for this formidable two-hander which she played with Charlotte Fryer.

I was in Wiltshire as I had a fund-raising dinner to attend. I rang Louie early the next morning and said that as I had been rather late the night before I was going to call the whole thing off and not go over to Portsmouth. Louie said she didn't think that was very fair on poor Christopher who would already be on his way down from London.

'Yes, I suppose so. Oh, all right.' And, dutifully, I drove to Portsmouth.

I could not understand what was going on. Everyone in the office was dressed to the nines. After a desultory conversation amounting to nothing, Neil thought we should go and do the photo call which, for some reason, was to be on a boat. Still the penny didn't drop – and it was only the appearance of Michael Aspel and his little red book that made me say, 'You can fuck off for a start.'

He looked very worried.

He and Louie had been cooped up in the cabin for half an hour while the pretence of taking the photographs was happening on deck.

'Is it going to be all right?' he had asked her.

'I don't know. He's always said he wouldn't do *This Is Your Life*.'

No wonder the poor man looked worried.

Louie came to the rescue with a glass of champagne and some murmured persuasions like, 'Everyone's worked so hard, I think it would be a pity if . . .' I relented and went with the flow.

Louie told me afterwards that when she had first been approached and knowing my reservations, she had spoken to my daughters and they had, to a woman, insisted that she gave *This Is Your Life* the go ahead.

'We'll never speak to you again if you don't.'

Now that was an awesome threat from a new family of five daughters.

It was a great evening. I think what I treasure most is how Louie loves my girls and how they love her. In Matt O'Casey they have found a brother and he, poor man, five sisters.

Simisola was as happy a production of 'The Ruth Rendell Mysteries' as any. Jim Goddard directed with great pleasure and flair and the whole team were back in their familiar places. It was like going home. Our special guests were Jane Lapotaire and two fine black actors, George Harris and Ellen Thomas.

The rest of 1994 passed in riding on Salisbury Plain, writing a radio play and adapting *Road Rage*, another 'Ruth Rendell Mystery', for Blue Heaven. Ruth had had Dora Wexford kidnapped and it gave Louie a chance to step out of the 'doormat Dora' syndrome and do some lovely acting. Bruce MacDonald was our new director and an exceptional one he proved to be too.

I had bought a young horse, Obe, which Chris Davies – in whose yard I had kept all my horses and who had shown them as eventers – was to make for me (or break in, as it used to be called). The thinking was that I could have fun for a few years and then, as I got into my dotage, Obe would have settled down into an old man carrier. The end of the story must take its turn.

Louie had taken over the family health and, being a doctor's daughter, she was horrified that I had not been near a doctor for years. Dr Barbara Gompels was equally horrified to find there was no history on their computer; in fact, nothing but my address. My sleeve was up and blood pressure taken in a matter of minutes, a list of my past illnesses was entered on to the computer there and then, and I was admonished to lose weight.

This was not enough for Louie. As I had begun paying into BUPA when I started work on the Wexfords in 1987, she thought it would be sensible now for me to have a full medical check. Secretary Sally made the appointment and, to humour them both, I went to the BUPA centre in Bristol in November 1998. It appeared that my PSA (prostate specific antigen) count was rather high and I was told to go to the Royal United Hospital in Bath for a biopsy.

To take my mind off the regrettable intrusion of urological instruments up my bum, I toyed with some ideas for a production of *Uncle Vanya*. Up to a point it worked but it failed to work at the point of pain.

It was New Year's Eve when I heard that I had virulent cancer of the prostate. Louie was in the waiting-room, growing more and more anxious as the minutes ticked by. When the specialist, Graham Howell, realised that she was outside, he called her in so that she could know at first hand what was happening.

My daughter Sarah and her husband, Mark, had come down to West Lavington with a friend to celebrate the passing of the old year out. Louie and I decided, therefore, that mum should be the word. I got on with cooking the dinner, the wine flowed and a good time was had by all – well, on the surface.

Louie and I had grown very close and were now at the beginning of a final journey which we knew might take days, weeks, months or years. This cancer made us look at the reality of dying. I had seen it with Sal and my mother and brother, my father and many others. Louie had seen it with her mother and father. We had serious business to confront in our marriage. To love each other through the pain that was still very much there, for I thought of Sal most days, and find strength in love for the pain that was to come.

I had the most exceptional treatment and advice from the consultant, the radiologist and the surgeon. I was told very clearly what were the options, the upsides and the downsides of what was available.

I could ignore it, in which case I would have four years at the most to live.

I could have a radical prostateoctomy. The result of this would be the end of sexual activity as I had known it. But, after all, Louie and I were in our late sixties and, whilst sad at its passing, sex was not of prime importance.

If I had chemo or radiotherapy, there could not be any guarantee of complete success. And having had chemo or radiotherapy I could not then change my mind and have surgery.

If, during surgery, the cancer split, there could be no guarantee of complete success. The opposite, in fact; the cancer would spread.

After a long talk with Graham Howell, I opted for radical prostateoctomy. It was to be done as quickly as possible. But there were further complications: I had been seeing a surgeon about the disintegration of my knees. He had the winter flu that was prevalent at the time and gave it to me. I ran a high temperature and the flu was so bad that I could not have the anaesthetic for the cancer operation. Graham Howell was concerned about any delay and finally the anaesthetist decided that, on balance, it was better to chance the anaesthetic than the tumour.

The operation was on 22 February 1999. And, as I write, so far all seems to be well.

But I have never fully recovered my continence. I have to make sure I know where the loos are, not drink too much alcohol and not get emotional. If I can survive a long evening fund-raising and speaking for cancer research, then it can't be too bad.

If it were not for my wife I would either be dead or be dying.

And I must tell you, loving is a gift from the gods and a radical prostateoctomy can only kill procreation, not diminish joy.

I was persuaded that I should talk about my cancer in the hope that other men might get themselves tested on a regular basis. I talked about my experience at many cancer seminars and other gatherings but it was the article by Lynda Lee-Potter in the *Daily Mail* that brought the greatest return.

A man ran up to me in Hampstead saying, 'Thank you, thank you for the article. It saved my life.' And this has been repeated on many occasions.

It beats acting. Acting can enhance but it can't life save.

Mr Pozo removed the cartilage from both my knees, but told me that the left knee would eventually have to be replaced. It took an age for the general anaesthetic to leave my body but in the end I was riding again. Obe was not the easiest of horses and, being a youngster, needed a great deal of exercise. Chris Davies had had an operation on his ear which had damaged his balance so he was not able to exercise the horse himself. We found people to work him but it was not enough.

About six weeks before we started *Harm Done*, the last Wexford, I was exercising him in the school. I thought this would be one of the last rides before I started filming, so I decided not to take him up on to the plain because I didn't want to risk a fall.

The horse was restless; he was bored with the school but hubris made me take him round once more. I had placed three poles for him to trot over and now he decided to show me what he could do. He took a ginormous flying leap. As we were whizzing through the air I thought it quite exciting, but he gave a buck on landing which put me on his neck. When he saw how close he was to the fence, he went hard left and I went right, hard, into the wooden fence.

As I surfaced, I moved my neck and thanked God it was not broken.

The date of my fall was 22 February 2000, exactly a year since the cancer operation.

My secretary, Sally, drove me to hospital. I had multiple fractures back and front on six ribs on my right side, multiple fractures on my shoulder blade, my shoulder broken in three places and my shoulder socket broken. I had fluid between the ribs and the lung. If you want to know the meaning of exquisite pain, it is when a doctor makes an incision in order to put a drain into the cavity, without an anaesthetic, but because of the fractures to the ribs he can find no way through and has to shove his little finger into your ribs to make the cavity big enough to take the pipe. That is exquisite pain.

I should say, however, that the treatment I received at Odstock Hospital was exceptional in every department.

There wasn't much time to get better; I had to film in five weeks. I asked the surgeon, John Carvell, what the chances would be.

'I have never seen such horrific injuries except in a car smash, but you can make it if you need to.'

I needed to. Neil and I decided not to tell Graham Benson, the executive producer, in case it worried him. And I made it. It was a wonderful shoot and I was pampered and coddled by the crew because they were determined to see that I got through with as little discomfort as possible.

The wonderful thing about the career I chose so randomly as a small boy in Bulgaria is that as long as your memory serves you and your limbs obey, there is no need to stop acting. I have continued and will continue to continue.

The last Wexford has been made. Senior policemen are retired in their early fifties; I shall soon be seventy-two. I think that says everything. Detective Chief Inspector Wexford, *in memoriam*. Thanks for the wonderful journey. It was a great way to go.

Postscript

AFTER A MATINÉE OF *TOWARDS ZERO* AT THE OPERA HOUSE, MANCHESTER, IN 1956, I WAS APPROACHED BY A YOUNG MAN WHO WANTED MY AUTOGRAPH. I gave it to him. He asked me if I would send him a signed photograph of myself and gave me a stamped addressed envelope.

This was to be the beginning of a very great friendship.

Ernie Turner was a theatre buff. Being a clerk with British Rail in Warrington, he had the opportunity to travel cheaply and indulge his passion for theatre across the length and breadth of the country. When a man has travelled to Aberdeen to see a matinée, the least you can do is have a cup of tea with him between the shows. He was never obtrusive, always gentle and very much liked by my three wives. When the twins were born, he gave us two very practical sets of baby clothes. 'You can rely on Ernie to be thoughtful and practical. What a friend!' said Julia. That summed him up.

We were sitting in a café in Manchester one day when he produced an orange volume labelled 'George Baker – his work in films and theatre'.

I was somewhat surprised that anyone should take the trouble to delve back into my career, starting at the time when I was with the Salisbury Rep. It was an immaculate piece of work, noting time and place, the play, author and director and, of course, the cast. Sometimes he had even been able to get notices from local papers. Since I have never been able to keep notices or photographs of productions I have been in, Ernie was a godsend.

I used to ring him up and ask him what I was doing in June 1954, for instance.

'Hold on a minute, George.' He would look it up.

'*Our Family* with Geoffrey Palmer and Rosemary Dunham at the Grand Theatre, Croydon.'

In due course and most fortuitously, he sent me copies of the four volumes he had completed up to 1975. They were a wonderful help in writing this book. We became ever greater friends; he was at Sally's funeral and at my wedding to Louie.

He died two years ago, in 2000, just after I had smashed myself up in the riding accident so I was not able to get to his funeral. This saddened me a great deal.

Like the meticulous man he was, he had put all the rest of the volumes on my career, together with tapes, notices and photographs, into a box in a corner of his bungalow, with a strict injunction to his brother that they were to be sent to me. His niece rang me and told me about the box, but I was still nursing my broken bones and could not get up to Warrington to collect it. It was clearly labelled 'to stay' but the house clearance men didn't have time to read that. It went with everything else. All that part of Ernie's diligent work and friendship was gone.

That's not the end of the story. I received two albums of photographs that Ernie had taken of my children when young. The albums had been found under a hedge near Ellesmere Port. Then some weeks later, a tape containing *The Moonraker* and *Tread Softly, Stranger* was sent to me by a woman who had bought them in a car boot sale. How kind people are to bother. If anyone else found any of the other material and still has it, I would love to have it back.

How did the woman know where to send the tape? Ernie had written my name and address on the sleeve, along with message: 'Just in case you haven't got them.' Thank you, Ernie.

Index

Note: 'GB' indicates George Baker.
Subheadings are filed in chronological order.

Keen, Diane 318
Keith, Penelope 293
Kelly, Cassie 110, 113–14, 115, 122
Kelly, Dermot 255
Kemp, Jeremy 203
Kennedy, Jackie 238
Kent, Nick 245, 247, 248
Kent, William 200
Kerr, Fraser 233, 244
Khrushchev, Nikita 208
King, David 210
King, George 215
King, May 215, 216
King Solomon's Carpet (Rendell) 292
Kingsley, Ben 262, 264
Kingston, Mark 210, 293
Kissing the Gunner's Daughter (television) 319
Kitson, Ken 292, 318
Klaus (friend of brother Frank) 27
Knight, Colonel 65–6, 71
Kodak 8
Kossoff, David 168
Kounka (cook) 25
Krummnagle (Ustinov) 283
Kurnitz, Harry 222, 224

Lacey, Catherine 253
Lady Audley's Secret (stage) 112
Lady's Not for Burning, The (stage) 255–6, 278–9
Lamb, Larry 283
Lambda, Peter 213
Lamont, Duncan 113
Lancelot and Guinevere (film) 225, 248
Lancing College 65, 68–9, 72–3, 75, 76
Land, Gillie 319
Land, Peter (*stage name of* Peter White) 275, 319, 323
Landis, Harry 173
Lange, Di 300–301
Lapotaire, Jane 278, 292, 326
Larbey, Bob 257
Last, Jimmy 265
Last, Ruth 265
Last Troubadour, The (television) 179–81, 182
Laurence, Charles 173
Lavender, Ian 258
Law, Mary 176
Law, Phyllida 254
Law, Sir Horace 8
Lawson, Wilfrid 186
Lazenby, George 248–9
Le Mesurier, John 97, 99
Leach, Mrs (landlady) 149
Leaver, Don 254
Lee, Annie 206
Lee, Belinda 171
Lee, Bernard 161–2
Lee-Potter, Lynda 328
Leech, Richard 172, 190, 241
Leeman, Andrea 259, 260, 261

Leigh Fermor, Paddy 22
Leigh-Hunt, Barbara 292, 300, 301, 302, 303, 305, 306
Leister, Frederick 176
Lennard, Bob 153, 158, 159
Leonard, Hugh 237
Leonid (student) 24, 25
Lester, Richard 258
Levin, Bernard 219
Levy, Benn W. 94, 142, 251
Lewis, Duncan 226
Lewis, Ronald 173
Lidderdale, Alice 233, 240, 241
Life with the Carters (stage) 96
Lind, Gillian 226
Linklater, Dick 235
Linstead, Hilary 276, 277
Lipman, Maureen 323
Lisemore, Martin 267
Little Farringdons 76–8
Little Lord Fauntleroy (television) 22, 324–5
Little Sisters of the Poor 12
Litvak, Anatole 197
Livesey, Roger 252
Lloyd, Marie 230
Löhr, Marie 148–9, 150–51
Longhurst, Jeremy 255
Longman, Mark 107–8
Longman, Richard 107
Lonsdale, Frederick 113, 147, 148
Look After Lulu (stage) 86, 192–4, 195–6, 198
Loren, Sophia 187–8
Love, Bessie 113
Love Life (television) 237
Lovejoy (television) 315
Lowe, Arthur 245
Lowe, Barry 173
Lowry, Dick 279, 324
Lowry, Nina 279, 324
Loy, Myrna 197
Lucan, Lady 157–8
Lucan, Lord 158
Lucas, Mrs (landlady) 93
Lyle, Viola 247
Lynford Rees, Mr (psychiatrist) 220, 221
Lynn, Vera 74
Lynne, Gillian 275, 322

Macbeth (stage) 205, 206–7, 209
McCallum, John 255
McCloran, George 33
McCloran, Olga 33
MacCormack, John 179
McCowen, Alec 81, 205, 253
MacCrea, John 270, 274, 275
McDermott, Avie (aunt of GB) 35, 39, 62–3, 285, 294–6
McDermott, Bella (*née* Turner, grandmother of GB) 6, 7, 86
McDermott, Eva *see* Baker